NUMBER 254

THE ENGLISH
EXPERIENCE

ITS RECORD IN EARLY PRINTED BOOKS
PUBLISHED IN FACSIMILE

JOHN WILSON

THE ENGLISH MARTYROLOGIE

N. P. 1608

DA CAPO PRESS
THEATRVM ORBIS TERRARVM LTD.
AMSTERDAM 1970 NEW YORK

The publishers acknowledge their gratitude
to the Curators of the Bodleian Library, Oxford,
for their permission to reproduce
the Library's copies: Shelfmark: Douce M. 571
and the pages: B1 v, B2 r, B3 v, B4 r + last unsigned leaf recto
from another copy, Shelfmark: Wood 296.

S.T.C. No. 25771
Collation: $*^8$, A - Z^8, Aa^8, unsigned [1]

Published in 1970 by
Theatrum Orbis Terrarum Ltd.,
O.Z. Voorburgwal 85, Amsterdam

&

Da Capo Press
- a division of Plenum Publishing Corporation -
227 West 17th Street, New York, 10011
Printed in the Netherlands
ISBN 90 221 0254 8

THE ENGLISH

MARTYROLOGE

CONTEYNING

A SVMMARY OF THE LIVES
of the glorious and renowned Saintes
of the three Kingdomes,

ENGLAND, SCOTLAND, AND
IRELAND.

COLLECTED AND DISTRIBVTED
into Moneths, after the forme of a Calendar,
according to euery Saintes feftiuity.

VV HERVNTO
Is *annexed in the end a Catalogue of thofe, who haue fuffered
death in England for defence of the Catholicke Caufe, fince King
Henry the 8. his breach with the Sea Apoftolicke, vnto this day.*

By a Catholicke Prieft.

Ecclef. 44.
Nomen eorum viuet in generationem & generationem.
Their memory fhall liue from generation to generation.

Permiffu Superiorum. Anno 1608.

Ecce *Regni Angliæ dulcis patriæ excidiũ dolendũ &c. Martyribus, Confessoribus, &c.* Behould the lamentable destruction of England so pleasant a Countrey &c. An Iland so shining with Martyrs, Confessours, and holy Virgins, that scarcely shall yow passe by any famous Village or streete, where yow shall not heare the glorious Name of some new Saint or other &c. *Matth. Paris, in Hist. Angl. Anno 1. Gul. Conquest.*

NUsquam *gentium, vt opinor, reperies. &c.* No where, I supose, shall yow find so many incorrupted bodyes of Saintes *(as in England)* resembling that their euerlasting incorruptibility. Which by diuine prouidence, I thinke, to be therfore so ordayned; that a Nation situated almost out of the world, should by cõsideration of their incorruption, be more confidently animated to the hope of eternall Resurrection &c. *Author Continuat. Hist. Ven. Bedæ l. 2. cap. 30.* Vixit anno 1110.

EVery corner of S. *Augustines* Monastery at Cãterbury lieth full of the bodyes of Sayntes, and those of no small Name or merit; but euen of such, as one wherof alone were sufficient to make England famous. &c. *Idem eodem lib. cap. 33.*

TO THE
CATHOLICKS
OF
ENGLAND, SCOTLAND, AND IRELAND.

H E N I had almoſt brought this little worke to an end, (deare Catholicke Countreymen) I began to thinke with my ſelfe, to whome, among many ſo dearely affected, I might make bold to dedicate the ſame, therby the better to patronize that, which ouer bold preſumption had cōceyued. And though the thing it ſelfe needed none other Patrons or Protectors then the glorious Saintes themſelues, of whome we are now to treat: yet becauſe I might not ſeeme, in a manner, to defraude any heerin of their right & intereſt, which I imagined; at laſt I thought it moſt conuenient, that YOW, whoſe hartes and myndes are firmely fixed in the honour and veneration of ſo glorious and elected wightes, and for the imbra-

cing

cing wherof yow daily fuffer fo great and many
perfecutions, fhould take vpon yow this Protection, for whofe comfort and confolation
principally (next after the honour of the Saintes
themfelues) the fame is publifhed. I do not
heere offer vnto yow any new thing (which
is alwayes commonly the cuftome of fuch to do
who dedicate their workes to others) but that
which fo many ages fince, hath by a certaine
inheritance, as it were, of your forfathers, defcended ftill, by good right and title, vnto yow,
and fhall heerafter vnto your, and all pofterity.
Only this, that I haue heere gathered togeather,
and reftored vnto yow againe, that which the
iniury of tymes had violently taken from yow,
and fought to abolifh all memory therof : humbly prefenting the fame, as a duty of my loue
towards yow, & my deareft Countrey. Wifhing
yow to take in good part, what my poore endeauours haue byn able to produce heerin for
your fpirituall confolation, in thefe your fo great
afflictions and preffures : with defyre to be
made partaker of your good prayers. This firft
of October. 1608.

Yours wholy deuoted.

I. W. Prieft.

IANVARY

1 **M**idwyne Conf.
Eluane Bish.
2 A Thousand holy Martyrs
3 Meltorus Mart. *
4 Croniacke Conf. *
5 Edward King.
6 Peter Conf. *
7 Ced Conf.
8 Guithelme Bishop
Transl. William
Brituald Bishop
9 Adrian Abbot.
Transl. Iudocus
10 Sethrid Virg. *
11 Egwyne Bishop
12 Benedict Abbot.
13 Kentigerne Abbot
14 Beno Confessour *
15 Alfred King *
16 Henry Ermite
17 Milwyde Virg.
Deicola Abbot.
18 Vlfride Bishop *
Wolstan Bishop
19 Henry Bishop.
20 Elfred Virg. *
21 Malcalline Abbot.
22 Brituald Bishop *
23 Boysill Abbot. *

24 Sophias Bishop.
Cadocke Mart.
25 Conuersion Paul.
Eoglodius Conf *
26 Theorithgid Virg. *
27 Palladius Bish. *
28 Arwaldi Broth. Mart. *
29 Gildas Abbot.
30 Amnichade Conf.
31 Adaman Conf.

FEBRVARY

1 **B**Rigit Virgin
2 Laurence Bishop
Burchard Bishop.
3 Wereburge Virgin
4 Gilbert Conf.
Liephard Bish.
5 Ihn. Indractus Mart. *
6 Inas King. *
Richard King
7 Augulus Bishop
Transl. Helena
8 Edelfled Virg. *
9 Merigold Mart.
10 Transl. Wilfrid Bishop.
William Bish.
11 Caroch Conf.
12 Edilu ald Bishop *
Ermenild Queene
13 Transl. Kilian B.

14 *Conwane Conf.* ✳
15 *Sigfride Bishop.*
16 *Tancone Bishop.*
17 *Finan Bishop.*
18 *Iohn Bishop.* ✳
19 *Acca Bishop.* ✳
20 *Mildred Virgin* ⎫
   Vlfricke Ermite ⎭
21 *Cymbert Bishop.* ✳
22 *Transl. Gudwall Bishop.*
23 *Transl. Milburge Virg.*
24 *Ethelbert King* ⎫
   Berectas Conf. ⎭
25 *Transl. Furseus Abbot*
26 *Iohn Bishop.* ✳
27 *Sexulfe Bishop.* ⎫ ✳
   Alnoth Martyr ⎭
   Oswald Bishop.

MARCH

1 **D**uid *Bishop.* ⎫
   Switbert Bish. ⎭
2 *Chad Bishop.* ⎫
   Willeicke Abb. ⎭
3 *Wenlocke Abbot*
4 *Furseus Abbot*
5 *Wilgise Confeff.* ✳
   Frodoline Abbot ⎫
   Kinifdred Virg. ⎬
   Kinifwide Virg. ⎭

7 *Deifer Ermite.* ✳
8 *Felix Bishop.*
9 *Bofa Bishop.* ✳
10 *Himeline Conf.*
11 *Transl Ofwyn King.*
12 *Gregory Pope.* ⎫
   Fethno Conf. ✳ ⎭
13 *Vigane Conf.* ✳
14 *Ceolnulph King* ✳
15 *Ariftobulus Bishop.*
16 *Alred Abbot.* ✳
17 *Patricke Bishop.*
18 *Edward King* ⎫
   Chriftian Bish. ⎬
   Alkmund Mart. ✳ ⎭
19
20 *Cuthbert Bish.* ⎫
   Hercbert Conf. ⎭
21 *Ifenger Bishop.* ✳
22 *Hamund Bishop.* ✳
23 *Egbert King.* ✳
24 *Lanfrancke Bishop.*
25 *William Martyr*
26 *Many holy Martyrs.* ✳
27 *Archibald Abbot.*
28 *Transl. Fremund King.*
29 *Baldred Conf.* ✳
30 *Pattone Bishop*
31 *Transl. Adelme Bishop.*

APRIL.

1	Sadocke. ⎱ Adrian. ⎰ Mart. *
2	Ebba Abbesse. *
3	Richard Bishop . ⎱ Burgundofora Virg. ⎰
4	Guter Priest. *
	Tigernake Bishop ⎱
5	Gotebald Bishop.* ⎰
6	Celsus Confessour ⎱ Ethelwold King.* ⎰
7	Sigene Abbot. *
8	Duuianus Conf. *
9	Frithstan Bish. *
10	Paternus Confess. ⎱ Eschillus Bishop. ⎰
11	Guthlacke Conf.
12	Hugh Bishop ⎱ * Mechtild Virg. ⎰
13	Elsled Virgin. *
14	Ethelnulph King. *
15	Eleua. Oswald Bishop
16	Transl. Alban Protom.
17	Marianus Conf. *
18	Oswyn Conf. *
19	Elphege Bishop
20	Ceadwall King. ⎱ Transl. Aldar B. ⎰
21	Anselme Bishop
22	Birstan Bishop. *
23	George Martyr. ⎱ Etheldred King ⎰
24	Mellitus Bishop. ⎫ Egbert Abbot. ⎪ Inuent. Iuo B. ⎬ Tran. Wilfrid B. ⎭
25	Obodius Conf.*
26	Modan ⎱ Midan ⎰ Confess.*
27	Walburge Virgin
28	Kortill Bishop *
29	Senan Conf. *
30	Erconwald Bishop.

MAY

1	Assaph Bish. ⎱ Vltan Abbot ⎰
2	German Bishop. ⎱ Piran Conf. * ⎰
3	Walter Abbot
4	Etheired King. *
5	Algiue Queene ⎱ * Scandalaus Conf. ⎰
6	Edbert Bishop ⎱ Tran. Dubritius ⎰
7	Iohn Beuerley Bish.
8	Wyre Bishop.
9	Beatus Conf.
10	Transl. Bede Priest

11	Fremund King Martyr
12	Remigius Bishop
13	Merwyne Virg.*
14	Edith Virg. *
15	Dympna Virg.
16	Symon Confeſſ. ⎫ Tranſl.Alban ⎬ Brandan Abbot. ⎭
17	Tranſl.11000. Virgins
18	Sewall Bishop.
19	Dunſtan Bishop. ⎫ Alcuine Abbot ⎬
20	Ethelbert King Mart.
21	Godricke Ermite ⎫ Conſtātine Emper. ⎬
22	Henry King.
23	William Martyr
24	Edgar King *
25	Adelme Bishop.
26	Auguſtine Bishop ⎫ Fugatius Conf. ⎬ Damianus Conf. ⎭
27	Bede Prieſt
28	Ionas Abbot. *
29	Burien Virg. *
30	Hieu Virg. *
31	Wolſtan Martyr

IVNE.

1	Rufin ⎱ Vlſade ⎰ Mart. *
2	Malcolme King *
3	Eleutherius Conf. *
4	Patrocke Bishop . *
5	Boniface Bishop ⎫ Eboam Bishop. ⎪ Adlar Bishop ⎪ Vintruge Prieſt ⎪ Walter Prieſt ⎪ Abelhere Prieſt ⎬ Mart. Hamunt Deacō ⎪ Boſo Deacon ⎪ Gunderhere M. ⎪ Wilhere Monke ⎪ Adolph Monke ⎭
6	Gudwall. Biſh
7	Robert Abbot ⎫ Tranſl. Wolſtan ⎬
8	William Biſh. ⎱ Diſibode Biſh. ⎰
9	Columbe Abbot
10	Tran.Edmund King ⎫ Margaret Queene ⎬ Ithimar Bishop ⎭
11	Ediluald Conf. *
12	Agatha Virg.*
13	Elerius Abbot *
14	Tranſl Brandan Abbot

Ead-

	Eadburge Virg. ⎫
15	Transl. Menigold ⎬
	Mayne Abbot ⎭
16	Transl. Richard Bishop. ⎫
	Leofgar Bishop. Mart. ⎭
17	Botulph Abbot.
18	Dunstan Abbot *
19	Iohn Bishop. *
20	Transl. Edward K. ⎫
	Transl. Oswald K. ⎭
21	Engelmund Mart.
	Alban Protomart. ⎱
22	Souldiar Mart ⎰
	Transl. Ortrude V.
23	Ediltrude Virgin.
24	Rumwald Bishop.
	Amphibale Mart.
25	Adalbert Conf.
	Transl. Lebuine Conf.
26	Nine hundred Mart. *
	Iohn Conf. ⎫
27	Transl. Leuine B. ⎭
28	Columbane Monke *
29	Peter & Paul Apost. ⎫
	Ethelwyne Bishop * ⎭
30	Deusdedit Bishop.

IVLY

1	Ivlius & Aaron ⎫
	Goluin Bishop. ⎭

2	Swithin Bishop. ⎫
	Oudocke Conf. ⎭
3	Transl. Lanfranke B. ⎫
	Guthagon Conf. ⎭
4	Odo Bishop
5	Modwene Abbesse ⎫
	Transl. Anselme Bishop ⎭
6	Sexburge Abbesse
	Tran. Thom. of Cant. ⎱
	Hedda Bishop.
7	Willebald Bishop.
	Edilburge Virg.
	Ercongote Virg.
	Grimbald Abbot. ⎱
	Kilian Bishop
8	Colman Mart.
	Totnam Mart.
	Erwald Mart. ⎰
9	Edilburge Queene
10	Etto Bishop.
11	Dronston Conf. *
12	Luane Abbot *
13	Transl. Mildred Virg.
14	Marcheline Conf.
	Transl. Swithin ⎱
	Bishop of Winch.
	Plechelme Bishop
15	Eadgith Queene
	Harrucke Bishop
	Dauid Abbot. ⎰
16	Transl. Osmund Bishop

17	Kenelme King Mart. Iohn Abbot Fridegand Conf.	5	Oswald King.
			Henry Bishop
18	Edburge Virgin Transl. Odilia	6	Alexander Conf. *
19	Diman Conf. *	7	Maude Queene *
20	Ethelwide Queene *	8	Fagane Confess. *
21	Arbogastus Bishop	9	Hugh Bishop
22	Wilfrede Queene. *	10	Malcus Bishop . *
23	Vodine Bish.Mart. *	11	Gilbert Confessour *
24	Transl. Lewine Virg.	12	Bertelme Conf. *
	Wiaman	13	Wigbert Mart. *
25	Vnaman Mart. * Sunaman	14	Transl. Werenfrid Conf.
		15	Margaret Prioresse *
26	Christian Virgin	16	Thomas Monke *
27	Ioseph of Arimathia Hugh Martyr	17	Thomas Conf. Ieron Martyr
28	Sampson Bishop Lupus Bishop	18	Helen Empresse.
		19	Clintanke King.
29	Owen Conf. *	20	Oswyne King
30	Lesrone Abbesse Tacwine Bish.	21	Richard Bishop. *
		22	Arnulph Conf. *
31	Neoth Conf.	23	Iustinian Mart. *
		24	Alice Prioresse *
	AVGVST	25	Ebba Martyr Thom. of Hereford
		26	Pandwyne Virgin *
		27	Decuman Mart. *
1	Ethelwold Bishop Transl. Wenlock	28	Rumbald Conf. Agnes Virg. Mart. *
2	Alicke Ermite *	29	Sebbe King Transl. Edwold
3	Domitius Conf. *	30	Fiaker Conf.
4	Transl. Walburge Virg.		

Aidan

Aidan Bishop
31 Cuthberge Abbesse
Transl. Eanswide

SEPTEMBER

1 Elphege Bishop *
2 Adaman Abbot *
3 Transl. Foillan Bish.
4 Tran. Cuthbert Bish.
  Marcellus Bishop.
5 Altho Abbot *
6 Bega Virgin *
7 Transl. Dunstan Bish.
8 Ethelburge Queene *
9 Queran Abbot
  Wulfhild Virg.
10 Otger Deacon Conf.
11 Bather Abbot *
12 Eanswide Abbesse
   Quemburge Virg. *
13 Werenfrid Conf.
14 Bernard Conf. *
15 Chineburg Queene *
16 Ninian Bishop
   Edith Virgin
17 Stephen
   Socrates Martyrs
18 Transl. Winocke Abb.
19 Theodore Bishop
20 Cibthacke Confessour *

21 Edilhun Conf. *
22 Higbald Abbot *
23 Hereswide Queene *
24 Transl. Winibald Abb.
25 Ceolfride Abbot
26 Wulsy Abbot
   Iotaneus Conf. *
27 Sigebert King *
28 Lioba Abbesse
29 Cogan Abbot. *
30 Honorius Bishop.

OCTOBER

1 Roger Bishop
  Tran. Guthagō
  Wasnulph Conf.
2 Transl. Thom. of Hereford
3 Ewaldi Martyrs.
4 Edwyn King Mart.
5 Conwalline Abbot *
6 Ywy Conf.
  Comine Abbot *
7 Osith Virg.
  Transl. Hugh B.
8 Transl. Eloquius
  Keyna Virgin
9 Robert Bishop.
  Gislen Conf.
  Pauline Bishop
10 Iohn Conf.

Edil-

11	Edilburge Abbeſſe / Canake Abbot	29	Eadſine Bishop / Moniſer Conj.*
12	Wilfrid Bishop.	30	Egelnoth Bishop
31	Tranſl. Edward K. / Colman Martyr	31	Foillan Bishop
14	Tranſl. Burchard Bishop.		**NOVEMBER**
15	Tranſl. Oſwald B. / Tecla Abbeſſe	1	Tranſl. Boniface B. / Richard Ermite *
16	Lullus Bishop. / Gallus Abbot	2	Vulganius Bishop.
17	Ethelbrit Mart. / Ethelred Mart. / Tran. Ediltrude	3	Weneſiae Virgin / Tran. Eaith Virg.
18	Mono Martyr	4	Clare Martyr.
19	Frideſwyde Virgin / Tranſl. Willebrord / Ethbyn Abbot	5	Malachy Bishop.
		6	Winocke Abbot.
20	Wendelin Abbot.	7	Willebrord Bishop. / Florentius Bishop.
21	Vrſula Virgin	8	Willehade Bishop
22	Mellon Bishop / Cordula Virg. / Donatus Bish.	9	Congilla Abbeſſe * / Iuſtus Bishop
23	Syra Virgin *	10	Iohn Bishop
24	Maglore Bish. / Maxentia Virg.*	11	Bertuine Bishop.
25	Ardwine Conj.*	12	Liuinus Bishop / Lebuine Conf.
26	Eatta Bishop. / Albuine Bish.	13	Kilian Bish. Conf. / Tran. Erconwald
27	Tranſl. Romwald B.	14	Laurence Bishop / Dubritius Bishop
28	Symon Apoſtle / Alfred King.	15	Macloue Bishop
		16	Edmund Bishop / Margaret Qu.

Hugh

	Hugh Bishop⎞	7	Odwald Abbot. ⎱
7	Hilda Abbeſſe ⎰		Gallanus Conf. ⎰ *
8	Fulke Confeſſ. *	8	Conception of B.Virg. ⎞
19	Ermenburge Queene		Agatha Queene * ⎰
20	Edmund K. Mart. ⎞	9	Ethelgine Abbeſſe *
	Humbert Bishop. ⎰	10	Chined Ermite *
21	Columban Abbot	11	Geruadius Bishop *
22	Oſmane Virgin *	12	Elfred Virg. *
23	Tathar Ermite *	13	Iudocus Ermite ⎞
24	Eanflede Queene *		Edburge Virgin ⎰
25	Telean Bishop *	14	Mimborine Abbot *
26	Egbert Abbot *	15	Tranſl. Hilda Virg.
27	Oda Virgin	16	Bean Bishop ⎞
28	Edwold Conf.		Tibbe Virgin * ⎰
29	Barucke Ermite *	17	Tetta Abbeſſe *
30	Withbuge Virgin *	18	Winibald Abbot
		19	Macharius Abbot *
	DECEMBER	20	Comogel Abbot *
		21	Edburge Abbeſſe *
1	Daniel-Confeſſ. *	22	Hidelide Virgin *
2	Weede Virgin *	23	Inthware Virgin *
	Lucius King ⎞	24	Ruthius Conf. *
3	Birine Bish. ⎰	25	Gregory Conf. *
	Eloquius Conf. ⎰	26	Ethelfrede Virg. *
	Oſmund Bishop ⎞	27	Gerrard Confeſſ. *
4	Emerita Virg. ⎰	28	Tranſl. Elphege Bishop.
5	Chriſtine Virgin *	29	Thomas of Canterbury
6	Congellus Abbot ⎞ *	30	Euſtach Abbot *
	Florentina Virg. ⎰	31	Eternane Conf. *

AN

ADVERTISMENT
OF THE AVTHOR
to the Catholicke Reader.

WHERAS all Bookes (good Reader) of what subiect soeuer, that are publisled to the view of the world, must passe the censures and iudgments of many sortes of people; I haue thought it not amisse, before thou enter any further into the contentes, to giue thee two or three short aduertisments in this place; aswell therby to preuent all occasions of misconstruction or cauill, that any man, perchance, may take against this little worke or Sanctiloge of myne; as also the better to informe thy vnderstanding, concerning diuers doubtes or other difficultyes, that in the reading therof may happily occurre vnto thee.

1. First then I would haue thee to vnderstand, that what I haue heere set downe in this ensuing Martyrologe concerning the liues and miracles of these glorious and renowned Saintes of our *Great-Britany*, and of the Ilands belonging therunto; I haue done the same with all truth, sincerity & conscience, to my knowledge : not contenting my selfe with bare wordes and relations only; but haue in the margents quoted also the bookes and places of the Authors, out of whome I haue gathered al that is heere alleaged. Neyther haue I vsed any other Authors herin, but such as are approued by the Sea Apostolick, or at leastwise permitted by the same: reiecting all Apocryphall Legends or other fabulousHistoryes, that may be any way suspected of the least note of falsity or errour whatsoeuer.

2. Secondly I haue not taken vpon me in this Catalogue or Calendar to make an vniuersall Martyrologe, but haue gathered togeather only the ancient Saintes, Martyrs, Confessours & Virgins of our three Kingdomes, *England, Scot-*

land & *Ireland* : Yet for that, besides these of our owne, there are some others also of foraine Nations, by whome out said Countreys haue receyued some notable or peculiar benefit, either publicke or priuate ; as hauing byn our Apostles or Patrons, eyther by way of preaching, teaching, protection, or otherwise in the cooperation to our Conuersion, and consequently to be by vs honoured and reuerenced for such, as all our Cath. Ancestours and forfathers haue done before vs, and as we see all other Catholicke Countreys round about vs to do the like in the same case : These (I say) I haue thought good, to accompt as our owne, & togeather with our owne to place thē on their proper festiuall dayes, to the end we may as well with due honour obserue their Memoryes and Solemnityes ; as also therby auoyd the vngratefull obliuion of so great & inestimable benefits receyued by them and their merits.

3. The third Aduertifement may be, that wheras it hath pleased God to giue vnto our little Dominions so many glorious Saintes, both Martyrs, Cōfessours & Virgins (besides these later of our dayes, whose Names I haue also put downe in a Catalogue a part by thēselues, in the later end of this booke) who may be more then sufficient, to make a whole and complete Calendar, throughout euery Moneth, placing on euery day one ; yet for that a great number of our ancient Saintes haue no proper festiuityes in our English Catholicke Church, and many of them forgotten and almost out of memory, by this vnfortunate fall of our Countrey, frō the true and ancient Catholicke faith, and vnion of the Sea Apostolicke : I haue thought it most conuenient for the more full accomplishing and perfecting of a Martyrologe, that where any day falleth out to be altogeather voyd, there to place one or more of the forsaid ancient Saintes, whose publicke celebrity hath not byn hitherto kept, & therof to make a Commemoration only (which in the Roman & other Martyrologes is often vsed) noting the same with the signe of an Asteriske or Starre in the Margent, to the end it may be knowne and obser-

ued of the Reader. And where none of thefe forfaid Markes, fo noted, is to be found; then vpon that day is put the true feftiuity of the Saint, whome there thou fhalt find placed.

4. And laftly, I do not meane by this enfuing Martyrologe to introduce any other publicke obferuation or feftiuity of any of the Saintes heerin by me fet downe, then that which the Catholicke Church of England hath in former tymes, and doth alfo at this prefent celebrate: but only my intention is to lay forth the fumme of their liues and miracles as briefly as I may, for the increafe of deuotion in the Catholicke people, and for the duty and reuerence I owe vnto them both; leauing the reft to euery mans priuate and particular deuotion, as he fhall, by reading the fame, be affeĉted to their glorious veneration. Wifhing hartily all fuch Catholickes of our faid Coũtreys, to whofe hands this little worke may chance to come; that if they haue any other notes, concerning thefe our ancient Saintes lying by them, they would vouchfafe, eyther to impart the fame vnto me, or be pleafed themfelues, by reuiewing this fmall labour of myne, to publifh the fame anew, and amend my imperfeĉtions heerin, if any fhalbe found; as well for the honour of the glorious Saintes themfelues, as the publike vtility of thefe our Kingdoms and Countreys. Farewell.

I. W.

ERRATA

THE

THE
MONETH
OF IANVARY.

A   *The first Day.*

A T *Glaſtenbury - Abbey* in *Somerſetſhire* the Comme-moration of the Sayntes *Midwyne* and *Eluane* Con-feſſors , who being two noble auncient Britans by byrth , were ſent by King *Lucius* or *Britany* to *Rome* to Pope *Elutherius*, to treat of his Conuerſion to Chriſtian faith, and being there both baptized by the ſaid Pope, & *S. Eluane* made a Biſhop, they were ſent backe againe into Britany, togeather with *Fugatius* and *Damianus*, who baptized the King and the greateſt part of his Nation, in the yeare of our Lord 183. And after they had much laboured in teaching and inſtructing the new flocke of Chriſt in our Iland for many yeares, full of

*

Baron. in Annal. Eccl. an. 183. ex antiquis monum. Eyſeng. cent. 2 . p. 6 . diſt. 6 Io. Capgrau. in Catal. Sanctor. Britan. Regiſtr. Monaſt. Glaſcon.

A   ſanctity

sanctity of life, and venerable old age, they both ended their happy dayes, about the yeare of Chrift, an hundred nynty and eight, & were buried at *Glaftenbury*, as the ancient Records of that Abbey do witneffe.

And in other places of many holy Martyrs, Confeffors, and Virgins; to whofe prayers and merits, we humbly commend our felues.

This laft claufe is alwayes thus to be repeated in the end of euery day.

B   *The fecond Day.*

AT *Lichfield* in *Staffordshire* the Commemoration of *A thoufand holy Martyrs*, of the Britifh Nation, who newly conuerted to the faith of Chrift, and being Difciples and followers of S. *Amphibale* Prieft, that fuffered in the perfecution of *Dioclefian* Emperour, and prefent at his Martyrdome neere vnto the towne of S. *Albanes* in *Hartfordshire*, fled thence for feare of like torments; but being ouertaken at *Lichfield*, they were all in hatred of Chriftian Religion, there moft cruelly put to death, by commandement of the Prefident of *Brittany*, about the yeare of Chrift three hundred and foure. The place where they fuffered, was afterward called *Cadauerum campus*, which is as much to fay as *Lich-field* in Englifh, & where the for-

said

*
Bed. l. 1.
hift. An.
c. 7. in
fin. Mat.
VVeft-
monaft.
in hiftor.
Anglic.
Io. Roufe
de nomi-
ne Ciuit.
Lichfel-
diæ.
Humfr.
Lhuide
in fragm.
defcrip.
Britan.

said Citty is now built, and therof taketh his auncient name and denomination. *And in other places of many holy Martyrs, Confeſſors, and Virgins, &c.*

C   *The third Day.*

IN *Cornwall* the Cōmemoration of *S. Meliorus* Martyr, ſonne to *Melianus* Duke of that Prouince, who being his Fathers only ſonne and heyre, and ſecretly made a Chriſtian, was by a brother-in-law of his called *Rinaldus* a pagan, cruelly murdered, partly in hatred of his faith and Religion, and partly to inioy his inheritance. He firſt cut of his right hand, and then his left legge, and laſt of all his head, about the yeare of Chriſt foure hundred and eleuen. His body was buried in an old Church in *Cornwall*, wherat in ſigne of his innocency, it pleaſed God forthwith to worke many miracles; where alſo his reliques were kept with great honour and veneration, euen vntill our dayes.

Io. Caprau. in Catalog. Sanctor. Britan. Anno Domini 411. ex antiquis monum. Prouinc. Cornub.

D   *The fourth Day.*

IN *Scotland* the Commemoration of *S. Croniacke* Confeſſor, who borne of a very no-

ble

Io. Lef-
læus E-
pif. Rof-
fen. l. 5.
hift.Scot.
Arnold.
Wion in
addit. ad
lib.3.Lig.
vitæ lit.
C.

ble parentage in that Kingdome , tooke a
Religious habit, and became a Monke of
the venerable Order of S. *Benedict*, where
in all kind of fanctity of life, and Monafticall difcipline, he ended his bleffed dayes
about the yeare of Chrift, fix hundred and
fifty. His memory is yet very famous a-
mongft the Catholickes, afwell of the
Scottifh, as the Irifh Nation; in both which
Kingdomes in former tymes , many
Churches and altars haue byn dedicated in
his honour. It is heere, and in many other
places to be obferued , that the *Irish* and *Scot-*
tish Hiftoriographers do oftentymes difagree
about the natiue Contrey of diuers Saintes
mentioned in this Martyrologe ; For that
in aunciét tymes the Iland of *Hybernia* being
called *Scotia*, hath caufed a great confufion,
efpecially amongft forrayne wryters, who
for want of knowledge heerin , do often
confound the one nation with the other.

E   *The fifth Day.*

Alred.
Rieuall.
in eius
vita.Pol.
Virgil.l.

AT *VVeftminfter* by *London*, the depofition
of *S. Edward* King and Confeffour, who
being yet in his Mothers wombe, was elected, crowned, and annoynted King by
S. Peter the Apoftle, as it was miraculoufly
reueyled to *S. Brituald* Bifhop of *VVinchefter*,

that

that liued at the fame tyme. He was very famous for working of miracles, efpecially in curing a difeafe of fwelling in peoples throtes, which was afterward therof called the Kinges-euill. His body being taken vp thirty fix yeares after his death, was found as flexible and vncorrupt, as when it was firft buryed. He was Canonized for a Saint by Pope *Alexander* the third, in the yeare of Chrift, one thoufand one hundred three-fcore and three. His tranflation was wont to be kept holy-day throughout England vpon the thirteenth day of October: of whome in that place we haue fet downe a larger Narration.

8. Matt. Parif. an. 1069. Surius tomo 1. vit. Sanct. hac die. Petr. in Catal. Rom. Martyr. & alij.

F   *The fixt Day.*

✳

AT *Bologne* in *France* the Commemoration of S. *Peter* Confeffor, who being by S. *Auguftine* our Englifh Apoftle ordayned Abbot of a new Monaftery neere vnto *Canterbury*, which K. *Ethelbert* of *Kent* had founded, and going ouer into *France*, was by tempeft of fea, drowned neere to the coaft of *Bologne*, where the Inhabitãts finding his body, buryed it in an obfcure place: but a certaine miraculous light from heauen being feene euery night to fhine theron, the people began to inquire further what he

Ven. Beda lib. 1. hiftor. Gent. Angl. cap. 33. Arnold. VVion in appẽd. ad lib. 3. lig. vitæ.

A 3   was;

was; and at laſt hauing intelligence from *England*, that it was the forſaid Abbot, they tooke vp his body, and tranſlated it with great ſolemnity to *Bologne*, and there with due veneration placed it in a Church, wherat in ſigne of his ſanctity and holines of life, miracles are ſaid to haue byn forthwith wrought. This happened about the yeare of Chriſt, ſix hundred and ſeauen.

G   *The ſeauenth Day.*

Beda lib.
L. hiſt.
Angl.
cap.21.22
23.24.25.
Et lib. 4.
Cap.3.
Catal.
Epiſco.
Lodinenſ.
apud �श̃
l.2.lig.
vitæ.

AT *London* the feſtiuity of S. *Ced* Confeſſor and ſecond Biſhop of that Sea brother to S. *Chad* of *Lichfield*, who by his continuall preaching to the *Mercians* and *Eaſtſaxons*, conuerted many thouſands to the faith of Chriſt, and is worthily called their Apoſtle. The Sea of *London* being voyd for many years after the death of S. *Mellitus*, he was at length conſecrated therto, at the interceſſion of *Sigebert* K. of the *Eaſtſaxons*, who was newly conuerted to the Chriſtian faith. And afterwards building a goodly Monaſtery at a place called *Leſtinghen* in the Prouince of the *Deires*, and repleniſhing the ſame with many monks, at laſt in great ſanctity of life, full of venerable old age, he ended his bleſſed dayes, in the yeare of Chriſt, ſix hundred fifty and foure, and was buried

in

in his forfaid new Monaſtery, where he
deſceaſed. *S. Bede* recounteth, that when
afterward his brother *S. Chad* died, his foule
was feene to deſcend from heauen, with a
troupe of Angells, to accompany the fame
to paradiſe.

A   *The eight Day.*

AT *London* the depoſition of *S. Guithelme*
Biſhop and Confeſſor, who borne of a
noble bloud in our Iſlad, & in the Primitiue
Church of Britany ordayned Archbiſhop of
London, was very famous for preaching the
Chriſtian faith to the Pagans of our nation:
And after a moſt Saintly life, full of miracles,
in a good old age, he moſt bleſſedly depar-
ted this world, about the yeare of Chriſt
foure hundred and threeſcore.

Matth.
weſtmo-
naſt. an
Domini
435.
Gauf.
Monum.
l. 6. cap.
4. & 5.

THe fame day at *Yorke* the Tranſlation of
S. VVilliam Confeſſor and Biſhop of that
Sea, kinſman to K. *Stephen* of *England*, who
after he had moſt patiently endured many
iniuryes and wrongs, yea and baniſhment
alſo from his biſhopricke and flocke, being
againe reſtored by *Pope Anaſtaſius* the fourth,
in great holines of life, he ended his bleſſed
dayes, in the yeare of Chriſt, one thouſand,
one hundred, fifty and foure. His venerable
body being, after many yeares, taken vp

Calendar
ſecundū
vſu Sarū
hac die.

on this day , was with great folemnity
tranflated to a more eminent place of his
owne Cathedrall Church of *Torke*, wherat,
in figne of his innocency , through his
merits, it pleafed God to worke miracles.

B   *The ninth Day.*

AT *Canterbury* the depofition of *S. Bri-*
tuald Bifhop and Confeffor,who being
conftituted the firft Abbot of the Monaftery
of *Rheaculfe* in *Kent* , now called *Reaculer*,
which holy K. *Ethelbert* of that Prouince
had founded foone after his Conuerfion,
was thence promoted to the Archbifhop-
ricke of *Canterbury*, and fucceeded *S. Theodore*
in that Sea, which when he had gouerned
for almoft fourty yeares , in great fanctity
and holines of life , full of venerable old
age, he gaue vp his foule to reft , about the
yeare of Chrift, feauen hundred and thirty;
and was buryed at *Canterbury.*

THE fame day and fame place the depofition of *S. Adrian* Abbot, who borne in
in *Africke*, and fent into England with *S.*
Theodore of *Canterbury* aboue named , by *Pope*
Vitalian; after he had taught the Chriftian
faith in our Iland for nyne and thirty yeares
togeather ,full of fanctity of life & miracles,
he   departed to our Lord, in the yeare of
                                                        Chrift

Bed.l.5.
hift. cap.
9. Ioan.
Tritem.
de vir.
Illftr.
Polid.
Virgil. l.
4. & 6.
biftor.
Angl.

Beda l.4.
cap.1. &
2. & l. 5.
cap. 21.
Molan.
in addit.
ad vfuar.
Sigebert.
in Chron.

Chriſt, ſeauen hundred and ten, and was buryed in S. *Auguſtines* Church at *Canterbury.*

THE ſame day alſo at *Pontoiſe* in France the Tranſlation of S. *Iudocus* (cōmonly called in Engliſh S. *Ioyce*)who deſcended of a noble *Brittiſh* bloud, forſooke the world, and became an Ermite in *France*, where in all kind of moſt godly life and conuerſation, he ended his bleſſed dayes. His body being taken vp, on this day, threeſcore yeares after his death, was found as flexible and vncorrupt, as if it had byn buryed the day before. And being put into a coſtly ſhrine, was placed in a more eminent roome of the ſame Church, about the yeare of Chriſt ſeauen hundred and thirteene, wherat it pleaſed God to worke many miracles.

De hac Tranſl. vid. Calend. ſec. yſum Sarum, hac die.

C   *The tenth Day.*

AT *Brige* neere *Paris* in *France*, the Commemoration of S. *Sethird* Virgin and Abbeſſe, daughter to *Annas* King of the *Eaſtangles*, and ſiſter to S. *Edilburge* Virgin, who in her yong yeares went ouer into *France* and became a Religious womā there in a monaſtery at the forſaid towne of *Brige*, vnder the care of her ſaid ſiſter that then gouerned the ſame; after whoſe death, ſhe was made Ab-

beſſe

Catal. Abbatiſ. Monaſt. Brigenſ.

*

Bed. l. 30
cap. 8.
hift.
Angl.

beſſe of the whole Monaſtery; where in very
great ſanctimony of life, ioyned with
moſt godly Conuerſation and Monaſticall
diſcipline, ſhe yielded vp her bleſſed ſoule
to her heauenly ſpouſe, about the yeare of
Chriſt, ſix hundred and threeſcore : And
was buryed in the ſame place.

D　　*The eleuenth Day.*

AT *VVorceſter* the depoſition of *S. Egwine*
Confeſſor, & third Biſhop of that Sea,
who being a man of very auſtere life , made
a payre of iron-ſhackles , locked them cloſe
about his legges , then caſt the keyes therof
into the Riuer of *Seuerne*, an ſo went to
Rome with *Offa* King of *Mercia*; deſiring of
God , that the ſaid ſhackles might not be
looſed from his leges, vntill he had made
ſatisfation for all the ſynnes of his youth-
full yeares: and in his returne backe, as he
came ouer the ſea, vpon a ſuddayne a fiſh
leaped into the ſhippe , wherin he ſayled;
which being taken and killed , the forſaid
keyes of the ſhackles that he had throwne
into the riuer , were found in the fiſhes
belly; the which being brought to the
Bleſſed Biſhop , he forthwith applyed
them to the ſhackles that were about his
legges, and ſtraight vnlocking them, to the

Ranulph
Ceſtrenſ.
in eius
vita.
Matth.
VV eſt.
anno. 712
Florent.
VVigor.
in Chron.
anno 708
Mol.vi.
in addit.
ad V ſua.
hac die.
& alii.

admi-

admiration of the behoulders, he came ioyfully home to his Bishopricke. He founded
the famous Abbey of *Euesham* neere *VVorcester*,
& endowed it with great reuenewes & possessions, procuring from *Rome* diuers priuiledges and franchises for the same, of *Pope*
Constantine, by the meanes of *K. Coenred* and
K. Offa, that then resided in that Citty for
deuotion sake. And after many other workes
of piety, famous for miracles, he ended his
blessed dayes, about the yeare of Christ,
seauen hundred and sixteene: and was buried
at *Euesham*.

E   *The twelfth Day.*

AT *VVire-mouth* in the Bishopricke of
Durham, the deposition of *S. Benedict*
Abbot, surnamed *Biscopus*, who being descended of a noble parentage in our Iland, went
Rome, and after his returne thence, built a
goodly Monastery at the Riuer-banke of
VVire in the Kingdome of the *Northumbers*,
wherin our famous *S. Bede* was afterward
brought vp. He founded there also a goodly
Church, dedicating the same to the Blessed
Apostles *S. Peter* and *S. Paul*. And after a
second voyage to *Rome*, to procure priuiledges for his said Monastery, full of sanctity
and holinesse of life, he ended his venerable

Bed. l. 4.
cap. 4. &
l. 5. cap.
20. Mat.
Paris. &
VVestm.
anno
Domini
703.
Molan.
in addit.
ad Vsua.

dayes,

dayes, about the yeare of Chriſt ſeauen hundred and three, and was buryed in the forſaid Church which himſelf had built, wherat it pleaſed God to worke many miracles.

F   *The thirteenth Day.*

Io. Leſl. Epiſ. Roſ. l. 4. de geſt. Sco. Chron. Britan. & VV iõ in Mart. Benedict. hac die Molan. in addit. ad vſuar. & alij.

AT *Glaſco* in *Scotland* the depoſition of *S. Kentigerne*, Abbot and Confeſſour, Sonne to King *Eugenius* the third of *Scotland*, who being created Biſhop of *Glaſco*, ſoone after reſigned that dignity, and built himſelfe a Monaſtery in the ſame Kingdome, gathering togeather ſix hundred Monkes, whome he inſtructed in all kind of vertue and good learning, and was a myrrour to the Chriſtian world. And when he had thus cõtinued for very many yeares, full of venerable old age, ioyned with ſanctity of life and miracles, he gaue vp his bleſſed ſoule to reſt, about the yeare of Chriſt, ſix hundred and eight, and was buryed in the ſame place.

G   *The fourteenth Day.*

✶

Acta S. Wen e-

IN *North-wales* the Commemoration of *S. Beno* Prieſt and Confeſſor, who leading an Eremiticall life in the Weſt part of *England*

land, was by an angell admonished to go into *VVales* to a noble man called *Trebuith, S.VVenefrides* Father, who gaue him a part of his lands and possessions to build a Monastery, as also his daughter *VVenefride* to be instructed and brought vp in a Religious manner: whose head being soone after cut of by *Cradocus* sonne to *Alane* King of the same Contrey, for not yielding to his vnlawfull lust, he miraculously set on againe, she liuing fifteene yeares after. He ended his venerable life full of sanctity and miracles, about the yeare of Christ, six hundred and threescore: whose body hath alwayes byn had in very great reuerence in our iland, especially of the Ancient Britanes of *VVales.*

fridæ apud Surtom.6.3. Nouemb. Breuiar. sec. vsum Sarum in lect. S. Wenefridæ. & R. B. in eius vita M. S. in Collegio Angl. Audomarop.

A   *The fifteenth Day.*

AT *Mailros* in the Kingdome of *Northumberland,* the Commemoration of Blessed *Alfred* Confessour, and eighteenth King of that Prouince, who being a most vertuous Prince, in the one and twentith yeare of his raigne, contemning all worldly pompe and honour, to the admiration of all Christendome, both he and his wife the Queene, with mutuall consent entred into Monasteryes, & became Religious, she being veyled a Nunne at a place called *Dormundcaster,* two

✳

Bed. l. 5. cap. 13. Wernerus Rolwincke in fasciculo temporũ. VVion. lib. 4. ligni vitæ.

miles

Paulus Morigia ord. Iesu. de Vir. Illuftr. Monac. Plat. l. 2. de bono ftat. Rel.

miles from *Peterburrow* ; and he taking the habit of a Monke in the forfaid Monaſtery of *Maylros*, where in great fanctity of life & obſeruance of Monaſticall diſcipline, he ſpent the reſt of his dayes, and finally repoſed in our Lord, about the yeare of Chriſt, ſeauen hundred and twenty, and was buryed in the ſame place.

B   *The Sixteenth Day.*

AT *Tyn-mouth* in *Northumberlãd* the depoſition of *S. Henry* Confeſſor and Eremite, who borne in *Denmarke* of very honourable parents, came ouer into England, and obtayned leaue of the Prior of *Tyn-mouth* to lead a ſolitary or Eremiticall life in the Iland of *Cochet*, where he liued many yeares with only bread and water, and afterward he came to eate but thrice in the weeke, and three dayes alſo a weeke he kept ſylence. On a tyme he would haue gone to *Durham*, *Vita eius extat in veter. Codice Antuerpiæ, in cuſtodia cuiuſdam Nobilis viri,* but had no boate to paſſe ouer the riuer of *VVire*; Wherfore being ſolicitous how to get ouer, a boate that was faſtened on the other ſide of the water, brake looſe, and of it ſelfe came ouer vnto him, wherin he paſſed. Towards the end of his dayes, he got a ſwelling in one of his knees, through ouer much praying, which growing to an vlcer, at laſt

brake

brake , and when certayne little wormes
crept therout , he would take and put them
in againe , saying : *Go into your inheritance,
where you haue byn nourished, &c.* And so per-
seuering in a most godly and Saintly life for
a long tyme, when the houre of death drew
neere, he went into a little Chappell in the
same iland , and taking the belrope in his
hand , when he had rung it, he departed
this life. A monke of the next Monastery
hearing the bell ring, made hast thither, and
found him dead , sitting vpon a stone with
the belrope in his hand, and a candle stan-
ding lighted by him , which did yield so
cleere a light that it dazeled the eyes of the
behoulders. His body was brought to
Tyn-mouth, and there buried in the Church
of our *B. Lady* , neere to the body of *S. Oswyn*
King and Martyr , in the yeare of Christ
1120. which yeare also he died.

*vbi festi-
uitas eius
ponitur
hac die.*

C   *The seauenteenth Day.*

AT *Canterbury* the Commemoration of
S. Milwyde Virgin, daughter to *Merualdus*
King of *Mercia* , and sister to the Saintes
Milburge and *Mildred* Virgins, who contem-
ning all pleasures and delightes of this
world , became a Religious woman in a
Monastery in *Kent* , neere vnto *Canterbury*,

*Matth.
VVest.
an. Dom.
676.*

which

Pol.Vir.
l.4.hist.
Angl.
Ranulph
Cestrens.
lib.4 cap.
18.& alij
antiquio-
res.

which holy King *Ethelbert* of blessed memory had foūded, where in great sāctimony of
life and pious conuersation, she yielded her
soule vp to her heauenly spouse, about the
yeare of Christ, six hundred threescore and
sixteene. She had also a brother called *Meresine*, a man of great holynes of life, liuing
about the same tyme, of whome there is
made often mention in our ancient Histo-
riographers of Britany and England.

D   *The eighteenth Day*.

Petrus in
Catalog.
l.2.cap.
88. Vin-
cent.in
speculo.l.
23.cap.2.
3.4.& 5.
Molan.
& Mart.
Rom.hac
die.

*

Adam
Bremens.
in hist.
Suetica.l.
2.cap.22.

AT *Sutrium* in *Tuscany* the Deposition of
S. Deicola Abbot and Confessor, who
borne in *Scotland* of a noble parentage, and
hearing of the vertues and sanctity of *S. Columbane* the *Great*, then liuing in *Italy*, went
ouer vnto him, became his disciple, and
was afterward made Abbot there of a new
Monastery, called *S. Martins*, erected in a
towne of *Tuscany*, commonly named *Sutrium*,
where in great sanctity and holines of life,
he ended his blessed dayes, about the yeare
of Christ, fiue hundred fourscore and e-
leuen.

THE same day in *Suetia* the Commemoration of *S. Vlfride* Bishop and Martyr,
who being an English man by byrth, and
of great learning & knowledg in the scrip-

tures

tures, went ouer into the low Countreyes firſt, and thence into *Suetia* to preach the Chriſtian faith, which when he had done moſt feruently, and with great fruite of his holy labours for ſome yeares, he was there finally put to death, by the enemyes of Chriſt, and ſo obtayned a palme of martyrdome, about the yeare of Chriſt, one thouſand thirty and foure.

Cranʒ. in Metrop. & Baron.in Annal. ad annū citat.

E   *The ninteenth Day.*

AT *VVorceſter* the depoſition of *S. VVolſtan* Biſhop and Confeſſour, who being brought vp from his youth in the Abbey of *Peterburrow*, and afterward made a monke in the Monaſtery of *VVorceſter*, was finally created Biſhop of the ſame Citty in the tyme of K. Edward the Confeſſour, but being after depoſed, through falſe & ſlaunderous accuſations, by *K. VVilliam* the Conquerour, and Biſhop *Lanfranke*, was by a miracle that himſelfe wrought at *S. Edwardes* body in *VVeſtminſter*, in the preſence of many people, againe reſtored to his Biſhopricke, where in very great ſanctity and holines of life, he perſeuered to the end of his venerable dayes, which happened in the yeare of Chriſt, one thouſand nynty and fiue, and was buryed in his owne Cathedrall Church of *VVorceſter*.

Matth. VVeſt. an. 1095. *& Mat. Pariſ. eodē an. Pol.Vir. l.* 9. *Sur tom.* 1. *Malmeſ. &Florēt in hiſt. Calend. ſec. vſū Sarum hac die, & alij omnes.*

B   This

This day was afterward cōmãded to be kept
holy, in his memory, throughout England.

THE fame day in *Suetia* the paſſiō of *S.He-*
ry Martyr & Biſhop of *Opſlo*, who going
out of England,to preach the faith of Chriſt
in thoſe partes,was honourably intertayned
of the King of *Suetia*, by whoſe counſell &
direc̃ion he made war againſt the *Finlanders*
& ſubdued thē,wherby the whole coūntrey
of *Finland* was cōuerted to the Chriſtiā faith
& he became their Apoſtle. He was afterward ſlayne by the Pagā people of the ſame
Countrey, being ſtoned to death , about the
yeare of Chriſt , one thouſand, one hundred
fifty and one. His body was afterward
tranſlated to *Opslo* , and there kept in his
Cathedrall Church vntil the dayes of *Martyn*
Luther , when as his ſacred Reliques were
prophaned,beatē to duſt,& caſt into the ayre

F   *The twentith* Day.

AT *Ramſey-Abbey* in the Ile of Ely the Cōmemoratiō of *S.Elſled* Virgin & Abbeſſe,
who deſcēded of a noble family,& daughter
to *Ethelwold* an Earle in the Preuince of the
Eaſt-Angles, after her Fathers death,contēned
all worldly & tranſitory prefermēts,& became a Nunne in the Monaſtery of *Ramſey*,
which her ſaid Father had lately founded,
vnder the Gouermēt of *S. Merwyne* then Ab-

beſſe

beſſe therof, after whoſe deſceaſe, & *Eluyne*
that ſucceeded her, ſhe was choſen *Gouerneſſe*
of that houſe,& confirmed in office by holy
King *Edgar* of bleſſed memory,wherin ſhe ſo
excelled in all kind of vertue , workes of
mercy , & Monaſticall diſcipline, that her
name was famous throughout Englād,both
aliue & dead. It happened vpō a tyme,before
ſhe was choſen Abbeſſe, that being in the
Church at Mattins,before day,with the reſt
of her ſiſters,& going into the middeſt according to the cuſtome, to read a leſſon , the
candle wherwith ſhe ſaw to read,chāced to
be put out,& therupon wanting light, there
came frō the fingers of her right hād ſuch an
exceding brightneſſe vpō the ſuddaine, that
not only herſelfe,but all the reſt of theQuire
alſo might read by it. Another time alſo
it fell out (her charity being ſo exceeding
great & bountifull towards the poore) that
through the large reliefe of the needy, her
coffers were greatly emptied,in ſo much that
the Procuratour of the houſe,did checke her
ſomwhat ſharply for exceſſiue lauiſhnes. She
with many teares,was ſilent & made moane
to her ſupreme Lord, crauing his aſſiſtance
herin : And her prayers were not in vayne.
For the empty cheſtes were againe miraculouſly filled as before by Gods gracious re-
compence & approbation of her charitable
beneficence & liberality . She died in all

Monaſt.
Ramſ.
in vitis
SS.
Mulierū
Angl.
*pag.*242.

ſan-

sanctimony and holines of life: about the
yeare of Chrift nyne hundred fourfcore
and twelue,& was buryed in our B. Ladye
Church of the fame Monaftery, which he
Father had alfo built.

G   The one and twentith Day.

A T *Virdune* in *France* the depofition o
S. *Malcalline* Abbot and Confeffour
who being an Irifhman by byrth, and de
fcended of a noble ftocke, went ouer int
France in his youth; and there entring int
a Monaftery, became firft a monke of the
order of S. *Benedict*, and afterward was mad
Abbot of *Michells* at *Virdune*, where in ver
great fanctity of life and other vertues, ef
pecially in the exercife of Monafticall difci
pline, in a good old age, he gaue vp hi
foule to reft,about the yeare of Chrift, nyn
hundred threefcore and eighteene.His bod
was buried in the fame Monaftery, wher
the fame is yet preferued with great honou
& veneration of the inhabitants therabout

A   The two and twentith Day.

A T *VVinchefter* in *Hampshire* the Comme
moration of S. *Brituald* Confeffour an
Bifhop of that Sea, who of a monke of the
venerable order of S.*Benedict*, was ordayne

                                    Bifho

Side notes (left margin):

Append.
ad Cron.
Frodoar.
Abb.
Arnold.
VVion
l.3. ligni
vitæ in
Mart.
Bened.
hac die.

*

Matth.
VVeft.
an.1045.
in hift.
Angl.

Bishop of *VVinchester*; In which dignity after he had continued for many years, full of singular vertue and holines of life , he ended his venerable old dayes, about the yeare of Christ, one thousand and fourty . He liued in the beginning of King *Edward* the *Confessors* raigne ; of whome it is wrytten, that he had a miraculous reuelation , how that he saw the said King *Edward*, being yet in his Mothers wombe , elected King, crowned and annoynted by *S. Peter* the Apostle , and ordayned to raigne foure & twenty yeares, & finally to dy without issue. Moreouer in that vision he seeming to demaund of *S. Peter*, who should raigne next after him , it was answered him againe, *That the Kingdome of England was Gods Kingdome, and he then would prouide a King for it.* His body was buried at *VVinchester*, wherat many miracles , by his merits , are recorded to haue byn wrought.

Pol. Vir. l. 8. Arnold. VVion l.2. ligni vitæ in Catalog. Episcop. VVintonienfium.

B *The three and twentith* Day.

AT *Mailros* vpon the Riuer-banke of *Tyne* in the Kingdome of the *Northumbers*, the Commemoration of *S. Boyfill* Confessour and Abbot of that famous Monastery, wherin *S. Cuthbert* was brought vp, and vnder whome he first put on his Religious habit, whofe great holynes of life , and fin-

✱

Ven. Bed. in vita S. Cuthber. cap. 6. & 8.

gular

Et lib. 4.
cap. 27.
& lib. 5.
cap. 10.
hist.
Angl.

gular vertues especially in the gift .of Prophesy , haue byn famous in tymes past throughout our whole Iland. And when he had for many yeares most exemplarly gouerned that Monastery , being by an angell admonished of his death, he ioyfully departed this transitory life, about the yeare of Christ, six hundred threscore and ten and was buryed in the same Manastery. *Cuthbert* succeeding him in his office.

C   *The foure & twentith* Day.

Io. Capg.
in Catal.
Sanctoru
Britan.
Antiq.
Monu-
meta Ec.
Beneuet.
Triuph.
Eccl. Col.
Anglic.
Roma.

AT *Beneuentum* in *Italy* the passion of *S. Sophias* Bishop & Martyr, who being a noble Britan by birth & sonne to *Guelleicus* King of *North-wales*, became first a moke, & then Abbot of a Monastery , which himselfe had built in *Vales* with his owne inheritace; and lastly hauing byn three tymes at *Hierusalem* to visit the holy sepulcher of Christ, & seauen tymes at *Rome* on pilgrimage, was for his knowne vertues and innocency of life, created Bishop of *Beneuentum* in *Italy*, where stading at the altar at Masse, was by a wicked fellow in hatred of Christian beliefe thrust through the body with a laúce , & so receyued a crowne of Martyrdom about the yeare of Christ , foure hundred & nynty, & in the raigne of King *Arthur* of *Brittany*, whose

Kinsman

Kinſeman he is ſaid to haue byn.

THE ſame day in *Monmouthſhire* , the feſtiuity of *S. Cadocke* Martyr , nephew to
Bragham King of *Brecknocke*, and Coſyn to *S.*
Dauid Biſhop of *Meneuia*, whoſe memory is
famous, euen vntill this day in our Iland of
Great Brittany, eſpecially in the forſaid Prouince of *Momouth* in *South-VVales*, where there
are yet remayning Churches & Chappells
dedicated in his honour. He ſuffered about
the yeare of Chriſt 500.

Ex anti.
Monum.
Prou.
Monum.
& in vita
S. Keyn.
Virg.
apud R.
Bucklād,
de vit.
SS. Mu-
lierum
Angl.

D   *The fiue & twentith Day.*

THE Conuerſion of the glorious Apoſtle
S. Paul, by whome our Iland of great
Brittany hath receyued no ſmall fauour.
For that according to diuers ancient wryters , in the fourth yeare of *Nero* the Emperour his raigne (the Iewes being by his *Edict*
baniſhed *Rome*)he perſonally came into *Brit-*
tany , and there preached the faith of Chriſt.
Venantius Fortunatus a moſt holy and learned
mā wryting aboue a thouſand yeares agone
of *S. Paules* perigrination, ſaith of him:

> ⎧ *Tranſijt Oceanum , vel qua facit Inſula* ⎫
> ⎨   *portum,*   ⎬
> ⎩ *Quaſque Britannus habet oras, atque vltima* ⎭
>   *Thule .*

After this he returned againe to Rome

Theodo-
ret.in
Epiſt.
ad Tim.
& in
Pſal. 116.
& lib. 9.
de curād.
Græc.
affect.
Sophron.
Serm. de
Natal.
Apoſt.
Arnol.
Mirma
in Theat.

where at laſt both S. *Peter* and himſelfe, on one, and the ſelfe ſame day, receiued the reward of their labours, by Martyrdome, in the yeare of Chriſt, threeſcore and nyne.

THE ſame day in *Ireland* the Commemoration of *S. Eoglodius* Monke and Confeſſour, who deſcended of a noble parentage in that Kingdome, and diſciple to *S. Columbe* the *Great*, came with him ouer into *Scotland*, and was his coadiutor in teaching and preaching the Chriſtian faith to the *Pictes*, that then inhabited that Countrey, where famous for ſanctity of life, and other vertues, finally reſted in our Lord, about the yeare of Chriſt, foure hundred fourſcore and ſeauen.

E   *The ſix and twentith* Day.

AT *Barking* in *Eſſex* the Commemoration of *S. Theorithgid* Virgin, who deſcended of a very noble Brittiſh ſtocke, became a Religious woman in the Monaſtery of the forſaid towne of *Barking* vnder the care of *S. Edilburge* the firſt Abbeſſe therof, & ſiſter to *S. Erconwald* Biſhop of London, who had newly founded that Abbey; where in great ſanctimony of life, and feruour of ſpirit, ſhe gaue vp her bleſſed ſoule to her heauenly ſpouſe, about the yeare of Chriſt, ſix hundred ſeauenty and eight: vnto whome S. *Edil-burge* appearing, as ſhe lay on her death-bed, told her, with moſt ſweet and comfortable words, that the tyme now drew neere, that ſhe ſhould be deliuered out of the priſon of this world, into the ioyes of eternall bliſſe.

F *The ſeauen & twentith Day.*

IN *Scotland* the Commemoration of S. *Palladius* Biſhop and Confeſſour, who being a Roman by birth, was ſent thither in the yeare, foure hundred and eleuen, by *Pope Celeſtine*, to reduce that Nation from certaine errors and hereſyes, which *Pelagius* the Brittan had ſowed among them; where being ordayned Biſhop and Primate of *Scotland*, he inſtructed the people for many yeares in all good learning and other Catholicke cerimonyes, according to the Roman vſe; and laſtly full of venerable old age, in great ſanctity and holines of life, he gaue vp his ſoule to reſt, about the yeare of Chriſt, foure hundred and fourty.

Proſp. in Chron. an.Dom. 431 . & 434 Bed. l. 1. cap. 13. Barō. tom . 4. Annal . an 429.

*

G *The eight & twentith Day.*

IN the ile of *VVight* in Hampſhire, the Commemoration of the Saintes called *Arwaldi*, Brothers and Martyrs, who being

*

two

Vē. Beda
lib. 4.
Hiſtor.
Angl.
c. 16.
Matth.
VVeſt.
an. 687.

two noble yong men , defcended of the
bloud Royall of the South Saxons, & brothers to the King of that Iland , were taken
prifoners by *Ceadwall* King of the *Geuiſſes* &
VVeſtſaxons who being but newly baptized,
were by him commanded to be ſlaine in the
yeare of Chriſt , ſix hundred fourfcore &
ſeauen.Their bodyes were decently,interred
in a Church of that Prouince by *S.Cymber* Ab
bot of *Redford* in *Hampſhire* , by whome they
had a little before byn baptized&inſtructed
in the Chriſtian faith , wherat in ſigne of
their Innocency , it pleafed God forthwith
to worke miracles.

A   *The nine & twentith* Day.

Pol.Vir.
l.1.hiſt.
Angl.
Gul.
Neubrig.
in hiſt.
Mart.
Rom.
Molan.
in addit.
ad vſuar.
& alij
hac die.

IN *Cornwall* the depofition of *S.Gildas* Confeſſor and Abbot of *Bangor* in *North-wales* ,
who after he had written many famous
bookes as well for the illuſtratiō of the Vni-
uerſall,as our Primitiue Church of *Brittany*,
became an Eremite , & lead a moſt ſtrict,
and feuere kind of life in the mountaynes of
Cornwall, where full of venerable old yeares
he reſted in our Lord, about the yeare of
Chriſt 581.He is famous yet among the *Cor-*
niſhmen ofEnglād efpecially for his writings,
amongſt whome alſo there haue byn many
Churches & altars dedicated, in his honour.

B

B   *The thirtith* Day.

AT *Fulda* in the higher *Germany* the deposition of *S. Annichade* Confeffour,
who defcended of a noble parentage in *Scotland*, forfooke the world, went ouer the fea,
and trauailing into *Germany*, at laft became a
monke in the Monaftery of *Fulda*, which
had byn founded by *S. Boniface* an Englifhman, for the Scottifh nation;where liuing a
moft Godly and exemplar life , when he
was ready to die , a great light was feene,
and Angelicall voyces heard in his Cell, the
which continued a long tyme after at his
Sepulcher, and were heard of all that came
to vifit it . He died about the yeare of
Chrift , one thoufand fourty and three: and
lieth buryed at *Fulda* in the forfaid Monaftery.

*Io.Trit.
de vir.
Illuftr.
ord. D.
Benedict.
l.3. cap.
244.Pet.
Cratepol.
de Epif.
Germ.
VVion
in Mart.
Bened.*

C   *The one & thirtith* Day

IN *Scotland* the Commemoration of *S.
Adaman* Prieft and Confeffour , who
being Prefect of the Monaftery of Nunnes
in the towne of *Coludon* (now called
Coldingham) in the Marches of *Scotland*,
was of fuch rare and fingular aufterity

*Bed. l.4.
hifto.
Angl.
cap. 25.*

of

Tritem.
de Vir.
Illuſtr. l.
3. cap,
124. Ioã.
Leſt. Epi.
Roſ. l. 4.
de geſt.
Scot.

of life, that it is wrytten of him, that he taſted meate but only twice in the weeke, to wit, Sundayes and Thurſdayes; and often ſpent whole dayes and nights in prayer and contemplation, vntill his dying day; which happened about the yeare of Chriſt, ſix hundred and fourſcore. This man is different from the other *S. Adaman* of the ſame name, that inſtructed the Scottiſhmen, about the obſeruation of Eaſter, whoſe feſtiuity is put downe afterward vpon the ſecond day of September.

T H E

THE
MONETH
OF FEBRVARY.

D   *The first Day.*

Laur.
Dunel.
in eius
vita apud
Sur.tom.
1. Catal.
Scripto.
Britan.
Marian.
Scotus in
Chronic.
Girald.
Cambr.
in Histor.
Chron.
Hyber.
Rom.
Martyr.
Mol. &
alij om-
nes hac
die.

N *Ireland* the depofition of *S. Brigit* Virgin, borne in the County of *Kildare* in a towne called *Fochart*, who in teftimony of her virginity, touching the wood of an Altar, the fame prefently in the fight of many people, became greene againe, and began to bud forth a frefh: and a ter many other miracles done, in figne of her fanctimony and innocency of life, fhe gaue vp her foule to her heauenly fpoufe about the yeare of Chrift, fiue hundred and fourty. There was a fayre Church erected in her honour in the Citty of *London*, which vntill this day is yet remayning, commonly called *S. Brides*, as alfo many others both in

Eng-

England, *Ireland* and *Scotland*. And in the ile of *Man*, where it is recorded that somtymes she liued, there is an ancient Towne & Church of her Name, ftill retayning the vulgar denomination of *S. Brides*. Her body was interred at the Towne of *Dunne*, in the Prouince of *Vlfter*, in the tombe, togeather with the venerable bodyes of *S. Patricke* and and *S. Columbe*, which was afterward miraculoufly reueyled to the Bifhop of that place, as he was praying one night late in the Church, about the yeare of Chrift 1176. ouer which, there fhined a great light : Of whome one wryteth thus.

* A liter.
Hi tres
in Du-
no, &c.

$$\left\{ \begin{array}{l} In \text{ * } Burgo\ Duno, tumulo\ tumulantur\ in\ vno, \\ Brigida, Patricius, at\acute{q}ue\ Columba\ pius. \end{array} \right\}$$

The fame Monument was afterward deftroyed in the raigne of *K. Henry* the eight, by the Lord *Leonard Gray* Viceroy or Deputy of that Kingdome, to the great lamentation of all *Ireland*.

E   *The fecond Day.*

Sigeb. in
Chron.
Bed. l. 2.
hift.
Angl.
cap. 4. 6.

AT *Canterbury* the depofition of *S. Laurence* Confeffour and Bifhop of that Sea, who comming into England with *S. Auguftine* and his fellowes to preach the Chriftian faith, fucceeded him in his Sea of *Canterbury*, which when he had gouerned ied moſt worthily, for diuers yeares, in ʒreat ſanctity and holines of life, he reſted n our Lord, about the yeare of Chriſt, ſix ıundred and ſeauenteene, and was buryed in the Porch of the Church at *Canterbury*, ıeere to the body of *S. Auguſtine*, at whoſe ːombe, it pleaſed God afterward to worke many miracles.

THE ſame day at *Hohemburge* in the higher Germany, the depoſition of *S. Burchard* Biſhop & Confeſſour, brother to *S. Swithin* of *VVincheſter*, who being firſt a mōke in England, went ouer into Germany to *S. Boniface* Archbiſhop of *Mentz*, and thence to *Rome*, where by Pope *Zachary* he was conſecrated Biſhop of *VVirtzburgh* in *Franconia*, and ſent to that Sea : where after he had ſpent fourty yeares in propagating the Chriſtian faith, ended his bleſſed dayes in a monaſtery at *Hohemburge*, which himſelfe had founded, about the yeare of Chriſt, ſeauen hundred fourſcore and eleuen.

& 7.
Matth.
VVeſt.
in hiſt.
Pol.Vir.
l.2. cap.
4. 6. 7.
Sur.tom.
1.de vit.
SS.

Egilwar-
dus in
eius vita
apudSur.
tom.5.14
Octob.
VVion
in Notis
ad Mart.
Bened.14
Octob.

F   *The third Day.*

AT Hamburge neere *Ely* in *Cambridgshire*, the depoſition of *S. VVereburge* Virgin, daughter to *VVulherus* King of *Mercia*, who deſpiſing all worldly delightes, became a

Re-

Author Cōtinua. hiſt. ven̄. Bed.
Vincent. inſpec. l. 5.cap.28.
Rob. Buckl. in eius vita lib.
M. S. de vitis SS. mulier.
Angl. Stous in Annal. ſub Gul. Rufo. anno. 5.

Religious woman in the Monaſtery of Nunnes at *Ely*, vnder *S. Audry* her aunt, and Abbeſſe therof, where in all kind of exemplar good life and ſanctimony, ſhe gaue vp her ſoule to her heauenly ſpouſe in the yeare of Chriſt, ſix hundred ſeauenty & fiue. Vpon her death-bed ſhe commanded her body to be buryed at *Hamburge*, but contrary to her will it was carried to the Monaſtery of *Trickingham*, where the gates faſt locked, the ſame was kept and watched very carefully. But ſee a wonder. They which were appointed to watch the ſame, fell into a deepe ſleepe, ſo as the people of *Hamburge* comming in the night for the body, the gates, both of the Monaſtery and Church, were opened of themſelues without mens hands; and taking it away without any reſiſtance, they interred it at *Hamburge*, as before her death ſhe requeſted. The ſame being taken vp againe, nyne yeares after her death, was found altogeather vncorrupt, her very garments not ſo much as any whit periſhed: where God teſtifying her Holines by many miracles, was therby greatly glorified in this his Virgin. It is recorded that her body was afterwards tranſlated to *Cheſter*, where in the tyme of K. *VVilliam Rufus* was erected a goodly Monaſtery in her honour, by Syr *Hugh Lupus* Earle of *Cheſter*, and *S. Anſelme* Archbiſhop of *Cāterbury*, in the yeare of Chriſt 1092

The

G   The fourth Day.

AT *Sempingham* in *Lincolneshire* the depoition of *S. Gilbert* Confeffour, who defcended of an honourable parentage, was the firft founder of the Order of Religous men in England called *Gilbertines*, where he built thirteene Monafteryes of that order, to wit, eight of women, and fiue of men. And after a moft godly and fainctly life, full of venerable old yeares, he departed this world, about the yeare of Chrift one thouland one hundred and fifty. His body was buryed in the faid Monaftery of *Sempingham* neere *Deeping* in *Lincolnfhire*, where for a long tyme it was kept with great veneration, for the often Miracles that were wrought therat:

THE fame day at *Huncourt* in the Territory of *Cambray* in *Hennalt*, the paffion of *S. Liephard* Bifhop and Martyr, who borne in our iland of Great Brittany, and there made Bifhop in her primitiue Church, wét on pilgrimage to *Rome*, and in his returne honward foure miles from *Cambray*, was flayne by certayne pagan theeues. His feaft is celebrated in the Church of *Cambray* on this day with an office of three leffons.

Molan.
in addit.
ad 1 fuar.
Gul.
Neubrig.
l.1.cap.16
Arnold.
W*ion in*
Martyr.
Bened. &
alij ones
hac die.

Molar. in
addit. ad
1 fuar. &
in Indic.
SS. Belgij
Hereb. in
faftis SS.

C   A

A   The fifth Day.

Hereber-
tus in
fastis
SS. hac
die.

AT *Lewis* in *Suffex* the depofition of *S.*
Iohn Conteffour, of the Order of Chanons-Regular, whofe integrity of life and
holy Conuerfation hath byn famous in
tymes paft, both at home and abroad. His
life is extant in wrytten hand in a Monaftery of the *Low-Countreys*, as teftifieth the
Reuerend Father *Herebertus Rofweydus* of the
Society of Iefus in the preface to his worke
intituled, *Fafti Sanctorum*, whofe feftiuity he
putteth downe on this day.

Gul.
Malmef.
in eius
vita.
Io. Capg.
in Catal.
SS. Bri-
taniæ.

THe fame day at *Glaftenbury* in *Somerfetshire*
the Comemoration of S. *Indractus* Martyr, who defcended of the bloud-royall of
Ireland and coming thence on pilgrimage to
Glaftenbury in England, with a further intention to vifit *Rome*, was with nyne other
Companions, and his owne fifter, called
Drufa, flayne at *Stapwich* in the fame Prouince
by certayne wicked fellowes of the VVeftfaxons, about the yeare of Chrift, feauen hundred & eight, whofe bodyes, being brought
to *Glaftenbury* Abbey with great folemnity,
were there very honorably interred, wherat
it pleafed God, in token of their Innocency
to worke Miracles.

B

B   *The sixt Day.*

AT *Rome* the Commemoration of Blessed *Inas* King of the *VVestsaxons* and
Confessour, who leauing the care of his
Kingdome to his kinsman *Ethelhard*, went
to *Rome*, where he erected a Schole for the
English nation, as also a fayre Church therto
belonging in honour of our blessed Lady,
neere to the hospitall of *Sanctus Spiritus*, in
the *Burgo* or suburbes of *S.Peters*, both which
were afterwards consumed by fire. He
was the first King of our nation, that ordayned throughout his Dominions, that
euery family should once a yeare giue a
penny to the Church of *Rome*, in honour
of *S. Peter* the Apostle, which contribution
continued euer synce, euen vntill our dayes,
commonly called by the name of *Peter-pence.*
He founded the Abbey of *VVells* with the
Cathedrall Church, dedicating the same to
God and *S. Andrew* the Apostle. He new
builded also the Abbey of *Glastenbury*, which
was the fourth building of that Monastery.
Besides, the said Godly King did there in
like manner, erect a Chappell, plated all
ouer with siluer and guilt, with ornaments
also and vessels (saith the Story) of gould
and siluer. To the building of which Chap-

*Pol. Vir.
l.4.histo.
cap.5.
Matth.
VVest.
an.Dom.
727.Guli
Malmes.
de rebus
gestis Re-
gū Ang.
in Ina.
Arnol.
VVion
l.4. ligni
vitæ.
Io. Sto.
in Anna.
Angl.
de regno
VVest-
saxonum.
Tabulæ
Eccl. S.
Petri
Romæ.*

*

pell, he gaue, in weight, two thouſand ſix
hundred forty pounds of ſiluer; and to the
aultar, two hundred threeſcore and foure
pounds of gold : A Chalice with the patin,
ten pound of gold : a Cenſar eight pound:
two candleſtickes, twelue pound and a halfe
of ſiluer : a couer for the Miſſall, or (as then
they vſed to call it) the Ghoſpell-booke,
twenty pounds : veſſels for wyne and water
to the altar, thirty pounds of gold : a holy
water pot, twenty pound of ſiluer : Images
of our Sauiour, our Bl. Lady, & the twelue
Apoſtles, one hundred threeſcore and fifteene pound of ſiluer, and twenty eight
pound of gold: A pall for the altar, and ornaments for the Monks of gold and pretious ſtones curiouſly wrought. All
which he gaue (ſaith the Author) to that
Monaſtery; but the ſame was afterward in
this laſt age, by commandement of K. Henry
the eight, defaced, ſpoyled, and robbed of
all the forſaid, and infinite other treaſure.
And after all this, the forſaid King Inas
going in perſon to Rome, and performing
the things aboue mentioned, tooke finally
vpon him the habit of a Monke, where in
great ſanctity and holines of life, he ended
his bleſſed dayes, about the yeare of Chriſt
727. and was there buryed in the entrance
of S. Peters Church, as the ancient Tables &
Records therof do declare.

C　　The seauenth Day.

AT *Luca* in *Italy* the deposition of S. *Ri-chard* King and Confessour, sonne to *Lotharius* King of *Kent*, who, for the loue of Christ, taking vpon him a long peregrination, went to *Rome* for deuotion to that Sea, and in his way homward, died at *Luca*, about the yeare of Christ, seauen hundred and fifty, where his body is kept vntill this day with great veneration, in the Oratory or Chappell of S. *Frigidian*, and adorned with an Epitaph both in verse and prose. That in verse is this.

Hic Rex Richardus *requiescit* Sceptrifer
　almus;
Rex suit Anglorum , *regnum tenet ille*
　Po*l-rum:*
Regnum dimisit, pro Christo cuncta reli-
　quit
Ergo Richardum *nobis dedit* Anglia
　Sanctum.
Hic genitor Sancta Walburgis *Virginis*
　alma,
Et Willebaldi *Sancti* , *simul* & Wini-
　baldi;
Suffragijs quorum det nobis regna Polorum.

THe same day at *Londo* the deposition of S. *Augulus* Bishop & Martyr, who in the per-

Sur tom.
1. vit.SS.
Democh.
l.2.de sa-
crif.Mis-
s.Mart.
Rom.
W*ion l.*
4. ligni
vita
Mola. &
alij ones
hac die.

Martyr Rom. Marcellin. l. 18. Calend. fec. vsum Sarū & Molan. hac die.

Sigeb. in Chron. 849. Almannus Monach. de eius Tranſlat. Molan in addit. ad Vſuard. hac die Mæna-log. Græ. 21. Maij.

ſecution of Dioclefian the Emperour, for peaching the Chriſtian faith in our Iland of Great Brytany, was put to death, by the enemyes of truth, about the yeare of Chriſt three hundred & fiue, a little after the death of S. *Alban.*

IN like manner the fame day at *Rhemes* in France the Tranſlation of S. *Helena* Mother to Conſtantine the Great, who borne in *Colcheſter* of Eſſex, according to the ancient traditions of the Britans, and daughter to *Coelus* Prince of Britany, was famous for building of Churches in honour of Chriſt, and his Saintes. She died at *Rome* when ſhe was fourſcore yeares of age, and was afterward on this day tranſlated to *Rhemes,* where her ſacred reliques are kept with great veneration. Her Memory hath byn very famous in tymes paſt in the Greeke Church, whoſe celebrity is there kept vpon the 22. of May, togeather with her Sonne *Conſtantine.*

D   *The eight Day.*

AT *Strenſhalt* in the Kingdome of the *Northumbers,* the Commemoration of of S. *Edelfled* Virgin & Abbeſſe, daughter to *Oſwyn* King of the fame *Prouince,* who, by her Father being dedicated vnto God for a fa-

mous

mous victory, which he obtayned againft the cruell *Penda* King of the *Mercians*, was cōmitted for her education to *S. Hilda* Abbeſſe of a Monaſtery amongſt the *Northumbers*, called *Hartefey*; and when ſhe came to riper yeares, ſhe founded for her ſelfe another *Nunry* in the ſame Kingdome, called *Strenshalt*, and was made Abbeſſe therof, where in all kind of profound humility & ſanctity of life, ioyned with other vertues, ſhe gaue vp her ſoule to her heauēly ſpouſe, about the yeare of Chriſt ſix hundred and ſeauenty. Her body was buryed in the ſame Monaſtery, wherat for many ages following it pleaſed God to worke wonderous miracles.

Bed. l. 4. cap. 26. VVion. l. 4. ligni vitæ. Ingulph. de Croyland. Hereb. Roſweyd in faſt. SS.

E   *The ninth Day.*

IN the territory of *Liege* in the lower *Germany*, the paſſion of *S. Menigold* Martyr, who borne in England, and deſcended of a very noble parentage, became firſt a Captaine in the French and German warres, & afterward an Eremite; vnto whome *Arnulph* the Emperour gaue a little territory neere to the banke of the riuer of *Mofa*, where he built himſelf a cottage or Oratory for his deuotion. And as he was going one day to the Church, was ſlaine in hatred of Chriſtiā

Molā. in Indiculo SS. Belgij & in addit. ad Vſuard, hac die.

faith,

faith, by certaine notorious malefactors &
enemyes therof, about the yeare of Chrift,
nyne hundred. His body was afterward
tranflated to *Huis*, neere *Cullen*, vpon the fifteenth day of Iune, where togeather with
the body of *S. Domitian* Bifhop, the fame is
kept with great veneration of the Inhabitants of that place.

F   *The tenth Day.*

+Wiccij

AT *VVorcefter* the Tranflatiō of *S. VVilfrid*
the fecond of that name, Confefſour &
Biſhop of *Torke*, whofe great fanctity and
holines of life it pleafed God to manifeft by
the incorruption of his body, which being
reueyled to *S. Ofwald* Bifhop of *VVorcefter* to
remayne interred in the Monaftery of *Rippon*
in *Torkeshire*, then decayed &deftroyed by the
Danes, was by him fought for & foūd whole
& incorrupt, togeather with the venerable
bodyes of fiue Reuerēd Abbots, *Tillert, Bornyn,*
Albert, Sygred and *VValden*; all which *S. Ofwald*
traflated to his Cathedrall Church of *VVorce-*
fter, & therewith great veneration and honour interred them, wherat it pleafed God
alfo in figne of their fanctity to worke miracles. He died about the yeare of Chrift
feauen hundred & thirty. This *S. VVilfrid* is
different from the other of the fame name,

Ven, Bed.
l. 5. cap.
24. & in
Epitome.
Sur. to .5.
in Vita S.
Ofwaldi
15. Octob.
& alij.

whofe

whofe feftiuity is kept vpon the 12. of *October*.

G *The eleuenth Day.*

AT *Tyre* in *Syria* the Commemoration of Bleffed *VVilliam* Bifhop and Confef-for, who being an Englifhman by byrth, became firft a monke of the venerable Order of *S. Benedict,* and was afterward fent into *Paleftine*, and made *Prior* of the Monaftery of the holy *Sepulcher* in *Hierufalem* : And in the yeare of Chrift one thoufand, one hundred & thirty, he was confecrated the firft Archbifhop of *Tyre* in *Syria* : which function when he had inioyed fix yeares, in all fanctity of life and vertuous conuerfation, he ended there his happy dayes, in the yeare of our Lord, one thoufand one hundred thirty & feauen.

Gul. Tyrius lib.13 cap.23. & l.4. cap. 11. Wion. l. 2. ligni Vitæ, in Catal. Epif. Tyrienfium.

THE fame day in *Brecknockshire* of *VVales* the Commemoration of *S. Canoch* Confeffor, who being fonne to *Braghan* King of *Brecknocke*, & great Vncle to *S. Dauid* Bifhop of *Meneuia*, was very famous for holines of life in thofe partes, about the yeare of Chrift foure hundred fourfcore and twelue ; and whofe memory is yet famous amongft the ancient *Britans* of our Iland, efpecially in *South-wales.* He had a brother called *S. Cadocke*, that was a Martyr, & a fifter named *S. Keyne*, who liued about the fame time, in great o-

Rob. Buckl. l. M.S. de Vitis SS. Mulieru̅ Anglic. in Vita S. Keynæ Virg. fol. 90.

pinion

pinion of fanctity, as the Records of their
liues yet extant, do demonitrate.

A   The twelfth Day.

T item.
l.4.d vir.
Illuftr.
ord.D.
Benedict.
cap. 179.
Matth.
VVeft.
an.738.
VVion.
2.ligni
vitæ.

AT Durham in the Bishopricke, the Commemoration of S. Edilwald Bithop and
Confeffour, who being firit a menke & then
Abbot of the Monaftery of Mailros in the
Kingdome of the Northumbers, was laftly
promoted to the Bithopicke of Lindisferne
(now tranflated to Durham)and fucceeded S.
Edbert in that Sea; which when he had gouerned, like a worthy paftour of his flocke
for almoft fourty yeares, in great fanctity of
life and vertues therto agreeable, full of venerable old yeares, he finally repofed in our
Lord, in the yeare of Chrift, feauen hundred thirty and eight: and was buryed at
Lindisferne.

B   The thirteenth Day.

Matth.
weft. an.
Do. 676,
Vincent.
in fpecul.

AT Ely in Cambridgshire the depofition of
S. Ermenild Queene, wife to VVulherw
King of Mercia, who after the death of her
husband, became a Religious woman in
the Monaftery of Ely, vnder her owne Mother S. Sexburge, who at that tyme was Ab-

beffe

beſſe therof and after her ſaid Mothers deſceaſe, ſhe was elected in her place, where
famous for ſanctimony and holines of life,
ſhe gaue vp her ſoule to her heauenly ſpouſe,
about the yeare of Chriſt, ſix hundred-
threeſcore and eighteene.

ALſo the ſame day at * *VVirtzburgh* in
Germany, the Tranſlation of *S. Kylian*
Biſhop and Martyr, who deſcended of the
bloud-royall of *Ireland*, for the loue he bare
to his neighbour-Countreyes, came thence
with three other Companiōs into *Flaunders*,
& ſo went into Germany, where he was ordayned Biſhop of *VVirtzburgh* : which Sea
when he had held for few yeares, diligently
attending to his flocke, he was ſlayne, togeather with his three forſaid Companions,
by the enemyes of Chriſtian faith in the
yeare of Chriſt, ſix hundred fourſcore and
ſeauenteene. His body being buryed at
VVirtzburgh, was afterward on this day taken
vp, and tranſlated to a more eminent place
of the ſame Church, where before it
lay; but his principall feſtiuity
is celebrated vpon the eight
day of Iuly.

*Litaniæ
ſec. vſum
Sarum.
Molā. in
addit ad
Vſuard.
hac die.*

* Herbi-
polis.

*Petrus
Gaſelin.
in ſuo
Marty-
rologio
hac die.
Democh
l. de ſacrif
Miſſæ
cap.35.
tomo 2.
wion in
Martyr.
Bened.*

C   The fourteenth Day.

Io, Lef.
Epif.
Roffenf.l.
4.de geft.
Scot.
Arnol.
Wion in
addit.
ad l. 3.li-
gni vitæ.

*

IN *Scotland* the Commemoration of *S. Conwane* Contessour, who borne in the same Kingdome, and descended of a noble parentage, despised all pleasures of this world, & retyring himself to a Monastery, became a Religious man of the Order of *S. Benedict* in one of the Ilands of *Orcades* neere *Scotland,* where in all kind of exemplar good life, learning and vertuous conuersation, in a good old age, ended his blessed dayes, about the yeare of Christ, six hundred and fourty. His memory hath byn famous, euen vntill these our dayes, throughout the whole Iland of Great Britany, but especially amongst the Scottish nation: amongst whome also, diuers Churches and altars haue in tymes past, byn erected and dedicated in his honour.

D   The fifteenth Day.

AT *Vexouia* in *Goth-land* the deposition of *S. Sigfride* Bishop and Confessour, who being Archdeacon of the Church of *Yorke,* was sent by King *Alfred* of *England* into *Gothia,* to preach to the pagan people of that

Con-

Countrey, whome he conuerted to the Chriſtian faith, togeather with their King *Olaus*, and ſo became their Apoſtle. He was afterward made Biſhop of *Vexouia* and *Metropolitan* of Gothia, which Sea when he had gouerned moſt worthily for many yeares in great ſanctity and holines of life, full of venerable old age, he went to reſt in our Lord, about the yeare of Chriſt, one thouſand and two, and was buryed in his owne Cathedrall Church of *Vexouia*, where his body was kept with great honour and veneration of that nation, for the myracles that were wrought therat, vntill theſe later yeares of ſchiſmes and hereſyes in thoſe Prouinces.

Ioan. &
Olaus
Magnus
in hiſt.
Goth.l. 7
cap.16.19
& 20.
Molan in
addit. ad
Vſuard.
hac die

E   *The ſixteenth Day.*

AT *VVerdt* in *Cleeu-land* the depoſition of *S. Tancone* Biſhop and Martyr, who borne of a noble bloud in *Scotland*, was firſt a monke, and then Abbot of a Monaſtery in the ſame Kingdome, called *Amarbaricke*, and being very deſirous to help his neighbour-Countreys for their ſoules health, went ouer into *Flaunders*, and thence into *Cleeu-land*, and there was made Biſhop of *VVerdt*, where preaching continually and propagating the Chriſtian faith, he was at laſt ſlayne by the barbarous and incredulous

Ioan.
Leſlæus
Epiſcop.
Roſ. l. 5.
de geſt.
Scot.
Cranʒ. in
Metrop.
cap.22.l.
1.VVion
hac die in
Martyr.
Bened.

people

people of that Prouince in hatred therof
about the yeare of Chrift, eight hundred
His body was buryed at *VVerdt*.

F   *The feauenteenth Day*.

A T *Lindisferne* in the Kingdome of the
Northumbers, the depoſition of *S. Finan*
biſhop and Confeſſour, who being firſt a
monke of *S. Columbes* Monaſtery in the Iland
of *Hoy* by *Scotland*, was ordayned Biſhop of
Lindisferne, and ſucceeded *S. Aidan* in that Sea,
where in all kind of godly conuerſation &
ſanctity of life, he ended his bleſſed dayes
about the yeare of Chrift, ſix hundred and
threeſcore. He is called the Apoſtle of the
Mercians (or middle Engliſhmen) by whoſe
endeauours in preaching, a great part of that
Kingdome was firſt conuerted to Chriſtian
faith , togeather with their Prince *Peda*,
ſonne to the notable perſecutor *Penda*, who
with many great Earles & Lords of *Mercia*,
was at the inſtance of holy King *Oſwyn* of
Northumberland , by him baptized , at
* *Barwicke*, as *S. Bede* and other Engliſh Hiſtoriographers do recount. There are many
Churches both in England and *Scotland* dedicated in his honour.

*Beda l. 3.
hiſt.
Angl.
cap. 21. 22
& 25.
Gul.
Malmeſ.
in hiſtor.
Martyr.
Rom.
Molan.
& alij
omnes.
hac die.*

**Ad Mu-
rum.*

G

G   The eighteenth Day.

AT *Saltzburge* in *Bauaria* the Commemoration of *S. Iohn* Confeſſour & Biſhop of that Sea, who being a monke of an old Monaſtery neere *VVinchelſea* in *Suſſex*, went ouer into *Germany* to *S. Boniface* Archbiſhop of *Mentz*, with whome he remained for a tyme, and after going to *Rome*, was by Pope *Gregory* the third created the firſt Biſhop of *Saltzvurge*, and ſent thither: which ſea when he had moſt worthily gouerned and preached the Chriſtian faith for fourteene yeares togeather, and brought many thouſands to the true worſhip of God, in great ſanctity of life and venerable old age, he ended his bleſſed dayes, about the yeare of Chriſt ſeauen hundred fifty and ſeauen, and was buryed in his owne Cathedrall Church of *Saltzburge*.

*

Ioan. Tritem. lib. 4. cap. 105. Wion l. 2. ligni vitæ in Catal. Epiſ. Saltzburg.

A   The ninteenth Day.

AT *Haguſtalde* in the Kingdome of the *Northumbers*, the Commemoration of *S. Acca* Confeſſour and Biſhop of that Sea, who being one of *S. VVillebrord* his coadiutors, and going ouer with him into *Saxony*
and

*

Bed. l. 5. cap. 21. 22. 23. & 24.

Math.
VVeſt.
an. 734.
& 792.
Molā. in
Indiculo
SS.Belgij

and *Frizeland* for the conuerſion of thoſe nations; was ſent backe againe into Englād to the Conſecration of *S. Switbert*, and there detayned and ordayned Biſhop of *Haguſtalde*, by *S. VVilſrid* the ſecond of *Torke* : which paſtorall function whē he had moſt worthily performed for many yeares, in great ſanctity of life and godly conuerſation, full of venerable old age, he repoſed in our Lord, about the yeare of Chriſt, ſeauen hundred thirty and ſix.

B   The twentith Day.

Pol. Vir.
l.4.biſto.
Angl.
Molan.in
addit . ad
Vſuard.
Rob.
Buckl.
in eius
vita l.M.
S. pag.
150.

IN the ile of *Thanet* in *Kent* the depoſition of *S. Mildred* Virgin, daughter to *Merualdus* King of *Mertta*, who contemning the vayne pleaſures of this world, went ouer, in her tender yeares, into *France*, and there dedicaed her ſelfe to God in a Monaſtery of Virgins, at *Kale*; but afterwards returning into *England*, and gathering togeather ſeauenty other Virgins, was conſecrated Abbeſſe of a new Monaſtery erected in the ile of *Thanet*, by *S. Theodore* Archbiſhop of *Canterbury*, where famous for ſactimony of life, & miracles, ſhe gaue vp her ſoule to her heauenly ſpouſe, about the yeare of Chriſt, ſix hudred threſcore and foure. The forſaid Monaſtery was afterward burned by the *Danes*, with many

others

others in our Iland. There is yet to be feene
a fayre Church dedicated in her honour in
London in the Poultry, commonly called *S.*
Mildreds ; as alfo an old Chappell yet ſtãding,
erected likewiſe in her honour in a village
of *Flaunders* called *Milàn*, three miles diſtant
from the Citty of *S.Omers*.

THE fame day at *Hafelburrow* in *VViltſhire*
the depoſition of *S.* †*Vlſricke* Confeſſor
and Eremite, whoſe wonderfull life in
prayer and abſtinence, togeather with working of Miracles, was very famous throughout England about the yeare of Chriſt, one
thouſand one hundred fifty and foure, about
which tyme alſo he died ; and was buryed
in a little Oratory at the forſaid village of
Hafelburrow, which himſelfe had built, at
whoſe body many miracles are recorded to
haue byn wrought.

> †aliter
> wilfrick.
>
> *Matb.*
> *weſt. &*
> *Pariſ. in*
> *hiſtorijs*
> *ad annũ*
> *Do.1154.*

C   *The one and twentith Day.*

IN the Ile of Wight in *Hampſhire* the commemoration of *S. Cymbert* Biſhop and
Confeſſour, who being a monke of the venerable Order of *S.Benedict*, & Abbot of the
Monaſtery of *Redſord* in the ſame Prouince,
was in the raigne of *Ethelhard* King of the
VVeſtſaxons ordayned Biſhop, and placed in
the Ile of *VVight*, where he confirmed the

> *

> *Vẽ. Beda*
> *l. 4. cap.*
> *16. Trit.*
> *l.4.c.178*

D   people

Arnol.
Vion l. 2.
ligni
vitæ.

people in the Chriſtian faith, which *S.*
VVilfride of *Yorke,* had there planted ſome
twenty yeares before, in the tyme of his baniſhment from that Sea, where in all kind
of moſt godly conuerſation and ſanctity of
li.e, he gaue vp his bleſſed ſoule to reſt,
about the yeare of Chriſt, ſeauen hundred
and thirty.

D   *The two and twentith* Day.

Molan.in
addit. ad
Yſuar. 6.
Iunij.
Sigeb. in
Chron.
an.958.
Sur.to.3.
in vit.SS.

AT *Gaunt* in *Flaunders* the Tranſlation of
S. Gudwall Biſhop and Cófeſſour, who
being a noble Britan by birth, & ordayned
Biſhop in that Primitiue Church, preached
inceſſantly the faith of Chriſt with great
profit in our Iland. He built many Monaſteryes and became himſelfe a Father of an
hundred and fourſcore monkes. And after
all this, thirſting the good of his neighbour-Countreyes, he went ouer into the
lower *Germany*, and there taught the Chriſtian faith in like manner, with no leſſe
profit then in Britany. And laſt of all, full of
venerable old age, in great ſanctity and holineſſe of life, he reſted in our Lord, about
the yeare of Chriſt, three hundred and
fourty, and was one of the firſt of our Iland
that preached the Chriſtian faith in *Flaun-*
ders. His body hauing byn brought into

England,

England, was afterwards on this day, in the second perfecution of the *Danes,* tranflated to *Gaunt* by *Arnulph* Earle of *Flaunders,* and *S. Gerard* Abbot, in the yeare of Chrift, nyne hundred and threefcore. Where the fame is ftill preferued with great veneration of the Inhabitants.

E *The three and twentith Day.*

AT † *VVenlocke* in *Shropshire* the Tranfla-tion of S. *Milburge* Virgin, daughter to *Merualdus* Prince of *Mercia,* whofe great fanctimony & innocency of life, it pleafed God to manifeft vnto the world, after her departure, by the manifold miracles wrought at her body, which being miraculoufly reuea-led to a certaine godly man, in the raigne of K. *VVilliam* the Coquerour, was takē vp, and found found & vncorrupt to the admiratiō of the behoulders; and being put into a coftly fhrine, was kept in the Monaftery of *VVenlocke,* which fhe had built with her owne inheritance, vntill the tyme of King *Henry* the eight, when the fame was de-ftroyed. She departed to our Lord about the yeare of Chrift, fix hundred threefcore and foure, vpon the fix and twentith day of May, but her feaft is commonly celebrated on this day, both in *England* and other Coun-treyes.

† Mona-sterium Feneloc-kenfe.

Gotzel. Monac. in eius vita. Ma. Weſt. an. Do. 676. Pol. Vir. l.4.hiſto. Vincent. in ſpecul. l.25. Petr. in Catal. Gul. Malmeſ. in hiſt. Angl. & alij omnes hac die.

treys. Her life is wrytten at large by *Gotze-lipus* a monke of the Monaſtery of *S. Bertin*, in the Citty of *S. Omers* in Artoys.

F   *The foure & twentith* Day.

Bed. in Epit. & in hiſt. cap. 25. *& deinceps. Item in hiſt.lib.* 1. *VVeſt. Martyr. Rom. Mola. & alij ōnes hac die.*

Gaſel. in catal. SS. et in M.S. Calendar. Wion *in Martyr. Bened.*

AT *Canterbury* the depoſion of *S. Ethelbert* King of *Kent* and Confeſſour, who firſt of all other Princes in our Iland, after the *Britans*, receyued the Chriſtian faith, by the preaching of *S. Auguſtine* and his fellowes, ſent from *Rome* by Pope *Gregory* the Great. He built many goodly Churches and Monaſteryes in his dominions, and among the reſt *S. Auguſtines* at *Canterbury*, *S. Andrewes* at *Rocheſter*, and *S. Paules* at *London*. He departed this life in the yeare of Chriſt, ſix hundred and ſixteene, and was buryed at *Canterbury*.

THE ſame day in *Scotland* the depoſitiō of *S. Berectus* Confeſſour, who leading a Monaſticall life in that Kingdome, was famous for ſanctity of life & working of miracles, about the yeare of Chriſt, ſeauen hundred and fourteene, about which tyme alſo he ended his bleſſed dayes, and was buryed in *Scotland*.

G The fiue & twentith Day.

AT *Perone* in *Picardy* the Tranflation of
S. *Furfeus* Abbot and Confeffour, fonne
to K. *Philtan* of *Ireland*, who comming into
England/to *Sigebert* King of the *Eaftangles*,
built there a Monaftery, and gathered many
monkes togeather, inftructing them in all
kind of vertue and good learning. And then
leauing the care therof to his brother, called
Fo'llan, he went ouer into *France*, and there
built another Monaftery at *Perone*, where in
his venerable old dayes, full of great fanctity and holines of life, he departed to our
Lord, about the yeare of Chrift, fix hundred
and thirty. His body was buryed in the
fame Monaftery, of whome the Monkes of
that place, haue many particular hymnes in
their Office : the which being taken vp
afterwards, was on this day tranflated to a
more eminent place of the forfaid Church
of *Perone*, where the fame is kept with great
veneration, for the miracles, that are recor-
to haue byn wrought therat.

Sur. to. r.
Bed. l. 3.
hift. c. 19.
Aymo de
geft, Fra.
l. 1. c, 18.
Trit. de
vir, Illuft.
Petr, in
Catal. l. r
cap. 130.
& alij.

A   The six and twentith Day.

Bellef. in
Cofmogr.
Democh.
de Sacr.
Miſſæ
caꞵ 35.
tomo 2.
Wion l. 2.
ligni vitæ
in Catal.
Epiſ.
Conſtant.

AT *Conſtance* in the higher *Germany* the Commemoration of *S. Iohn* Biſhop & Confeſſour, who borne in *Scotland*, and deſcended there of a noble parentage, became in that Kingdome firſt a monke of the Venerable Order of *S. Benedict*, and thence went ouer into *France* to *S. Gallus* Abbot, that then was famous in thoſe partes, of whome being throughly inſtructed in all kind of Monaſticall diſcipline, was at laſt ordayned Biſhop of *Conſtance*, where after many yeares of moſt approued vertue and ſanctity of life, he happily repoſed in our Lord, in the yeare of Chriſt, ſix hundred fifty and foure, and was buryed in his owne Cathedrall Church of *Conſtance*.

B   The ſeauen & twentith Day.

Beda l. 3.
hiſt.
Angl
Tritem.
l. 4 de Vir.

AT *Lichfield* in Staffordſhire the Commemoration of Bleſſed *Sexulfe* Biſhop and Confeſſour, who being the firſt Abbot of the Monaſtery of *Medshamſted* (now called *Peterburrow*) by whoſe perſuaſion *VVulferus* K. of *Mercia* had newly founded the ſame, was ordayned Biſhop of *Lindisferne* in the

King

Kingdome of the *Northumbers*, and afterward translated to *Lichfield* in the place of *VVinfrid* that was deposed by *S. Theodore* of *Canterbury.* In both which Seas, he most worthily behaued himselfe in teaching and instructing his flocke for many yeares: And at last full of venerable old age, ioyned with sanctity of life, he departed to our Lord, about the yeare of Christ, seauen hundred.

T H E same day in the Prouince of the *Eastangles* in the Diocesse of *Ely*, the Cō-memoration of *S. Alnoth* Martyr, who being heardsman to *S. VVereburge* Abbesse of the Nunry of *Ely*, became an Anchoret, leading a most strict and seuere recluse life for the loue of God: whome when he had so serued for some yeares, he was slayne by certaine wicked theeues in hatred therof, and so receyued his crowne of Martyrdome, about the yeare of Christ 670.

C *The eight & twentith Day.*

A T *Yorke* the deposition of *S. Oswald* Bishop & Cōfessour, nephew to *S. Odo* Archbishop of *Canterbury*, who being first made Chanon of *VVinchester*, & then Bishop of *VVorcester*, was lastly promoted to the Archbishopricke of *Yorke*, whose godly vertues and innocency of life, was after-

Illustr. ord. D. Benedict. cap. 158. Matth. VVest. an. 700.

*

Rob. Buckl. in vita S. Wereb. in libr. de vitis SS, Mulierū Anglic,

Senat, Brauon. in eius vita. Wion in Mart. Bened. hac die,

D 4 ward

ward declared by the manifold miracles wrought at his body. Amongst other works of Charity, he was wont euery day to giue dinner to twelue poore men or pilgrims, seruing them at table with his owne hands, wash their feet, giue them money in almes, and alwayes at Easter to giue them new apparrell. He died on this day in the yeare of Christ, nyne hundred fourscore and twelue, and was afterward translated to *VVorcester* vpon the fifteenth of October, on which day his principall festiuity is celebrated in our Catholicke Church of *England,* of whome also, in that place, we haue made a large Relation.

THE

THE
MONETH
OF MARCH.

D   *The first Day.*

T *Meneuia* in *Penbrookshire* the deposition of *S. Dauid* Bishop and Confessour, sonne to *Xantus* Prince of VVales, and Vncle to the valiant King *Arthur*, who was so famous for working of miracles in his life tyme, that he became a great pillar, and vphoulder of the British Primitiue Church, especially in extinguishing the Reliques of the Pelagian heresy. He translated his Bishopricke (which was at *Carleon* vpon *Vske*) vnto *Meneuia* (now called in the British tongue of his name, *Twy Dewy*, & in English S. *Dauids*) where finally after he had built twelue Monasteryes, and reple-

Gaufr. Monum. in hist. Britorū Pol. virg l. 3. Mat. west. an. 872. Gir. Cambr. in eius vit. Breuiar. sec vsū Sar. alijque omnes hac die.

nished

nifhed the fame with monkes, being of the age of an hundred fourty & fix yeares, he ended his bleffed dayes, & was buryed in his owne Church , about the yeare of Chrift, fiue hundred fourfcore & twelue. It is recorded by the Britifh antiquityes, that by his prayers, he obtayned the heate and vertue tnat the waters of *Bath* in *Somerfetshire* haue in curing and affwaging many defeafes, though others do affigne it to haue byn found out long before. He was afterward canonized for a Saint by *Pope Calixtus* the fecond.

Marty.
Rom.
Bed, l. 5.
cap. 21.
Sur.tom.
2. vit.SS.
Mola. in
Indiculo
SS.Belgij
Tritem.
de vir.
Illuftr.
Cranz.
Metrop.
l.2. & alij

THE fame day at *VVerdt* in *Cleeu-land* the depofition of *S. Switbert* Conreffour, and firit Bifhop of that Sea, Sonne to *Sigebert* Earle of *Nottingham*, who going ouer into the lower *Germany* and thence into *Saxony* & *Frizland* with S. *VVillebrord* and his company to preach the Chriftian faith, was there elected Bifhop of *VVerdt*, and fent backe into England to be confecrated ; and then returning to his Sea, after much fruite wrought in that harueft, in great fanctity and holines of life, he repofed in our Lord, in the yeare of Chrift, feauen hudred & feauenteene. His body is kept at *VVerdt*, where he died , with great veneration of the inhabitants. He was canonized by Pope *Leo* the third.

E   *The second Day.*

AT *Lichfield* in *Staffordshire* the deposition of S. *Chad* Confessour and Bishop of that Sea, whose most exemplar life, togeather with working of manifold miracles is yet famous throughout England. The Cathedrall Church (or Minster) of that Citty, is dedicated to our Blessed Lady and S.*Chad*. There is a so a *Well* neere to the same Church, commonly called S. *Chads Well*; In the bottome wherof, lieth, vntill this day, a cleere great marble stone, wheron S. *Chad* was wont to kneele and pray in his Oratory; the water of which Well, is very wholsome & soueraigne for many diseases. He died in the yeare of Christ, six hundred threscore and foure, and lieth buryed in his owne Cathedrall Church of *Lichfield*.

THE same day at *VVerdt* in *Cleeu-land* the deposition of S. *Willeicke* Abbot and Confessour, who going out of England with S *Switbert* and his company to preach the Christian faith to the Pagans of the lower *Germany* and *Saxony*, was constituted Abbot of a monastery at *VVerdt*, which S. *Switbert* had newly founded, where after the reaping of a fertile harueft in the conuersion of infinite soules to God, full of sanctity &

Beda in Epit. & in hist. l.3.cap. 28. & deinceps. Matth. VVest. an.657. Marty. Rom. & alij hac die.

Marcel. in vita S. Similberti cap.16. Molan.in addi: . ad Vsuar.et in Indic. SS.Belgij

mira-

miracles . repofed in our Lord, about the
yeare of Chrift 727.

☞   The third Day.

Sur,to.2,
Molan.in
addit . ad
Vfuar.et
in Indic.
SS.Belgij
wion bac
die, & alij

AT Tauracum in little Britany the depofition of S. VVenlocke Abbot and Confeffour, who defcended of the royall bloud of
of Great Britany, and nephew to Francanu
Viceroy of that Kingdome, went ouer into
litle Britany, and was ordayned Abbot there
of an ancient Monaftery called Tauracum,
whofe life replenifhed with fanctity and
miracles, was famous, afwell in our Kingdome, as in France and Flanders, about the
yeare of Chrift , foure hundred and fourfcore, about which tyme alfo he repofed
in our Lord. His body was afterward tranflated to Gaunt in Flanders in the Normã perfecution, and there is kept vntill this day
with great veneration of the Inhabitants
for the ofte miracles that haue byn wrough
therat.

G   The fourth Day.

AT Perone in Picardy the depofition of S.
Furfeus Abbot and Confeffour, fonne
to Philtan King of Ireland, who cõming into

Eng-

England to *Sigebert* King of the *Eaftangles*, built there a goodly Monaltery, and filled the fame with monkes, wherof himfelfe was ordayned Abbot. And then after a while leauing the care therof to his brother *Foillan*, he went ouer into *France* and built another Monaftery at *Perone*, where in moft godly and faintly exercife of life, he died on this day, about the yeare of Chrift, fix hundred thirty and fix. His body is preferued yet in the fame Monaftery with great veneration for the frequent miracles that haue byn wrought therat.

Sur. in eius vit. Bed. l. 3. cap. 91. hiftor. Aymo de geft.Fra-corum l. 1.cap. 18. wion hac die,&alij

A **The fifth Day.**

IN *Northumberland* the Commemoration of S. *VVilgife* Confeffour, a noble man of that Prouince, and Father to the famous S. *VVillebrord*, who cafting from him the cares of this world, became an Eremite, leading a folitary & feuere life in the Kingdome of *Northumberland*, where he built him a little Cottage or Oratory in honour of S.*Andrew* the Apoftle, in which when he had liued many yeares, in continuall fafting, watching and prayer, full of fanctity of life, and venerable old age, he finally went vnto our Lord, about the yeare of Chrift, feauen hundred thirty and fix. S. *Alcuine* Maifter to

*

Alcuinus in vita S. Wil-lebror. apud Sur.tom. 6.die 7. Noue ris & in eius vita.

Charles

Charles the *Great* ; wrote his life in Elegiacall
verfe , as himfelfe witneffeth in the life of
S. *Willebrord*, where alfo in the end therof, he recounteth a miracle wrought by
S. *Wilzife*, about the multiplication of
wyne.

B   *The fixt Day.*

Ioan.
Leflaus
Epifcop.
Rof. l. 4.
de rebus
Scoticis.
Petr.
Cratepol.
de Epif.
Germ.
Molã. in
addit. ad
Vfuard.
Gafel.hac
aie. & c.

A T *Secking* on the *Rhene* in the lower
Germany, the depofition of S. *Frodoline*
(otherwife called *Winfred*) Abbot and Conteffour , fonne to *Conranus* King of *Scotland,*
who going ouer into *Flaunders* and *German*
for the conuerfion of thofe people to Chrift,
was ordayned Abbot of a Monaftery , called
Secking, fituated vpon the riuer-banke of
Rhene, where after he had conuerted many
thoufands to the faith of Chrift, in all kind
of vertue and fanctity of life, he ended his
venerable aged dayes, about the yeare of our
Lord, fiue hundred threefcore and foure.

Math.
VVeft.
an.705.
Pol.virg.
l. 4. hift.

TH E fame day at *Dormundcafter* two
miles from *Peterburrow* in Northamp-
tonfhire, the depofition of the Saints *Kinif-*
dred and *Kinifwide*, Virgins and fifters, daughters to *Penda* K. of *Mercia*, who being dedicated to God, euen from their infancy, defpi-
led all worldly preferments , and er^tring
into a Nunry at the forfaid towne of *Dor-*

mundcaſter, there only ſtudied how to ſerue their Lord, in all kind of vertuous conuerſation and Sanctimony of life vntyll their dying day, which happened about the yeare of Chriſt, ſix hundred thirty and foure. Their bodyes were afterward tranſlated to *Peterburrow*, wheſe S. *Ethelwold* Biſhop of of *Wincheſter* built a goodly Monaſtery in their honour, about the yeare of our Redemption, nyne hundred and fourſcore.

Ranulph. Ceſtrenſ. l. 5.hiſt.cꜳ 18. Rob. Buck. de vitis earū hac die.

C *The ſeauenth Day.*

IN *North-wales* the Cōmemoratiō of *S. Deiſer* Conſeſſour, who borne of a noble britiſh ſtocke, contemned the vanityes of this world, and became an Eremite, leading for many yeares, a ſolitary and ſeuere kind of life, in all vertue and humility in the North of Wales; where among other miracles which he wrought, one is recorded, that by his prayers, he raiſed out of the ground a fountayne of cleere water very ſoueraigne for many diſeaſes. He died in great ſanctity and holines, about the yeare of Chriſt, ſix hundred threeſcore and foure, about which tyme alſo S. Wenefride was famous in thoſe partes for the miracles wrought at her body; and with whome this holy man *Deiſer* had byn very conuerſant, whilſt ſhe liued.

✱
Acta S. Wenefr. 3. Nouem. apudSur. & Breui. ſecſ vſum Sarum in lectio. S. Wenefr. & antiq. Monum. Cambriæ.

D   The eight Day.

AT *Dunwich* in *Suffolke* the depofition of
S. Felix bifhop & Confeffor, who comming out of *Burgundy* where he was borne,
was by *S. Honorius* Archbifhop of *Canterbu-*
ry fent to preach the Chriftian faith to the
Eaftangles, where he côuerted the whole Prouince, togeather with their King *Sigebert*; &
fo became their Apoftle : and laft of all was
ordayned Bifhop of an old Citty called
Dunmocke (otherwife *Dunwich*) which at
this day is more then halfe confumed by the
fea. This holy man founded in that Prouince, Monafteryes, Schooles, and Churches.
And after a moft Saintly life full of miracles, he finally repofed in our Lord ; about
the yeare of Chrift, fix hundred and fifty, &
was buried in the Abbey of *Soam* in *Cam-*
bridgshire, foure miles from *Ely*, from whence
in the Danifh perfecution, he was tranflated
to the Monaftery of *Ramfey*.

Vĕ. Beda
l. 2. cap.
25. & l. 3.
cap. 20.
VVeft.
an. 632.
Marty.
Rom.
Molan.
& alij.

E   The ninth Day.

AT *Torke* the Commemoration of *S.*
Bofa Confeffour and Bifhop of that
Sea, who being a monke of the Monaftery

of *Strenshalt* in the Kingdome , of the
Northumbers , was at the inftance of *Egfride*
King of that Prouince , ordayned Bifhop of *Yorke*, and placed in that Sea, in
the roome of *S. Wilfride*, who then liued in
exile in the Ile of *Wight*, being expulfed the
Dominions of *Northumberland* by the forfaid
King: which when he had gouerned moft
worthily for nyne yeares in all kind of
good learning and vertue , and *S. Wilfride*
reftored againe,he willingly returned to his
Monaftery,& there in great fanctity of life,
and heauenly contéplation he fpent the reft
of his dayes,and finally repofed in our Lord,
about the yeare of Chrift feauen hundred.

Vē. Beda
l.4.hifto.
Cap. 12.
Math.
Weft. *in*
flor.hifto.
Tritem.l.
4. *cap.*4.
*Wio n.l.*2.
ligni
vitæ in
Catal.
Epifcop.
Eboracēf.

F   *The tenth Day.*

AT *Viffenaken* in the lower *Germany* the
depofition of *S. Himeline* Confeffour,
who borne in *Ireland* and there defcended of
a noble bloud , and allied to the famous
Bifhop *S.Romwald* of that Nation, defpifing
this tranfitory world , went ouer into the
lower *Germany* and there led an Eremiticall
life in the Montaynes neere vnto *Thene* in
the Duchy of *Brabant* , where he was very
famous for fanctity of life and other vertues;
the fame being manifefted afterward , by
the manifold fignes and miracles at his

Molan.in
addit.ad
vfuar. &
in Indic.
SS.Belgij
Antiqua
Monum.
Hyber.

E   death,

death, which fell out about the yeare of Chriſt ſeauen hundred and threſcore. His memory is vntill this day very famous in the forſaid towne of *Viſſenaken*, where his body remayneth, and is greatly honoured by the frequent concourſe of ſuch as dayly come to viſit the ſame.

G   *The eleuenth Day.*

AT *Tyn-mouth* in the Kingdome of the *Northumbers* the Tranſlation of the venerable body of S. *Oſwyne* Martyr, and King of the *Deires* in the ſame Prouince, who being impiouſly ſlayne in hatred of Chriſtian faith by *Oſway* King of the *Bernicias*, it pleaſed God to maniſeſt his innocency, by the wonderfull miracles wrought afterward at his body, which being on this day found out, was taken vp, and with great ſolemnity and veneration tranſlated to a Church of our Bleſſed Lady in an old towne of the ſame Kingdome, now called *Tyn-mouth*, where afterward was a godly Monaſtery erected in his honour, and where his principall feſtiuity was wont in Catholicke time to be celebrated on the twētith of *Auguſt*, on which day he was Martyred in the yeare of Chriſt, ſix hundred fifty and one.

Ve. Beda in Epit. & l.3. hiſt. cap. 14. Weſt. an. 641. 745. & Pariſ.ibi. & alij.

A

A   The twelfth Day.

AT *Rome* the deposition of *S. Gregory*
Pope and Doctor, who for his admirable workes and labours in Gods Church,
was surnamed the *Great.* He sent *S. Augustine*
with other Monkes into England, for our
Couersion, who landing in the Ile of *Thanet,*
and intertayned by King *Ethelbert* of *Kent* of
blessed memory, within a while conuerted that Prouince to the faith of Christ, togeather with the said King *Ethelbert,* and
by little and little the whole Realme of
England. The memory of which our Apostle
S. Gregory, hath byn very famous in former
tymes in our Countrey, whose feast was
wont to be kept holyday, in diuers partes
of the Land, where also are many goodly
Churches and monuments yet remaining,
erected and dedicated in his honour. He
died in the yeare of Christ, six hundred and
foure; and lieth buryed in S. *Peters* Church
at *Rome.*

THe same day in *Scotland* the Commemoration of *S. Fethno* monke and Confessour, who being a disciple of *S. Columbe*
the Great of *Ireland,* came with him ouer
into *Scotlãd,* togeather with eleuē other Cõ-
panions, all Irishmen, to preach the Chri-

*Bed.l.2.
cap.13.
Paul.
Liac. de
gest.Lon-
gobard.
l.3.cap.11.
& 12.
Mart.
Rom.
Breuiar.
sec. Vsum
Sarum.et
alij ōnes
hac die.*

*

*Hect.Bo-
etius in
hist.Scot.
Ioã. Lesl.
l. 4. Ibid.*

ftian faith to the *Pictes* that then inhabited that Kingdome, where after their conuerſion from Idolatry to the true knowledge of Chriſt, famous for ſanctity of life and other vertues, he there ended his bleſſed dayes about the yeare of Chriſt 580.

B   *The thirteenth Day.*

✳

Arnol.
W*ion. l.*
2. *ligni*
vitæ. de
ſcript.
Ord. D.
Benedict.

IN *Scotland* the Cōmemoration of *S. Vigane* Confeſſour, who deſcended of a very honourable parentage in that Kingdome, became there a monke of the Venerable Order of *S. Benedict* , of the Congregation of *Cluniacke*, whoſe great learning and vertue, hath not only illuſtrated very much the Order of his Religion, but the whole iland alſo where he was borne. There is yet extāt in diuers libraryes of *Europe*, a famous worke of his, intituled, *Sermones ad populum*, which he wrote about the yeare of Chriſt, one thouſand and two, about which tyme alſo in great ſanctity of life and venerable old age he departed to our Lord, and was buryed in *Scotland.*

C The fourteenth Day.

AT *Lindifferne* in the Kingdome of the *Northumbers*, the Commemoration of *S. Ceolnulph* King of that Prouince and Confeffour, who leauing the care of his Kingdome to *Eadbert* his kinfman, and reiecting all worldly pleafures and titles, became a monke in the Abbey of *Lindisferne*, where in all kind of moft godly and exemplar good life he fpent the reft of his dayes, and finally in a good old age there gaue vp his foule to reft, about the yeare of Chrift, feauen hundred thirty and feauen. He was afterward buryed in the fame place, neere to the Venerable body of *S. Cuthbert* Bifhop of that Sea, at whofe tombe many miracles are recorded to haue byn wrought in witneffe of his fanctity.

Matt.
Weft.
an.Do.
733. Continuator
hift. Ven.
Bedæ l. 1.
cap. 9. &
in. Epit.
an. 737.

D The fifteenth Day.

AT *Glaftenbury* in Somerfetſhire the feftiuity of *S. Ariftobulus* Bifhop and Martyr, who being a noble Roman by birth, and one of the firft Chriftians of that Citty, as appeareth by *S. Paul* his falutation of him, in his Epiftle to the Romans, was crea-

Arnold.
Mirman.
in theat.
Conuerf.
Gentium
Doroth.
in fynopfi.

E 3   ted

Baron. i
ad not...ad
Martyr.
Rom.
hac die.

ted Bifhop by *S. Peter* the *Apoftle*,and fent by him into *Britany* to preach the Chriftian faith;whereafter he had brought very many erring fheep to Chriftes fould, moft glorioufly ended his bleffed dayes by Martyrdome, about the yeare of Chrift threfcore and ten. His memory hath byn famous in our Iland vntill thefe later tymes of fchifmes and herefyes, as being one of our firft Apoftles and Patrons.

E   *The fixteenth Day.*

*

Arnold.
Wion l.
2.de ligno
Vite in
Catal.
fcrip.
Ord. D.
Benedict.
& alij.

AT *Ridall-Monaftery* the Commemoration of Bleffed *Alred* Abbot and Confeffor, whofe great learning and vertue hath much illuftrated the Catholicke Church of Chrift, but efpecially our Iland of *Great Britany*, where he was borne,liued,and died. He was firft a monke of the venerable Order of *S Benedict* , and afterward became Abbot of an ancient Monaftery called *Rhieuallis*, (now vulgarly *Ridall*) where in great fanctity of life, he ending his bleffed dayes, repofed in our Lord, about the yeare of Chrift, one thoufand one hundred threefcore & foure. He wrote the life of King *Edward* the Cofeffour,befides very many other learned and pious bookes to the number of one and twenty : all which are yet extant to be feene in diuers Libraries, as well in *England,* as other Countreyes of *Europe.*

F *The feauenteenth Day.*

IN *Ireland* the depofition of *S. Patricke* Bifhop and Confeffour, Apoftle of that lland, who borne in the Territory of *Briftow* in *Somerfetshire,* & brought vp at *Glaftenbury,* went ouer, in his youth, into *France* to *S.Martyn* his Vncle then Bifhop of *Towers,* who was brother to *S. Patrickes* Mother, of whome he was inftructed in learning and other vertues: & afterwards going to *Rome,* was there confecrated Bifhop by *Pope Celeftinus,* and fent backe to preach the Chriftian faith in *Scotland,* which he did for a tyme with great fruit of his labour; and thence he went into *Ireland* (becaufe at that tyme the greateft part of the *Scotts* inhabited that Kingdome) where he conuerted the whole lland, and fo became their Apoftle, working wonderous miracles among them. He liued an hundred and two and twenty yeares, obtayning by his prayers, that no venemous creature fhould liue or breed in *Ireland,* and died in the yeare of Chrift, foure hundred fourfcore and one. His body was firft interred in the towne of *Dun,* in the Prouince of *Vlfter,* and afterward tranflated to the Arch-

Profp. Aquit. in fua hift.Mar. Scot. an, 432.Sige. in Chron, an.491. Guliel. Neubrig. l. 3. cap. 19. Ioan, Capgr. i.i Catal.SS, Britāniæ

bifhops

bifhops Sea of *Armachan* in the fame Kingdome, about the yeare of Chrift, one thoufand, one hundred, threefcore and feauenteene, as the ancient Records of *Ireland* do
declare.

G   *The eighteenth Day* .

Sur. in
eius vita.
tom. 2.
Pol. virg.
l. 6. hifto.
Angl.
Weft-
an. 978.
Martyr.
Rom. &
alij ōnes
hac die.

AT *Corfe-caftle* in the Ile of *Purbecke* in
Dorcetshire the paffion of *S. Edward* K. of
the *VVeftfaxons* and Martyr, who through
the trechery of his ftep-mother Queene *Al-*
fred (defyrous that her owne fonne *Ethelbert*
fhould be King)was flayne by certayne foul-
diers hired by the forfaid Queene to that
purpofe, whilft he was on hunting, in the
yeare of Chrift, nyne hūdred threefcore and
eighteene. His body was firft interred at
VVarham, and after at *Shaftesbury*, wherat it
pleafed God in witneffe of his Innocency to
worke many miracles. And laft of all the
fame was tranflated to Glaftenbury-Abbey
in the yeare of Chrift, one thoufand and
one.

Vincent.
in fpeculo
l. 29. c. 11.
& 12.
Wion .l.
2. ligni
vitæ.

THE fame day in *Ireland* the depofition
of *S. Chriftian* Bifhop and Confeffour,
who borne in the fame Iland, became there
firft a monke of the Order of *Cifterce*, and
fcholler to the famous *S. Malachy* Archbifhop
& Primate of that Kingdome, & afterward

Abbot

Abbot of *Mellifonte*, and laſt of all Biſhop, where in great ſanctity of life he ended his bleſſed dayes, about the yeare of Chriſt one thouſand one hundred fourty and eight, whoſe memory is yet famous throughout *Ireland*.

Bernard. in vita S. Malach.

A The ninteenth Day.

AT *Derby* the Commemoration of *S. Alkmund* Martyr, ſonne to *Alred* King of *Northumberland*, who being ſlayne in a battayle againſt the Duke of *VVilton* in the behalfe of the *Viceroy* of *VVorceſter*, named *Ethelmund*, that pretended to recouer certayne lands, that *VVolſtan* Duke of *VVilton* detayned from him wrongfully, his body preſently began to do miracles; which being ſeene, and witneſſed, the ſame was tranſlated to *Derby*, and there with great veneration interred moſt ſolemnly in a Church erected in his honour, and called afterwards of his name, *S.Alkmunds*, which in former Catholicke tymes, hath byn a famous pilgrimage, eſpecially for the Northerne people of *England*. He ſuffered in the yeare of Chriſt, eight hundred.

*

Ranulph. Ceſtrenſ. l.5.c.28. & alij noſtrat.

B   The twentith Day.

Ve. Beda
l. 4. cap.
26. 27. 28
29. & 30.
Abbo
Floriac.
inprolog.
ad vit. S.
Edmūdi
Regis.
Vincent.
in speculo
Sur. to. 2.
hac die eū
Mart.
Rem. &
alijs om.i
bus.

AT *Lindisferne* in the Kingdome of the *Northumbers* the depofition of S. *Cuthbert* B. fhop and Conteffour, who defcended of the Kings bloud of *Ireland*, became a monke firft of the famous Monaftery of *Mailros*, in the Marches of *Scotland*, and afterward was ordayned Bifhop of *Lindisferne* : which Bifhopricke, after he had gouerned fome two yeares, he refigned, and became an Eremite, leading a moft ftrict and feuere kind of life, in the Iland of *Farne*, and fo continued vntill his dying day: which hap-pened about the yeare of Chrift, fix hundred fourfcore and eight. He was very famous for fanctity and working of miracles both aliue and dead.

Bed. l. 4.
cap. 29.
hift.
Angl.

THE fame day, and fame place the depo-fition of Bleffed *Herebert* Prieft and Con-feffour, a man of great holineffe of life, who often repayring to S. *Cuthbert* aforfaid, al-wayes vfed his counfell and direction, for the affayres both of his body and foule And one day S. *Cuthbert* telling him, that himfelfe was fhortly to leaue this world & paffe to the other; *Herebert* fell downe at his feet, and importunely befought him that he might alfo paffe to the next life with him,

that

that had fo long inioyed his company
heere on eartn. At whofe earneft interçeſſiõ,
S. Cuthbert falling to his prayers, finally ob-
tanned the fame. And fo with in a while
after, they both falling ficke, went both
to our Lord vpon the one and felfe fame
day and houre, in the yeare of Chrift, 688.
and were both buryed at *Lindisferne*.

C   *The one and twentith Day.*

AT *VVerdt* in *Cleeu-land* the Commemoration of *S. Ifenger* Biſhop and Martyr,
who defcended of a noble Scottiſh family,
contemned the vanityes of the world, and
became firſt a monke in that Kingdome, of
the venerable Order of *S. Benedict*, and afterward Abbot there of the Monaftery called
Amarbarick, which whē he had gouerned for
diuers yeares, mooued with zeale of con-
uerting his neighbour-Countreyes, went
ouer into *Flanders* and *Germany*, and being
there ordayned B:ſhop of *VVerdt*, was a little
after flayne in defence of the Chriſtiã faith,
by the infidels of that Countrey, about the
yeare of Chrift, eight hundred twenty and
foure. His body being brought to *VVerdt*, &
there interred in his owne Cathedrall
Church, was kept for a long tyme with
great honour & veneratio of the Inhabitãtes.

*

Cranʒ.
Metrop.
l.1.cap.
29. Wion.
l.2. ligni
vitæ in
Catal.
Erif.
Wer-
denfium.

D

D   *The two and twentith* Day.

AT *Sherborne* in *Dorcetshire* the Comme-moration of S. *Hamund* Biſhop of that Sea and Martyr, who in the Daniſh perſe-cution vnder the Captaynes *Hingar* & *Hubba,* was for the Confeſſion of Chriſt moſt bar-barouſly ſlayne at *Merdune* , by thoſe Tyran-nicall Pagans, who in the vaſtation of England, ſpared neyther Eccleſiaſticall nor Religious perſon whatſoeuer. His Martyr-dome happened about the yeare of Chriſt, eight hundred threeſcore and eleuen, and in the raigne of *Alfred* King of the *VVeſtſaxons.*

E   *The three and twentith* Day.

AT *Lindisferne* the Commemoration of Bleſſed *Egbert* King of the *Northumbers* and Confeſſour, who after he had gouerned that Prouince moſt laudably for twenty yeares, conténed his Crowne & dignity of a King, leauing the ſame to his ſóne *Oſwulph,* & entring into the Abbey of *Lindisfern* afor-ſaid, became there a monke of the venera-ble Order of *S.Benedict* , where in very great ſanctity of life , humility, obſeruance of Monaſticall diſcipline and other vertues, he

finally

finally ended his peaceable dayes in our
Lord, about the yeare of Chriſt, ſeauen hundred threeſcore and eight. He endowed the
Archbiſhopricke of *Yorke* , whilſt he was
King, with great reuenewes, where alſo he
founded a worthy Library, and furniſhed
the ſame with all good Authors that could
then be gotten.

F *The foure & twentith Day.*

AT *Canterbury* the depoſitiõ of *S. Lanfráke*
Confeſſour, and Archbiſhop of that
Sea, who borne at *Pauia* in *Lombardy*, became
firſt a monke of the Abbey of *Becke*, & then
Abbot of *Cane* in *Normandy*, and afterward
ordayned Archbiſhop of *Canterbury*, at the
requeſt of King *VVilliam* the *Conquerour*;
whoſe moſt pious life, & good learning,
ioyned with extraordinary charitie to the
poore, and aſſiſtance of the Church of *England*, is yet memorable throughout the Chriſtian world. Of this man there is a ſtory
recorded, how that in his yõger dayes he trauayling by the way, & chãcing to be robbed
by theeues, tooke the ſame ſo impatiently,
that by no means he could be pacified for a
tyme: but at lẽgth cõming to himſelfagaine,
he brake forth into theſe words: *VVhat? haue
I ſo much learning & knowledge both in Philoſophy,*

*Math.
Weſt. an.
1089.
Pol. Vir.
Petr. in
Catal.
l. 6. c. 4. et
7. Vinc.
in ſpeculo
Tritem.
de Vi. .
Illuſtr. l.
2. & 3.*

Hier.
Platus l.
2. de bono
flatus
Religiofi.

Diuinity and Scriptures, and yet haue not learned to be patient in aduerfity? Surely, I will not ceafe vntill I fynd out that learning. And vpon this, he prefently went into France, and thence into Normandy, where comming to the Abbey of Becke, he lay fecretly for many yeares in that Monaftery, being reputed for an Idiot and fimple man, vntill at length his learning and wifdome being difcouered, he was made Prior of Becke, and prefently afterward Abbot of S. Stephens in Cane aforfaid, and finally Archbifhop of Canterbury. He died in the yeare of Chrift, one thoufand fourfcore and nyne, and was buryed in his owne Church at Canterbury.

G   The fiue & twentith Day.

Io.Capgr.
in Catal.
SS. Brită.
Cul.
Nubrig.
l.3.cap.7
8.9 Geor.
Lilius in
hift. anno
1235.
Vincent.
in fpecul.

AT Norwich in the County of Norfolke the paffion of S. VVilliam Martyr, who being a boy of the fame Citty of fome ten yeares old, was by his Father fet an apprentice to a glouer of the fame towne, whome the Iewes of Norwich fecretly ftealing away, crucified on a Croffe in defpite of Chrift & his bleffedMother, vpő the feaft of herAnnuciation. His body they caft into a wood or thicket, neere to the faid Citty, which being foűd & brought vnto the towne with a follemne proceffion of the Clergy, was placed

in

in the great Church, or Minſter of that Sea, and there was wont, to be kept with great veneration. His Martyrdome happened in the yeare of Chriſt, one thouſand one hundred forty and ſix, in the eleuenth yeare of the raigne of K. *Stephen.*

A   *The ſix and twentith*Day.

AT *Bardney* in *Lincolnſhire* the Commemoration of *Many holy Monkes* Martyrs, who in the firſt Daniſh perſecution in our Iland, were ſlayne by thoſe Pagan people in their owne Monaſteryes in hatred of Chriſtian Religion. At what tyme alſo the ſaid *Danes* ranging abroad the Countreyes, ſlew (ſaith the Story) the Abbot & the Monkes of the Monaſtery of *Croyland*, and fiered their Church, and houſes belonging thervnto. At *Peterburrow* alſo they made the like ſlaughter of Religious perſons ; and comming to the *Nunry* of *Ely*, they put the Religious Virgins all to the ſword without compaſſion,and ſo receyuing theyr Crownes of Martyrdome, they went vnto our Lord. All which happened in our Countrey, about the yeare of Chriſt, eight hundred threeſcore and ten.

*

Ingulph. de Croyland in hiſtor. *Io. Stous Annal. Angl de Reg. weſtſax. pag.* 100.

B The seauen & twentith Day.

Arnold.
Wion in
Mart.
Benedict.
& Gasel.
ex antiq.
Scotiæ
Monum.
hac die.

IN *Scotlād* the depositiō of *S. Archibald* Abbot & Confessour, descended of a very noble parentage in that Kingdome, whose rare life & conuersation togeather with the singular gifts of clemency towards the poore and orphanes, hath in former tymes byn famous both in *England* and *Scotland*. His feast is recounted to haue byn celebrated on this day, by the ancient Records of *Scotland* and *Ireland*: among both which Nations, many altars, and some Churches also, haue heertofore byn dedicated in his honour. He florished about the yeare of Christ seauen hundred and eight, about which tyme also he desceased.

C The eight & twentith Day.

Io. Capgr.
in Catal.
SS. Britā.
Molan.
in addit.
Vsuard.

IN the Marches of *VVales* the Translatiō of the glorious body of S. *Fremund* King and Martyr, sonne to *Offa* King of *Mercia*, who setting aside his crowne and kingdome for the loue of Christ, in the second yeare of his raigne, became an Eremite in a little Ilād of the Marches of *VVales*, called in the British tongue *Illesage*, where at last he was slayne by

Ofway the *Apostata*, in hatred of Christiā Religion, in the yeare of Christ, seaué hundred fourscore and sixteene. He being afterward canonized for a Saint in the yeare of our Lord 1157. and raygne of King *Henry* the third, his body was taken vp on this day, & translated to a more eminent place of the same Church where it lay before, wherat it pleased God to worke miracles. His principall festiuity is celebrated vpon the eleuenth day of May, of whome in that place, we haue made mention againe.

wion hac die in Mart. Benedict.

D *The nine & twentith Day.*

IN *Scotland* the Commemoration of *S. Baldred* Confessour, whose memory in ancient tymes hath byn very famous in that Kingdome. For that he hauing sometymes preached to the people of three villages neere adioyning one to the other in *Scotland,* called *Aldham*, *Tiningham* and *Preston,* was so holy a man of life, that when he was dead, the people of ech village, contended one with another which of thē should haue his body, in so much, that at last, they not agreeing therabout, tooke armes, and ech of them sought by force to enioy the same. And when the matter came to issue, the said sacred body was found all whole in three distinct

Io. Maior de gestis Scot. l. 2. cap. 7. ex antiq. Scot. Monum.

✱

F   stinct

ſtinct places of the houſe where he died:
ſo as the people of ech village comming thither,& carrying the ſame away, placed it in
their Churches, and kept it with great honour and veneration for the miracles, that
at ech place it pleaſed God to worke. He
liued in the tyme of S. *Kentigerne* and S. *Co-
lambe* the *Great*, about the yeare of Chriſt,ſix
hundred and ten, about which tyme alſo he
gaue vp his ſoule to reſt in our Lord.

E   *The thirtith* Day.

Io.Leſl.
l.5. hiſto.
Scot.
Albert.
Cranz.
Metrop.
li.c.20.
Wion in
Mart.
Bened.
hac die.

AT *VVerdt* in *Cleeu-land* the depoſitiõ of S.
Pattone Biſhop of that Citty and Conteſſour, who deſcended of a worthy bloud
in *Scotland*, was firſt made Abbot of the
Monaſtery called *Amarbaricke* in the ſame
Kingdome, and thence going ouer into
the lower *Germany* and *Saxony*, was at laſt
conſecrated Biſhop of *VVerdt*, where in
great ſanctity of life and other vertues, diligently attending to his flocke & preaching the Chriſtian faith among them, he
ended his venerable old dayes, about the
yeare of Chriſt, ſeauen hundred threſcore
and two, and was buryed in his owne Cathedrall Church at *VVerdt*, where his body
was wont to be kept with great veneration
of the Inhabitants.

F

F _The one & thirtith_ Day

AT _Malmefbury_ in _VViltshire_ the Tranflation of _S. Adelmus_ Bifhop & Confeffour
nephew to _Inas_ King of the _VVeftfaxons_,
who trauayling in his youth into _France_
and _Italy_, through his diligence in ftud-
dies, attayned to great learning, both in
the Greeke and Hebrue tongues, but efpecially in Diuinity. In the knowledg wherof, he was in his dayes accompted excellent.
After his returne into England, he firft became a monke of the Order of _S. Benedict_ at
Malmesbury, and then Abbot of the whole
Monaftery: and afterward going to _Rome_
with King _Ceadwall_, he was there created
Bifhop of _Sherborne_ by _Pope Sergius_, and
fent backe to that Sea: where after great
labours taken in the Gouernment therof,
and many notable bookes wrytten for
the inftruction of men in Chriftian life, he
finally repofed in our Lord, in the yeare of
Chrift, feauen hundred and nyne: whofe
body was afterward folemnly on this day
tranflated to _Malmefbury_, and there kept in
Catholicke tymes with great honour and
veneratiō, for the manifold miracles, that
are recorded to haue byn wrought therat.

Gul.
Malmef.
de pontif.
Angl.
Bed. l. 4.
cap. 19.
Calendar.
fed. vfum
Sarum
hac die.
Catal.
Epifcop.
Sirebur-
genfium.

THE
MONETH
OF APRIL.

G   *The first Day.*

In Vita.S.
Ricarij.
Abbatis
apud
Sur.to.2.
die 26.
Apr. de
vitis SS.

T *Pontoyse* in *France* the Commemoratiō of the Saintes *Sadoch* & *Adrian*, Prieftes & Confeffours, who being Irifhmen by birth, came ouer into *France* to preach the Chriftian faith to the people and inhabitants of *Picardy*, where they were honourably receyued and intertayned by *S. Richarius* a noble man of that Countrey, and afterward Abbot of *Pontoyse*. And when they had laboured in that new harueft for many yeares, and reaped therin moft aboundant fruite, in the conuerfion of infinite foules from their Idolatrous fuperftitiō to the true worfhip of one

God

God, they finally ended their happy dayes in a venerable old age, about the yeare of Chrift, fix hundred and forty. Their facred Reliques are kept vntill this day by the Religious men in the forfaid Monaftery of *Pontoyfe*, with great veneration of the Inhabitants.

A   The fecond Day.

AT *Coldingham* in the Marches of *Scotland* the Commemoration of *S. Ebba* Virgin and Abbeffe, daugher to *Ethelfride* King of *Northumberland*, and fifter to *S. Ofwald* and *Ofway* Kings of the fame Prouince, who côtêning the vanities of the world, became a Religious woman , and receyued the holy veyle of chaftity at the hands of Bleffed *Finan* Bifhop of *Lindisferne* : but afterward building two goodly Monafteryes of her owne, one vpon the riuer of *Derwent*, called of her name *Ebbecefter*, and the other at the forfaid *Coldingham* , fhe became Abbeffe of the later, and ruled the fame in all perfe-ćtion and holines of life, hauing very many noble and vertuous virgins vnder her; amôg whome, *S. Audry* Queene and flower of the Ile of *Ely* was one. And after fhe had heaped vp ftore of heauenly treafure, in a good old age, fhe went to her fpoufe, about the yeare

*

Rob.
Buckland
in eius
vita l.
man. Scr.
fol. 156. de
vitis SS.
mulierũ
Angl.

of Chrift, fix hundred fourfcore and foure, whofe memory hath in tymes paft byn very famous both in *England* & *Scotland*, where many goodly Churches and Chappels haue byn erected and dedicated in her honour; and one yet ftanding to be feene in *Oxford*, commonly called *S. Tabbes*; as alfo in the forfaid Marches of *Scotland* neere to *Coldinghā*, there is a little port or hauen in the promōtory of that Prouince, ftill retayning the name of *S. Tabbes-head*.

B   *The third Day.*

Matth.
Weft.&
Parif.
an. Dom.
1253.
Sur. to. 2.
Breu. fec.
vfum Sa-
rū. Mart.
Rom.
& alij.

AT *Chichefter* in *Suffex* the depofition of *S. Richard* Confeffour and Bifhop of that Sea, whofe wonderfull life and doctrine, ioyned with the greatnes of his miracles, hath byn fufficiently manifefted to the Chriftian world. He was borne at *VVich* in *VVorceftershire*, and died at *Douer* in *Kent*, the ninth yeare of his Prefulfhippe , and yeare of Chrift, one thoufand two hundred fifty and three. Whofe body being brought to *Chichefter*, fo fhined with miracles, that among others, it is recorded, that three dead men, were at the fame, by his meritts, againe raifed to life. He was canonized for a Saint, by Pope *Vrban* the fourth feauen yeares after his death, and of Chrift 1260.

THE same day at *Eureux* in *France* the deposition of *S. Burgundofora* Virgin and Abbesse, who descended of a noble Brittish bloud and disciple to *S. Columbane* the Great of *Ireland*, was by him sent ouer into *France* & there made Abbesse of a Monastery, which he had built at *Eureux*, where in great sanctimony of life she ended her blessed dayes, about the yeare of Christ, six hūdred & ten. *S. Bede* hath wryttē her life at large, wherin he recounteth many worthy and memorable actes of hers, especially for the obseruation of Monasticall discipline, wherin she excelled.

Bed.to.
3. Operū,
Sur.to. 3.
Vit . SS.
in vita S.
Columb.
Mart.
Rom. &
Molan.

C   *The fourth Day.*

IN *Cornwall* the Commemoration of *S. Guier* Priest and Confessour, who leading an Eremiticall, and seuere kind of life in that Prouince, and being companion to *S. Neoth* (by whose counsell the Vniuersity of *Oxford* was founded) that lined in those partes with him in the tyme of King *Alfred*, was very famous for sanctity of life, and working of Miracles both aliue & dead. His name is yet very memorable, and frequent among the *Cornishmen*, where in times past, haue byn many altars erected, and dedicacated in his honour. He died about the yeare

*
Matth.
Parif. in
hist. Ma-
iori ad
An. 871.
ex antiq.
monum.
Britan-
niæ.

of Chriſt, eight hundred threeſcore and eleuen.

D   *The fifth Day.*

*M*ⁿ*lan.in addit . ad Vſuard. hac die. Antiq. Monum. Regni Scotiæ.*

IN *Scotland* the depoſition of S. *Tigernake* Biſhop and Confeſſour, whoſe godly life, and doctrine, hath not only illuſtrated that Countrey, where he was borne, but his neighbour-Kingdomes alſo round about: And therfore his memory not vnworthy to be recorded among the other Saints of our Iland, that hath byn made worthy of ſo glorious a Patron. He died in all ſanctity & holines of life, about the yeare of Chriſt, ſeauen hundred and thirty, and was buryed in *Scotland*.

✱

Adam. Bremenſ. in hiſt. Gothorū l. 2 . cap. 29. Baro- nius to. 10. Annal.

THE ſame day in *Suetia* the Commemo- ration of S. *Gotebald* Biſhop and Con- feſſour, who being an Engliſhman by birth, went ouer into *Norway* and *Sueueland* and there propagated the Chriſtian faith with aboundant fruite of his holy labours, for many yeares;and finally in great holines of life, there reſted in our Lord, about the yeare of Chriſt, one thouſand and foure.

E   *The fixt Day.*

Mart.
Rom. hac
die.
Bernard.
in vita S.
Malach.

IN *Ireland* the depofition of S. *Celfus* Confeffour and Bifhop of *Connerthen* in the
fame Kingdome, whofe godly life, full of
fanctity and miracles, hath byn very famous
in former ages, both at home, and abroad.
He was predeceffour to S. *Malachy* in his
Bifhoppricke, and died in the yeare of
Chrift, one thoufand one hundred twenty
and eight.

*

T. Ie fame day at *Hexam* in *Northumberland*
the Commemoration of S. *Ethelwold*,
King of the fame Prouince and Martyr:
who being wickedly flayne in the Ciuill
warres among his owne fubiects, and his
body brought to the Church of *Hexam*,
it pleafed God in figne of his innocency in
that caufe, to worke many miracles therat;
which being feene, and diligently exami-
ned, the fame was with great folemnity &
veneration honourably reconded in the faid
Church as befeemed fo pretious a treafure.
He fuffered about the yeare of Chrift, nyne
hundred.

Gul.
Malmef.
l.1.de reg.
Angl.
Symon
Dunelm.
in chron.
788.
Affer
meneuëf.
an.789.

F

F   *The ſeauenth Day.*

IN *Scotland* the Commemoration of *S.*
Sigene Abbot and Confeſſour, who deſcended of a very noble parentage in that Kingdome , became a monke of the venerable Order of S. *Benedict,* in a monaſtery of one of the Ilands of *Orcades,* belonging to that Prouince , wherof afterward himſelfe was made Abbot. In which office he ſo behaued himſelfe in ſanctity of life, good learning and reformation of Monaſticall diſcipline, that his name was famous aſwell throughout *Scotland* at home, as in *England, Ireland* and other Countreyes abroad. He liued about the yeare of Chriſt, ſix hundred and threeſcore, about which tyme alſo he repoſed in our Lord.

Io. Leſl.
Epiſco.
Roſſenſ. l.
4. de ge-
ſtis Scot.
Wion in
addit. ad
l. 3. ligni
vitæ.

G   *The eight Day.*

AT *Glaſtenbury* in *Somerſetſhire* the Commemoration of S. *Duuianus* Confeſſour, & ſcholler to *S. Ioſeph* of *Arimathia,* who being a noble man of Britany ioyned himſelfe to *S. Ioſeph,* and lead a ſolitary life with him and his companions, in the Iland of *Auallonia* (now called *Glaſtenbury*) which King

Arui-

Aruiragus of *Britany* had graunted vnto them; where being very famous for sanctity of life and miracles in that first Primitiue Church of our Countrey, he finally reposed in our Lord, about the yeare of Christ, one hundred and eleuen. His body was buryed at *Glastenbury*, and there conserued with due veneration vntill the dayes of K. *Henry* the eight, in whose raigne that Monastery decayed. He was very nobly borne, and one of the first Christians of our Iland, that exercised a solitary or Eremiticall life, after the comming of S. *Ioseph* of *Arimathia* into *Britany*.

Ioan.de Kirkstat in Monasticis Eyseng. cent.2. part.3. dist. 4.

A   *The ninth Day.*

AT *VVinchester* in *Hampshire*, the Commemoration of S. *Frithstan* Confessour & Bishop of the same Sea, who forsaking the burden of that dignity, betooke himselfe to a solitary kind of life, in a village neere to the said Citty of *VVinchester*: In which he constantly perseuered in all sanctity and holinesse of life to his dying day, which happened in the yeare of Christ, nyne hundred thirty and three, and was buryed at *VVinchester*, where his body was wont to be kept in Catholicke tymes, with great honour and veneration. There is a story recorded, how

✳

Matth. West. an. D.932.& 935. Pol. Virgil.l. 6. Ranulph. Cestrensis l.6.c.6.de offic.& Missa defunctorū

that

that S. *Frithstane* was wont euery day to say masse, and office for the dead; and one euening as he walked in the Church-yard reciting his said office, when he came to *Requiescant in Pace*; the voyces in the graues round about, made answere aloud, and said *Amen*.

B   *The tenth Day.*

Ioan.
Tritem.
de Vir.
Illust.l. 3.
cap. 324.
Lest. l. 5.
hist. in
fine. Wion
in Mart.
Benedict.
hac die.

AT *Paderborne* in the higher *Germany* the deposition of S. *Paternus* Confeßour, who borne in *Scotland* of a worthy bloud & despising all wordly things, gate him ouer into *Germany*, and there became a Monke of the Order of S. *Benedict* in a Monastery of the forsaid towne of *Paderborne*, where, by diuine prophefy, he fortold the burning therof by casuall fire, wherin himselfe, being in his Cell, was also cōsumed to ashes, about the yeare of Christ, one thousand fifty and eight. His memory is very famous, vntill this day, both in *Germany*, where he liued, and in *Scotland* also where he was borne.

Ioan.
magnus
in hist.
Goth.
l. 18. c. 11.

THE same day in *Suetia* the passion of S. *Eschillus* Bishop and Martyr, who going out of *England* with *S. Sigfrid* and his Nephewes, to preach the Christian faith to the *Suetians*, after he had laboured for many yeares

incef-

inceſſantly in that kind, and brought many thouſands to the true worſhip of God, was by the incredulous Pagã people of that coũtrey, ſtoned to death, as he was preaching the word of liſe, vpon Good Fryday; And therby deſerued to be crowned with Martyrdome vpon the ſame day, that our Bleſſed Sauiour ſuffered for the Redemption of mankind This happened about the yeare of Chriſt one thouſand and ſixteene, and in the raigne of King *Edmund* of *England*, ſurnamed *Iron-ſide*. {*A nnales Sueuici & Breua. Sueu.*}

C   *The eleuenth Day.*

IN the Ile of *Crowland* in *Lincolnshire* the depoſition of S. *Guthlacke* Confeſſour and Eremite , who being in his youth a ſouldiour, and of good parentage, became weary of the world, and retyred himſelfe to the Monaſtery of *Ripendowne* (now called *Rippon*) in *Yorkshire*, where he tooke firſt the habit of a monke, & ſhortly after became an Eremite in the forſaid Ile of *Crowland*. In which kind of life he continued in ſo great auſterity of faſting , praying, & pennace , that he deſerued twice a day for fifteene yeares togeather to enioy the glorious ſight of his good Angell, working wonderfull miracles both aliue and dead . He departed this {*Fœlix Croland. Gul. Rameſius & Petr. Bleſenſ. in eius vit. Weſt. an.714. Sur.to.2. Pol. Vir. l.4. Mar. Rom. & Molan.*}

world

world in a venerable old age, about the yeare of Chrilt, feauen hundred and fourteene, and was buryed in Crou land-Abbey.

D   The tweluth Day.

AT Roane in France the Commemoration of Blelled Hugh Côicffour & Bilhop of that Sea, who being an Englilhmā by birth, & Abbot of Reading in Barkshire, was thence in the time of K. Henry the nrlt, promoted to the Bilhopricke of Roane; in which dignity he fo worthily behaued himfelfe for fix and thirty yeares togeather, that his name was famous in thofe dayes throughout all France. He died in great fanctity of life and miracles about the yeare of Chrilt, one thoufand one hundred threefcore and fix. This man is different from the other S. Hugh, Bilhop of the fame place, whofe feftiuall day is celebrated vpon the nynth of this moneth.

THE fame day at Alaxion, alfo in France, the Commemoration of S. Mechtild Virgin, who defcended of the bloud Royall of Scoilād, fled thēce fecretly, with her yōgeſt brother Alexander in bafe attire, into France, where placing him as a Brother in the Monaftery of Ciſtercian Mōkes at Fone, fhe wēt herfelf to a village nyne myles of, called Alaxion & there made her a little Cottage of ſtickes

Matth.
Weſt. in
hiſt. Maiori ad
an. Chri.
1130.
Chron.
Cluniacenſe &c.

*

Rob.
Buckland
in eius
vital. M.
S. de vit.
SS. Mulierum

and

and rushes, liuing in great seuerity and pennance, manteyning herself with the labour of her owne hands till her dying day, which happened about the yeare of Christ, one thousand and two hundred. The townesmen of *Alaxion* buryed her body with great solemnity and veneration, God glorifying the same by many Miracles.

Angl, ex antiq. monum. Galliæ.

E   The thirteenth Day.

AT *Glastenbury* in *Somersetshire* the Commemoration of S. *Elsled* Virgin, and Neece to King *Ethelstane* of England, whose wonderfull vertues, and holines of life, togeather with working of miracles, haue in tymes past, byn famous in our Iland. She built herselfe a little Oratory, by the counsell of S. *Dunstan*, neere to the Church of our Blessed Lady at *Glastenbury*, in which she liued in continuall prayer, watching and fasting, vntill her dying day. And when vpon a tyme her vncle K. *Ethelstane*, that was there on hunting, came to visit her, & with a great company, stayed and dined with her, she hauing but one little vessell of drinke (called meath) set the same before him and his trayne; of which when euery one had dronke his fill, the said vessell was notwithstanding as full as before. She ended

*
Osbert. Monac. in vita S. Dunstani apud Sur. to. 3. 19. Maij. west. an. Do. 929

her

her bleſſed dayes about the yeare of Chriſt, nyne hundred thirty and ſix, and was buryed at *Glaſtenbury.*

F   *The fourteenth Day.*

AT *VVincheſter* in *Hampſhire,* the Commemoration of Bleſſed *Ethelnulph* King of the *VVeſtſaxons* and Confeſſour, whoſe godly acts in propagating and increaſing the Chriſtian faith in our Iland, is not only famous to all poſterity, but may be an example alſo and myrrour to all other Chriſtian Princes of Europe. He made the tenth part of his Kingdome free from all tributes and and exactions, and gaue it to the Church in honour of our Bleſſed Lady, and other Saints of God; as alſo he ſent euery yeare three hundred Markes to *Rome,* one hundred to S. *Peters* Church, another hundred to S. *Paules,* and the third to be beſtowed in almes at the Popes diſcretion. And at laſt went thither himſelfe in pilgrimage, togeather with his yongeſt ſonne *Alfred,* whome he committed to Pope *Leo* for his education; And there among other deeds of Charity, he reedified the Engliſh-ſchoole that had byn a little before conſumed by fire. And ſoone after his returne backe into England in moſt godly wiſe, he repoſed in our Lord, about

Card. Baron. in Annal. tom. 10. Matth. Weſt. an. 854 & 857. Pariſ. an. 1257. Pol. Vigil. l. 5. hiſt. Gulielm. Malmeſ. de regib. Angl.

the

the yeare of Chriſt, eight hundred fifty and
ſeauen. *Matthew Paris* a monke of *S. Albans*, and
a very graue Author, numbreth him among
the canonized Saints of our Nation. His
body was with all ſolemnity & veneration
honourably reconded in the Cathedrall
Church of *VVincheſter*, where it yet remayneth among the Monuments of our Saxon
and Engliſh Kings.

G   *The fifteenth Day.*

AT *Yorke* the Eleuation of the glorious
& venerable body of S. *Oſwald*, Biſhop
of that Sea and Confeſſour, who trauayling
in his yonger dayes into *France*, became there
firſt a monke in the Monaſtery of *Floriacke*,
& returning into England, was afterwards
ordayned Biſhop of *VVorceſter*; and laſtly, at
the interceſſion of K. *Edgar*, preferred to *Yorke*
where in great ſanctity of life and miracles
he ended his bleſſed dayes, in the yeare of
Chriſt, nyne hundred fourſcore and twelue.
His body in the yeare 1002. was on this day
with all ſolemnity and reuerence taken vp
by *Aldulph* his ſucceſſour in that Sea, and ſet
in a more eminent place of the Cathedrall
Church of *Yorke*, but afterward tranſlated to
VVorceſter. He built the famous Abbey of
Ramſey in the ile of *Ely*, as alſo a goodly

Matth.
Weſt.
ait. Do.
1002.
Arnold.
wion in
Mart.
Benedict.
Calend.
ſec. vſum
Sarum
hac die.

G   Church

Church at *VVorcefter*, which he dedicated to our bleſſed Lady.

A   The ſixteenth Day.

AT *Cullen* in the higher *Germany* the Tranſlation of part of the venerable body of *S. Alban* Protomartyr of *Great-Britany*, which togeather with other Reliques being firſt carried thence to *Rome* by *S. Germā* Biſhop of *Auxier* in *France*, when with *S. Lupus* he came into *Britany* to expell the *Pelagiā* hereſy, was afterwards brought backe to *Cullen* by *Theophania* wife to the Emperour *Otho* the ſecond, and there very honourably placed in the Monaſtery of *S. Pantaleon*, where the ſame is yet kept with great veneration of the whole Citty. This *S. Alban* in his youth before his conuerſion to Chriſtian faith, being Lord of *Verolame* (now called *S. Albans*) went to *Rome*, and there made a Royall Chalége of Iuſtes for the honour of his Realme, where before all others he had the price, and thereupon was made knight of the Bath by the Emperour *Dioclefian*, and high Steward of the *Britans*, who were then vnder the ſubiection of the *Romans*. And after his returne home, being made a Chriſtian by *S. Amphibale* Prieſt, was for that cauſe ſhortly after apprehended, and

put

Hiſt.
Conuent.
S. Panta.
impreſſa
Coloniæ.
Io. Liag.
Monac.
Burierſ.
in eius
vita.
Molan.
in addit.
ad Vfua.
bac die.
Gerard.
Leigh
in rudi-
mentis
Infigniū
de Alba-
no.

put to death at the forſaid towne of *S.*
Albans in Hartfordſhire, about the yeare of
Chriſt, three hundred and three. *Fortunatus* in
his excellent Booke of Virginity ſpeaking
of Martyrs, among others, commendeth
S. Alban thus:

Albanum egregium fœcunda Britannia profert.
There was a goodly Church and Monaſtery
afterwards erected at *S. Albans* in his honour
by *Offa* K. of the *Merciãs*, wherin the ſaid body of *S. Alban* was placed; the which was in
our laſt age, deſtroyed by K. *Henry* the 8. his
commandement, with hundreds more in
our Iland.

B   *The ſeauenteenth Day.*

AT *Fulda* in the Dioceſſe of *Mentz* in the
higher *Germany*, the Commemoration
of *S. Marianus* Côfeſſour, who borne in *Scot-*
land, & deſcended of a good parentage in that
Kingdome, went ouer into *Germany* and
tooke firſt the habit of a Monke of the Order
of *S. Benedict*, in the Monaſtery of *S. Martins*
at *Cullen*, and afterward at the forſaid towne
of *Fulda*, in an Abbey, which *S. Boniface*
Archbiſhop of *Mentz* had ſometimes founded for the Scottiſh nation, where in great
holines and ſanctity of life, he repoſed in
our Lord, about the yeare of Chriſt, one

*
Arnol.
Wion. l. 2.
ligni vit.
de ſcript.
Ord. D.
Benedict.
Sixtus
Senenſ. in
biblioth.
lib. 4.

thoufand and threefcore, and raigne of K.
Edward the Confeffour of England . He
wrote many learned bookes which he left
behind him to pofterity , and are extant to
be read in diuers libraryes of Europe : The
Catalogue wherof yow may fee fet downe
by diuers Catholicke writers in print.

C　　*The eighteenth Day .*

IN the Marches or borders of *Scotland* the
Commemoration of *S. Ofwyn* Confeffour,
who defcended of a noble Britifh parentage, conténed the vanityes of this world,&
became a monke in an ancient Monaftery
called *Lefting* (which *S. Chad* of *Lichfield* had
fometymes founded) in the Kingdome of
the *Northumbers* , where giuing himfelf to
continuall fafting , prayer and other bodily
pennáce, famous for fanctity of life and miracles, he departed this tranfitory world,and
repofed in our Lord , about the yeare of
Chrift,fix hundred threfcore and ten,whofe
name and holineffe haue byn very memorable in former tymes in our iland of *Great
Britany*, efpecially among the Northerne
people, and borderers of *Scotland*.

*
*Io. Trit.
l.3.c.* 118.
Arnol.
Wion *in
Append.
ad l.3.
ligni vitæ*

D

D   The ninteenth Day.

AT *Green-wich* in *Kent* the paſſion of *S. Elphege* Biſhop and Martyr, who being firſt Abbot of an ancient Monaſtery neere *Bath* in *Somerſetshire*, was thence promoted to the Biſhopricke of *VVinchefter*, & after to *Canterbury*. And when the *Danes* came to inuade his Church of *Canterbury*, and demaunding of him three thouſand markes of money, he like a good Paſtour of his flocke, manfully reſiſted, refuſing to giue the ſaid ſumme from his Church. Wherfore after ſeauen moneths impriſonment, and diuers kinds of torments, he was finally ſtoned to death at the forſaid towne of *Green-wich* by the enemyes of truth, in the yeare of Chriſt, one thouſand and twelue ; whoſe body was firſt brought to *London*, and afterward tranſlated to *Canterbury*. About this tyme alſo (as it is recorded) were ſlayne by the ſaid *Danes*, for the Chriſtian faith, ſix and thirty monkes of S. *Auguſtines* Monaſtery in *Canterbury*, and eight thouſand of the lay people in other places of England.

Sur.to.3. hac die. Pol.Vir. l.7.Mar. Rom. & Molā. in addit. ad Vſuard. Ioan. Capgr. in Catal.SS. Angl. Breu. Sarū & alij ōnes hac die.

E   The twentith Day.

Vē. Beda
l.4.histo.
c.12.15.et
16. &
Epit. ad
an. Dom.
688.west.
an. 686.
687.688.
&689.

AT *Rome* the deposition of Blessed *Cead-wall* King of the *VVestsaxons* and Confessour, who before he was yet a Christian
himselfe, so much reuerenced the Christian Bishops, and Clergy of the Church of
England,that when he had subdued the Ile of
VVight, being Pagan, he gaue the fourth part
therof to *S. VVilfride* (at that tyme expulsed
from *Yorke*) wherin he caused him to preach
& plant the Christian faith; & afterwards
went himselfe to *Rome*,& was there baptized
by Pope *Sergius*, where within a few dayes,
being yet in his Albes, he departed to our
Lord on this day, in the yeare of Christ, six
hundred fourscore and nyne. His body lieth
buryed in the entrāce of *S. Peters* old Church
at *Rome*, as the ancient Tables and Records
therof do declare, wherof you may read S.
Bede more at large in his history of England,
where he setteth downe two Epitaphes en-
grauē ouer the forsaid Kings tombe,the one
in verse, the other in prose in memory of
so famous an act to all posterity. That in
verse is this.

Bed. l. 5.
hist. c. 7.

Culmen, opes, sobolem, pollentia regna, triumphos,
   Exuuias,proceres, mænia, castra; lares;

                                                    Quæ-

Quæque Patrum virtus, & quæ congesserat ipse
Ceadual Armipotens, liquit amore Dei.
Vt Petrum, *Sedemque* Petri Rex *cerneret hospes,*
Cuius fonte meras sumeret Almus aquas,
Splendisicumque iubar radianti carperet hausta,
Et quo viuisicus fulgor vbique fluit.
Percipiensque alacer rediuiuæ præmia vitæ.
Barbaricam rabiem, nomen & inde suum.
Conuersus conuertit ouans, Petrumque *vocari*
Sergius *Antistes iussit, vt ipse Pater.*
Fonte renascentis, quem Christi gratia purgans,
Protinus allutum vexit in arce Poli.
Mira sides Regis, Clementia maxima Christi,
Cuius consilium nullus aaire potest.
Sospes enim veniens supremo ex Orbe Britanni,
Per varias Gentes, per freta, perque vias,
Vrbem Romuleam *vidit, Templumque verendum*
Aspexit Petri, *mystica dona gerens.*
Candidus inter oues Christi socialibus ibit,
Corpore nam tumulum, mente superna tenet.
Commutasse magis Sceptrorum insignia credas,
Quam Regnum Christi promeruisse vides.

THE fame day at *Erford* in the higher
Germany, the Translation of *S. Adlar* Bishop and Martyr, who being an Englishman
by birth, and a monke in the Kingdome of
the *Northumbers,* went ouer into *Germany*
with *S. Boniface* to preach the Christian
faith to that Pagan Nation, where being
confecrated Bishop of *Erford,* he was, togea-

Petr.
Cratepol.
de Episc.
Germa-
niæ.

Trit. l. 3.
c. 173. &
l. 4. c. 183.
de vir.
Illuſtr.
Wion.
hac die.

ther with *S. Boniface*, and fifty others, ſlayne by the barbarous people, at a towne called *Dockam* in *Frizland*, for the defence of Chriſtian faith, in the yeare of Chriſt, ſeauen hundred fifty and foure. His body was afterward on this day tranſlated to *Erford*, and there is kept with great Veneration of the Inhabitants.

F *The one and twentith* Day.

Io. Trit.
de vir.
Illuſt. &
ſcript.
Eccleſ.
Syxt.
Senenſ. in
biblioth.
l. 4. Pol.
Virg. l. 11
hiſtor.
Mart:
Rom. &
Molan.
hac die.

AT *Canterbury* the depoſition of *S. Anſelme* Biſhop & Confeſſour, who borne at *Auguſta* in *Burgundy*, came thence into *Normandy* to the Abbey of *Becke*, and there became firſt a monke, then Prior, and laſtly Abbot of the ſaid Monaſtery. And being afterward promoted to the Sea of *Canterbury*, gouerned the ſame moſt laudably, vntill the tyme of King *VVilliam Rufus*, by whome he was baniſhed the Realme, but againe reſtored by King *Henry* the firſt. He celebrated two famous Councells at *London*. And after a moſt holy life ioyned with great piety & learning, full of venerable old age, he ended his bleſſed dayes, in the yeare of Chriſt, one thouſand one hundred & nyne, and ſixteenth yeare of his Gouerment : and was buryed in his owne Cathedrall Church of *Canterbury*, at the head of his predeceſſour

Lan-

Lanfranke, at whofe body it hath pleafed God to worke many miracles.

G   *The two and twentith* Day.

AT *VVinchefter* in *Hampshire* the Comme-moration of *S. Birftan* Confeffour and Bifhop of that Sea, whofe godly life and miracles, haue much illuftrated our Iland of *Great Britany*. There is a ftory recorded, how on a tyme after his death he appeared to *S. Ethelwold* his fucceffor in the Sea of *VVinche-fter*, togeather with *S. Birine* and *S. Swithin*, all in great glory, & told him: *That he who was made worthy of fo great glory in heauen, had no reafon to be defrauded of his honour on earth.* After which tyme *S. Ethelwold* caufed his body to be kept with more veneration & reuerence then before. He died in great fanctity and holyneffe of life, about the yeare of Chrift, nyne hundred forty and foure, and was buryed at *VVinchefter*.

Matth. Weft. in hift. ma-iori ad an. Do. 944. & 965.

A   *The three and twentith* Day.

THE Celebrity of *S. George* Martyr, whofe feaft, for that he is Patron of *England*, hath alwayes byn kept holy, and ferued with a double office throughout our whole

Mart. Rom. & ónes alij hac die.

Realme in former Catholicke tymes, according to the vſe of *Sarum.*

Sea.
Chrō. an.
Do. 872.
Ingulph.
de Cro-
land in
Liſtor.
Marian.
Scot. &
Io. Stous
in Anna-
libus.

THE ſame day at *VVimborne* in *Dorſetſhire* the Paſſion of *S. Etheldred* King of the *VVeſtſaxons* and Martyr, who in the Daniſh perſecution, was ſlayne by the Tyrannicall Pagans, in hatred of Chriſtian Religion, at an old Towne in the weſt part of *England* called *VVhittingham*, in the yeare of Chriſt, eight hundred threeſcore and twelue. His body was brought to the Monaſtery of *VVimborne*, and there entombed with great veneration, as is yet to be ſeene by his Epitaph, recorded by our Engliſh Hiſtoriographers, thus : *In hoc loco requieſcit corpus S. Etheldredi Regis VVeſtſaxonum Martyris, qui anno Domini octingenteſimo ſeptuageſimo ſecundo, vigeſimo tertio die Aprilis per manus Dacorum Paganorum occubuit.*

B   *The foure & twentith* Day.

Bed. l. 1. c.
20. & 30.
& l. 2. c. 2.
3. 7. Sigeb.
in Chron.
Mart.
Rom. &
alij omnes
hac die.

AT *Canterbury* the depoſitiō of S. *Mellitus* Biſhop & Confeſſour, who being ſent into *England* by S. *Gregory* the *Great*, with three other Cōpanions to aſſiſt S. *Auguſtine* in the harueſt of ſoules, was ſhortly after his comming firſt created Biſhop of *London*, and afterwards gouerned the Sea of *Canterbury*, where in all venerable ſanctity of life and

mi-

miracles, he ended his bleſſed dayes, about the yeare of Chriſt, ſix hundred twenty and foure: and was buryed neere to his predeceſſours S. *Auguſtine* and S. *Laurence*, in the North porch of his Cathedrall Church of *Canterbury*.

THE ſame day in the Monaſtery of S. *Columbe* in *Scotland*, the depoſition of S. *Egbert* Abbot and Confeſſour, who deſcended of a noble Britiſh linnage, ſent S. VVillebrord and his fellowes into *Flanders* and *Germany*, to preach the Chriſtiã faith; as alſo gaue inſtructions to the monkes of *Scotland*, about the obſeruation of the feaſt of *Eaſter*. And finally in great ſanctity of life and miracles repoſed happily in our Lord, about the yeare of Chriſt, ſeauen hundred twenty and nyne.

Bed.l.3.c. 27.& l.5. cap.3. Marcell. in vita S. Simibert. Molan. & alij.

ALſo the ſame day at S. *Iues* in *Hütington-ſhire* the inuétiõ of the venerable body of S. *Iuo* Biſhop & Confeſſour, who comming out of *Perſia* into Englãd, there preached the Chriſtian faith; & dying about the yeare of Chriſt, ſix hundred, was afterward on this day found out, and taken vp by *Alwyn* Earle of the *Eaſtangles*, and moſt honourably, and with great veneration entombed and placed in the Abbey of *Ramſey*, in the yeare of Chriſt, one thouſand and one, and raigne of King *Ethelred* of England.

Matth. Weſt. an. Dom. 1001. Andr. Leucãder & Got-zelin. in eius vita.

Moreouer

MOreour the same day at *Canterbury* the Trāslatiō of *s. VVilfrid* Bishop of *Yorke* and Confessour, whose body in the second Danish persecution, was on this day translated to *Canterbury*, from *Rippon* in *Yorkeshire*, where he was first buryed, by *s. Odo* Archbishop of that Sea, and there with great solemnity & veneration, placed in the Cathedrall Church of that Citty, about the yeare of Christ, nyne hundred fifty and seauen, wherat it pleased God to worke miracles. His principall festiuity is celebrated in our English Catholicke Church vpon the tweluth day of *October*.

Calend.
sec. vsum
Sarum.

C   *The fiue & twentith Day.*

AT *VVancourt* in the Territory of *Arras* in the lower *Germany*, the Commemoration of *s. Obodius* Confessour and Eremite, who descended of a very noble parentage in *Ireland,* and contemning the vanityes of the world, in his youth, went ouer into the Low-Countreyes, & there lead a solitary and Eremiticall kind of life in the aforsaid Territory of *Arras,* to the great edification of the Inhabitants of that place; where finally in great sanctity and holines of life, he ended his blessed dayes, about the yeare of Christ, seauen hundred; whose body is yet cōserued

＊
Chron.
Lamberti
de Loos
Monach.
Camerac.
ex antiq.
montium.
Eccles.
Wacor-
tens. &
Attreba-
tensis.

in

in the said towne of *VVancourt*, with great
honour and veneration of the people dwel-
ling therabout, as Patron of that Village.

D   *The six and twentith* Day.

IN *Scotland* the Commemoration of the
Saints *Modane* and *Midane* Brothers and
Confessours, who borne in the same Kingdome, and there descended of a worthy family, contemned the vanityes of the world,
and became Religious monkes of the venerable Order of *S. Benedict* in their owne
Countrey, where in all kind of good learning, vertue, and sanctity of life, they finally, in a good old age, reposed in our Lord,
about the yeare of Christ, eight hundred and
foure. Their memory hath in former Catholicke tymes byn famous throughout
Scotland and *Ireland*, where many aultars and
Oratories haue byn dedicated in their honour, as the ancient Records of those Kingdomes do declare.

*Io. Lesl.
Epis.
Rossensis
l.5.de
gest.Scot.
ex antiq.
monum.
Wion.in
addit. ad
l.3.ligni
vitæ.*

E   *The seauen & twentith* Day.

AT *Heydentine-Monastery* in the higher
Germany the deposition of S. *Walburge*
Virgin and Abbesse, daughter to S. *Richard*

King

Io. *Trit.*
de vir.
Illuftr.
Ord.D.
Bened. l.
3.c.250.
Anton.
Demo-
char. l. 2.
Sacrific.
Miffæ.
Arnold.
Wion *in*
Mart.
hac die.
Mart.
Romanū
die 1.
Maij.

King of *England*, who after the death of her Father, being fent for by *S. Bonifaee* Archbifhop of *Mentz* and her vncle, was by him made Abbeffe of the forfaid Monaftery of *Heydentine*, where in very great fačtity & working of miracles fhe gaue vp her foule to her heauély fpoufe, about the yeare of Chrift, feauē hūdred threfcore & fixteene Her body was afterward tranflated to *Eyft*, and there placed in the Cathedrall Church of that Citty (neere to the venerable body of S. *VVillebald* her owne brother;) out of which there diftilleth vntill this day, a moft fweet and pretious oyle, very foueraigne for many difeafes. Ouer whofe tombe is engrauen in marble this fhort Epitaph.

{ *Filia Regis erat, fed egenam fe faciebat,* }
{ *Diues vt Chrifto, regnaret femper in ipfo.* }

The feaft of this her Tranflation is celebrated in Germany vpon the firft of May with great folemnity and deuotion of the people of *Eyft*. She was canonized for a Saint by Pope *Adrian* the fecond.

F *The eight & twentith Day.*

AT *VVerdt* in *Cleeueland* the Commemoration of S. *Kortill* Bifhop and Martyr, who borne of a noble parentage in

Scotland, became firſt a monke in that Kingdome of the venerable Order of S. *Benedict,*
in an anciét Monaſtery there called *Amarba-*
ricke, wherof he being ſoone after made
Abbot , went ouer into the Lower *Germany*
and *Saxony* to propagate the Chriſtian faith
newly planted in thoſe partes; and being
there ordayned Biſhop of *VVerdt,* was a little
after in hatred of the ſame Chriſtian faith,
ſlayne by the incredulous and barbarous
*Saxons,*about the yeare of Chriſt,eignt hundred and twenty. His body was buryed at
VVerdt aforſaid, and there kept in former
tymes with great veneration.

Albert.
Cranz.
Metrop.
l.1.ca.26.
Wion l.
2.ligni
vitæ in
Catalog.
Epiſcop.
Werdēſ.

G　The nine *&* twentith Day.

IN *Northwales* the Commemoration of
S. *Senan* Confeſſour,who deſcended of an
ancient and noble Britiſh bloud, contemned the vanities of the world, and became
an Eremite, leading a ſolitary and ſeuere
kind of life in the North of *VVales* neere to
the Teritorry of S. *Wenefrides* Father, by
whome S.*Wenefride* her ſelfe was often viſi-
ted, and after her death lay many yeares buried neere to his body, vntill her tranſlation
to *Shrewsbury.* He liued in great ſanctity and
fame of miracles in the yeare of Chriſt , ſix
hundred and threeſcore,about which tyme

*
Acta. S.
Weneſr.
Virginis
in diuerſis
Codic. &
in. lectiō.
eiuſdem
Sanctæ,
in Bre-
uiar.Sar.

alſo

alſo he happily repoſed in our Lord. His memory hath in former Catholicke tymes byn very famous in our Iland of *Great-Britany*, but eſpecially among the *Welch-men*. And in *Cornwall*, there is yet a Village and Hauen of his name, commonly called S. *Senans*.

A   The thirtith Day.

Io. Trit.
l.4. de
vir. Illuſt.
Bed. l. 4.
biſt. c. 6.
Mart.
Rom.
Molan.
& omnes
hac die.

AT *London* the depoſition of S. *Erconwald* Confeſſour and Biſhop of that Sea, ſonne to *Offa* King of the *Eaſtſaxons*, who being firſt Abbot of *Chertſey* in *Surrey*, which himſelfe had built, was thence promoted to the Biſhopricke of *London*, wherin he ſo excelled in all ſanctity and holines of life, that it pleaſed God to manifeſt the ſame to poſterity, by the wonderfull miracles wrought by him both aliue & dead. He deſeaſed in the yeare of Chriſt, ſix hundred threeſcore and fiue, and was buryed at *London*. He founded another goodly Monaſtery of Nunnes at *Barking* in *Eſſex*, wherof he ordayned his owne ſiſter *Edilburge* Abbeſſe. The feaſt of his Tranſlation was wont to be kept in our Countrey in Catholicke tymes, with great ſolemnity, vpon

the

the fourteenth of Nouember (in which
place we haue againe made mention of
him) especially in the Diocesse of *London*,
where it was appointed holy-day, as
the ancient Recordes of *S.*
Paules Church do
declare.

* *
*

THE

THE
MONETH
OF MAY.

B *The first Day.*

Arnol.
Wion in
Mart.
Benedict.
ex Chrō.
Britan.
Molan.
in addit.
ad Vsua.

AT S. *Assaphs* in *Flint-shire* of *VVales* the deposition of S. *Assaph* Confessour and first Bishop of that Sea, who of a monke and disciple of S. *Kentigerne* Abbot of *Glasco* in *Scotland*, was ordayned Bishop of an old towne in Northwales named *Elgoa*, but afterwards called S. *Assaphes* of his owne name, where he excelled in all kind of vertue and singular holines of life vntill his dying day, which happened in a venerable old age, about the yeare of Christ, fiue hundred fourscore and sixteene.

THe same day at *Fossis* in the Territory of *Namures* in the lower *Germany*, the

depo-

depofition of *S.Vltan* Abbot and Confeffour, fonne to *Philtan* King of *Ireland*, & brother to S. *Furfens* and S. *Foillan*, who going ouer into *France* and *Flanders*, built a Monaftery or hofpitall for the intertaynment of poore pilgrims at a place called *Foßis* in the forfaid Territory of *Namures*, which he obtayned of S. *Gertrude* Abbeffe of *Niuelle*. And after infinite workes of piety and deuorion in that kind, he there finally went to our Lord, about the yeare of Chrift, fix hundred and threefcore, and was buryed at *Foßis*.

Bed. l. 3. c. 19. Sigebert. in Chron. Vincent. in fpecul. & Wion. hac die.

C   *The fecond Day.*

IN the lower *Germany* the feftiuity of S. *German* Bifhop and Martyr, who being an Englifhman by birth, went ouer into the low Countreyes to preach the faith of Chrift, where finally for his reward, he receyued a Crowne of Martyrdome. His life is to be read at large in wrytten hád, extant in a Monaftery of the Low-Countreyes, as teftifieth a Reuerend Prieft of the Society of *Iefus*, whofe feftiuity he appointeth on this day, in his booke intituled, *Fafti Sanctorum &c.*

Heriber. Rofweyd. Soc. Iefu in Tab. faft. SS. hac die.

THE fame day at *Padflow* in *Corn-wall* the Commemoration of S. *Piran* Con efour, who borne in *Ireland* of a Kings bloud,

*

for the loue of God contemned the world, and became an Eremite in that Kingdome, leading (for many yeares) a very strict and seuere kind of life, in so much that it pleased God to worke by him many miracles. Among which, one is recorded, that with the flesh of three kyne, he sustayned ten armyes of mē for eight dayes, as also rayfed diuers dead men to life. And after all this he came ouer into *England*, and liued at *Padstow* in *Corn-wall*, where in great sanctity of life, he finally reposed in our Lord, and where in like manner his body hath byn kept with great solemnity and veneration, in a Chappell of the forsaid towne of *Padstow*, which Chappell is there to be seene vntill this day.

Chron.
Hyburn.
& antiq.
n. on.m.
Eccles.
Padsto.

D   *The third Day.*

AT *Mailros* in the Kingdome of *Northumberland*, the deposition of *S. Walter* Abbot and Confessour, sonne to *Dauid* King of *Scotland*, who forsaking the dignities and honours of the world, and refusing the Archbishopricke and Metropolitan Sea of *S. Andrewes* in the same Kingdome, became a monke and afterwards Abbot of the goodly Monastery of *Mailros*, situated in the Marches of *Scotland*, in the Kingdome of the *Northum-*

Io. Mola.
in addit.
ad Ysuar.
Io. Lesl. l.
6. de gest.
Scot. in
Dauidem
Regem.

bers, where in very great fanctity of life and
working of miracles, he ended his bleſſed
dayes, about the yeare of Chriſt, one thoufand and one hundred. His memory is yet
famous throughout the whole Realme of
Scotland, where many Chappells and altars
haue in Catholicke tymes byn dedicated in
his honour, but now quite deſtroyed and
defaced by the enemyes of Gods truth, to
the great lamentation of the Chriſtian
world.

E   *The fourth Day.*

AT *Bardney* in *Lincolnſhire* the Commemoratiō of Bleſſed *Ethelred* Confeſſour,
and King of the *Mercians* (or middle Eng-
liſhmen)who after he had ruled that Kingdome moſt laudably for thirty whole yeares
togeather, left the fame to *Coenred* his Nephew, contemned the world, and tooke the
habit of a monke in the Monaſtery of *Bardney* of the venerable Order of S. *Benedict*, and
afterward became Abbot of the fame place,
where he fo greatly excelled in all kind of
vertue and fanctity of life, that his name
was very famous in thofe dayes throughout
England. He died about the yeare of Chriſt,
feauen hundred and ten, and was buryed in
in the fame Monaſtery.

✱
Bed.l.5.
hiſt. cap.
20. & in
Epito. ad
An. Do.
704.
Pol. Vir.
l.4. Mat.
Weſt.
an.692.et
705.

F   The fifth Day.

*

Matth.
Weſt.
an. Do.
943. &
955. &
974.

AT Shepton in Warwickſhire the Comme
moration of S. Algiue Queene, mothe
to King Edgar of bleſſed memory and Mo
narch of England, who ſo greatly excelled i
piety, deuotion, and other eminent vertu
whilſt ſhe liued, that her body in the yea
of Chriſt, nyne hūdred threeſcore and fou
teene (which was ſome thirty yeares aft
her death) being miraculouſly reueyled
Shepton, it pleaſed God to worke many mira
cles therat, in teſtimony of her holineſſe,
increaſe of deuotion in our Iland of Gre
Britany.

*

Hect.
Boet. de
geſt. Sco.
& Leſl.
ibid. l. 4.
hiſtor.
& alij.

THE ſame day in Ireland the Comme
moration of S. Scandalâus mōke & Cor
feſſour, diſciple to S. Columbe the Great of th
Nation, who comming ouer into Scotla
with a dozen other Companions in con
pany of the forſaid S. Columbe, for the Cor
uerſion of the Pictes, who then inhabite
that Kingdome, was famous for ſancti
and holines of life, about the yeare of Chri
fiue hundred and fourſcore, about whic
tyme alſo he repoſed in our Lord.

G   The ſixt Day.

AT *Lindisferne* in the Kingdome of the *Northumbers*, the depoſition of S. *Edbert* Confeſſour and Biſhop of that Sea, who taking vp the venerable body of S. *Cuthbert* eleuen yeares after his death, and finding it altogeather vncorrupt, put the ſame into a new coffin, and ſaid : *Happy were that man, who might lye in the old;* and within a few dayes after, full of ſanctity and holines of life, he being called out of this world, was himſelfe layd therin, according to his wiſh. At whoſe body it pleaſed God to worke many miracles in token of the innocency of his life. This happened in the yeare of Chriſt, ſix hundred fourſcore and eigh-teene.

Vẽ.Beda. l.2.c. 29. et in vita S. Cuthb. Mart. Rom. Molan. & alij omnes hac die.

THE ſame day at *Landaffa* in *Clamorgan-ſhire,* the Tranſlation of S. *Dubritius* Biſhop and Confeſſour, who being ſom-time Archbiſhop of *Carleon* vpon *Vſke* and Metropolitan of the *Britans,* reſigned the ſaid Sea to S. *Dauid,* & became an Eremite, leading a very ſtrict & ſeuere kind of life in the moũ-taynes of *VVales,* vntill his dying day; which happened about the yeare of Chriſt, fiue hundred and twenty. His body was firſt buryed in the Iland of *Bardſey,* & afterward

Matth. weſt. an. 507. Gaufr. Monum. l.9.c.4.et 13.hiſt. vet. Brit. Humfr J huide in frag. deſcript. Britan.

on this day tranflated to *Landaffa*, about the yeare of Chrift, one thoufand one hundred and twenty.

A   The feauenth Day.

Bed.l.5.c.
2.3.4. &
6.Trit.de
Vir.
Illuſtr.
Breu. ſec.
vſū Sar.
Mart.
Ror.
Molā. &
alij.

AT *Beuerley* in *Yorkeshire* the feſtiuity of S. *Iohn* Biſhop and Confeſſour, commonly called S. *Iohn* of *Beuerley*, who after he had gouerned the Sea of *Yorke* in great fanctity and holines of life, for the fpaceof tnree and thirty yeares, famous for miracles, he ended his venerable old dayes, in the yeare of Chrift, feauen hundred twenty and one. His body was firft buryed at *Yorke*, but afterward with great honour and folemnity tranflated to *Beuerley*, by Biſhop *Alred* his fucceſſour, and there interred in the Monaftery which himfelfe had built, where with great veneration the fame was preferued euen vntill our dayes, and vifited of many, efpecially for the great miracles that it hath pleafed God to worke therat by his merits. The forfaid Monaftery of *Beuerley*, was afterward, by licence of the Pope, made a Sanctuary, in the raigne of King *Ethelftane*, who placed a certaine Chayre of ftone in the Church, neere vnto S.*Iohns* body, vpon which, this infcription was engrauen: *Hæc fedes lapidea dicitur* Freed-ftoole,

Regiſtr.
Eccleſiæ
Beuerla-
cenſis.

Id eſt, Pacis Cathedra; ad quam reus fugiendo per-ueniens , omnimodam habet ſecuritatē. This feſti-uall day of his was afterward in a Coun-cell of Biſhops held at *London* in the yeare 1416. appointed to be kept holy-day in his memory throughout *England*.

B   *The eight Day.*

AT *Maeſtricht* in the Territory of *Liege*, the feſtiuity of *S. Wyre* Cōfeſſour, deſcēded of a noble bloud in *Scotland*, who being or-dayned Biſhop of the *Deiri*, in the Kingdome of the *Northumbers*, went ouer into the lower *Germany*, where he became Cōfeſſor to Duke *Pepin* of *Brabant*, labouring inceſſantly in teaching and preaching the Chriſtian faith. And finally in great ſanctity and venerable old yeares, he departed this life, at the Mo-naſtery of *S. Odilia* neere *Ruremond*, vpon the Riuer of *Moſa*, about the yeare of Chriſt ſeauen hundred thirty and one . His body was tranſlated afterward to *Maeſtricht*, and there with great veneration of the Inhabi-tants is kept in the Cathedrall Church of that Citty.

Marc. in vita S. Si-miberti apud Surium. Mart. Rom. Molā. in addit. ad Vſuar. et in Indic. SS. Belgij

C

C   The ninth Day.

B.Rhena.
in hist.
German.
l.3.Eysen.
Cent. 2.
part. 5.
Mart.
Rom.
Vsuard.
Annales
Heluet.

AT *Vindecine* among the *Zwitzers* in the higher *Germany* the deposition of S Beatus Confessour and Apostle of *Zuizerland* who being sonne to a noble man of *Britany* wet to *Rome* in the primitiue Church, partly on pilgrimage, & partly to be better instructed in the Christian faith. And as he returned backe, he began to preach to the *Zwitz* zers in *Heluetia*, and conuerted many of then to the faith of Christ, wherby he becam their first Apostle. He died there in an Oratory which himselfe had built, where als his body was buryed, and many miracle wrought therat, about the yeare of Christ one hundred and eleuen, and was the fir Saint of our Nation we read of, that die out of *Britany.*

D   The tenth Day.

AT *Durham* in the *Bishopricke* the Tran lation of the venerable Body of S. Be Priest and Confessour, by whose wryting the Christian world hath byn much illu strated. When he was but seauen yean old, he was committed for his educatio

to S. *Benedict*, Abbot of the Monaſtery of
VVyremund, and afterward became a moke in
the ſame place , ſeruing God therin all the
dayes of his life, as himſelfe teſtifieth in the
end of his fifth booke of the hiſtory of *England*. And being at laſt admoniſhed of his
death , by an Angell, when the tyme drew
neere , which was on the feaſt of our Sauiours
ours Aſcenſion , kneeling downe vpon the
pauement of his Cell, and ſinging, *Gloria pa-
tri , & filio, & ſpiritui ſancto* &c . he haue vp
the ghoſt, about the yeare of Chriſt, ſeauen
hundred threſcore and ſix. His body was
afterward on this day tranſlated to *Durham,*
and there with great veneration placed in
the Tombe togeather with S. *Cuthbert,* with
this old inſcription or Epitaph:

Beda Dei famulus, Monachorum nobile ſydus,
     Finibus e terra profuit Ecclesia.
Soles iſte Patrum ſcrutando per omnia ſenſum,
     Eloquio viguit, plurima compoſuit.
Annos in hac vita ter duxit vita triginta,
     Presbyter officio , vtilis ingenio.
Iunij ſeptenis viduatus carne Kalendis
     Angligena , Angelicam commeruit patriam.

His principall feſtiuity is kept in our Engliſh Catholicke Church vpon the 27. of
this moneth according to the vſe of *Sarum,*
on which day he died.

Matth.
Weſt.
an.737,
Author
Cötin.
eius hiſt.
l.1.cap.7.
Trit .de
vir.Illuſt.
Molan.
hac die.
Arnol.
Wion l.
5.ligni
vit.cap.
101.
ex antiq.
monum.
Eccleſ.
Dunel-
menſ.

E

E   The eleuenth Day.

Ioan.
Capgr. in
Catal. SS.
Britan.
Molā. in
addit. ad
Vſuar.
Matth.
Pariſ. de
eius Ca-
noniʒat.
an. Do.
1257.

IN the Marches of *VVales* the paſſion of *S. Fremund* King and Martyr, ſonne to *Offa* King of the *Mercians* (of Middle Eng-liſhmen) who after a yeare and a halfe, that he had ruled his Kingdome, left the ſame, and for the loue of Chriſt became an Ere-mite in the Marches of *VVales*, in a little Iland there, called in the Britiſh tongue *Ilke-ſage*, where togeather with two ver-tuous prieſts he liued a very holy and exem-plar kind of life, vntill King *Oſway*, that was fallen from the Chriſtian faith, in ha-tred therof, ſecretly killed him, in the yeare of Chriſt, ſeauen hūdred threeſcore & nyne. He was afterward canonized for a Saint in the yeare, one thouſand two hundred fifty and ſcauen, and raigne of King *Henry* the third of England; whoſe memory in Ca-tholicke tymes, hath byn very famous in our Iland, eſpecially among the ancient Britans of *North-VVales.*

F   The tweluth Day.

AT *Lincolne* the depoſition of S. *Remigius* Confeſſour and Biſhop of that Sea, fa

mous

mous for fanctity of life and learning. He departed this world in the yeare of Christ, one thousand fourscore and eleuen : whose body being on this day interred with great solemnity and veneration, in his Cathedrall Church of *Lincolne*, it pleased God in testimony of his holynes to worke wonderous signes therat, especially in the raigne of King *Henry* the third, when as all England went on pilgrimage thither, for the great miracles that were the dayly wrought. He built two famous Monasteryes by the help of King *VVilliam* the *Cōquerour*, the one at *Battaile* in *Suffex*, the other at *Cane* in *Normandy*, which later he consecrated to S. *Stephen* the Protomartyr. And was the first that trāflated the Bishopricke of *Dorchester* to *Lincolne*, where he built a goodly Cathedrall Church, and adorned the same (saith *Stow*) with Clarkes that were approued both in learning and manners.

Matth.
Weft.
an. Do.
1091. Pol.
Vir. l. 10.
hiftor.
Mat Par.
an. 1253.
& 1255
Sto. in
Annal.
in vita
Guliel.
primi an.
1086.

G   The thirteenth Day.

AT the Monaſtery of *Ramfey* in the Ile of *Ely*, in the Prouince of the *Eaftangles*, the Commemoration of S. *Merwyne* Virgin, who being a womā of great fanctimony & holineſſe of life, was by King *Edgar* of bleſſed memory, conſtituted Abbeſſe of a new

✳

Matth.
Weft. in
hist. ma-
iori ad
An.Do.
967. &
de eius
Electione
ibid.

Monaftery, which by the help of *Alwyn* Earle of the *Eaftangles*, *S. Ofwald* Bifhop of *Yorke* had newly founded at *Ramfey*, where in all vertuous conuerfation and exemplar good life, efpecially in the obferuation of Monafticall difcipline, full of miracles, fhe gaue vp her foule to her heauenly fpoufe, about the yeare of Chrift, nyne hundred and fourfcore, where her body was alfo interred, and kept for a long tyme with great veneration. This forfaid Abbey of *Ramfey* is different from another of the fame name, which in tymes paft hath byn alfo very famous in our Iland, being fituated in *Wiltfhire*, where vntill this day the ruines therof are remayning to be feene.

A   The fourteenth Day.

*
Acta. S.
Edithæ
iunioris
apud
Sur.to. 5.
die 16.
Sept.
Matth.
Weft. in
hift. &c.

AT *Pollefworth* in *VVarwickfhire* the Commemoration of *S. Edith* Virgin, and fifter to holy King *Edgar* of bleffed memory, who being a woman of rare vertue, was ordayned Abbeffe of a Monaftery at the forfaid place of *Pollefworth*, which S. *Modwene* of *Ireland* had built with the goods of her owne inheritance; where in all kind of fanctimony of life, and godly conuerfation, full of miracles, fhe ended her bleffed dayes, about the yeare of Chrift, nyne hundred & four-

fcore.

score. This woman is different from another S. *Edith* of the same name, whose festiuall dayes are celebrated vpon the sixteenth of *September*, and third of *Nouember*, and was daughter to the forsaid *Edgar*, and Abbesse of *VVilton*, commonly called by the name of *Edith* the yonger, and Neece to this, of whome here we haue made mention.

B   *The fifteenth Day.*

AT *Ghele* in *Brabant* the festiuity of S. *Dympna* Virgin and Martyr, daughter to a pagan King of *Ireland*, who being secretly instructed in the Christian faith by S. *Gereberne* a Priest of her owne Nation, after the death of her mother the Queene, her Father would haue married her, and made her his wife: which thing the holy Virgin abhoring, stole priuily away into the lower *Germany*, whither her Father following her, and finding her out, cut of her head, with his owne hands, togeather with the head of S. *Gereberne* in hatred of Christian Religion, about the yeare of Christ, 600. Her body is honourably reconded at *Ghele*, and there is kept with great veneration, wherat it hath pleased God to shew infinite miracles, in signe of her innocency, especially in casting out Diuells, as

Sur.to. 3. de vit.SS. hac die. Molā. in addit. ad Vsuar. et in Indic. SS.Belgij Rob. Buckl. in eius vita. Mart. Rom. & alij omnes.

well

well to his owne glory, as increafe of deuotion in the Chriſtian world, & eſpecially in
the low Countreys. *S*. *Gereberns* body was
interred at the towne of *Santen* vpon the
riuer of *Rhene*, and there his Reliques were
kept, whiles that place was Catholicke,
with great veneration of the dwellers therabout.

C   *The ſixteenth Day.*

Speculum
Fratr.
Carmelit.
Io.Molā.
in addit.
ad Yſuar.
hac die.

AT *Burdeaux* in *Gaſcoyne* of *France* the depoſition of S. *Symon* Confeſſour, an
Engliſhman by birth, and Generall of the
Religious men called *Carmelites,* who as he
prayed to the bleſſed Virgin, ſhe appeared
with a troupe of Angells, holding vp the
Scapulare or Coole of his Order in her hāds,
and ſaid : *That whoſoeuer died in that habit ſhould*
be ſaued. He deſceaſed at *Burdeaux* in the viſi-
tation of his Generallſhip, about the yeare
of Chriſt, one thouſand, fifty and two,
where his body is yet kept with great veneration, God hauing, through his merits,
adorned the ſame with many miracles.

THE ſame day at the towne of S.
Albans in *Hartfordſhire,* the Tranſlation of
S. Alban Lord of *Verolame,* knight of the *Bath,*
high Steward of the Britans, and the firſt
Martyr that ſuffered for Chriſt in our Iland.

Whoſe

Whofe body was on this day by *Offa* King
of the *Mercians,* in the yeare of Chrift 794.
taken vp and tranflated to a Church, that
he had newly built in his honour, without
the towne of *S. Albans.* In which place alfo
he founded a goodly Monaftery, & endowed
it with great lands and poffeffions. This
King *Offa* went after in perfon to *Rome,* and
procured S. *Albans* Canonization, and priuiledges for the faid Monaftery, of Pope
Adrian the firft : As alfo gaue to the Sea of
Rome a certaine tribute of his Kingdome, gathering yearly, of euery family of his dominions, certayne money for the fame, commonly called *Peter-pence,* which tribute continued in our Iland vntill King *Henry* the 8.
when firft the breach began with the fea
Apoftolicke.

Matth.
Weft.
an.794.
& 796.
Pol. Vir.
l.4. hift.
Ioan.
Lidgate
Monac.
Burieſis
in eius
vita. vid.
Reſponſ.
ad D.
Cooke an.
1606. edi.
c.6.n.70.

THE fame day in like manner in *Scot-*
land the depofition of *S. Brandan* Abbot
and Confeffour, whofe life and miracles
haue byn famous in tymes paft in our Iland
of *Great-Britany.* He flourifhed in the yeare
of Chrift 570. about which tyme alfo he
died.

Rom.
Mart.
Molan.
& alij
omnes
hac die.

D   *The feauenteenth Day.*

AT *Elnona* in the higher *Germany* the
Tranflation of the venerable bodyes of

I   *Three*

Three of the *eleuen thousand Virgins*, martyred with *S. Vrsula*, who being of the Britiſh Nation, ſuffered death for defence of their virginity and Chriſtian Religion, at *Cullen* in *Germany*, with the forſaid *S. Vrsula*, and her companions, about the yeare of Chriſt, three hundred fourſcore and three. From whence on this day, three of their said glorious bodies were tranſlated to *Elnona*, and there very honourably and with great veneration reconded ; wherat it hath pleaſed God to worke miracles, as well for the increaſe of deuotion in the people, as alſo for confirmation of Catholicke Religion in thoſe partes.

Io. Mola.
in addit.
ad yſuar.
Regiſt.
Eccleſiæ
Elnonēſ.

E   *The eighteenth Day.*

AT *Yorke* the depoſition of S. *Sewall* Confeſſour and Archbiſhop of the ſame Sea, ſometyme ſcholler in *Oxford* to S. *Edmund* Archbiſhop of *Canterbury*, whoſe integrity and innocēcy of life, togeather with his admirable patience in aduerſity, was ſo acceptable to God, that it pleaſed his diuine Maieſty in ſigne therof, to worke miracles by him both aliue and dead : and among other, it is recorded, that lying on his death-bed, he turned water into wyne, by only bleſſing it. He ended his venerable old

Matth.
Pariſ. in
hiſt. Ang.
an. 1255.
1256.1257
& 1258.
Catal.
Epiſco.
Eboracēſ.

dayes

dayes, after much forrow and tribulation, in great fanctity and holineffe of life, in the yeare of Chrift, one thoufand two hundred fifty and eight, vpon the day of our Bleffed Sauiours Afcenfion, deferuing to receyue the Crowne of his labours, on the fame day, that Chrift our Sauiour, after his bitter paffion heere on earth for the Redemption of mankind, entred into the glory of his eternall Father. His body was buryed in hisowne Cathedrall Church of *Yorke*, and there kept and vifited with great veneration of the Northerne people, euen vntill the tyme of King *Henry* the 8. for the Miracles that had byn wrought therat.

F   *The ninteenth* Day.

AT *Canterbury* the depofition of *S.Dunstan* Bifhop and Confeffour, who being firft Abbot of the ancient and goodly Monaftery of *Glaftenbury* in *Somerfetshire*, was thence promoted to the Bifhopricke of *VVorcefter*, and after to *London*, and laft of all to *Canterbury* : whofe godly workes of piety, togeather with the multitude of his miracles, are manifeft to the Chriftiá world. He died in the yeare of Chrift, nyne hundred fourfcore and eight, and was buried at *Canterbury*, where his body was wont, in Catho-

Sur.to.2.
hac die.
Gul.
Malmef.
in hift.
Angl.
Petr. in
Catal.
l. 8 Pol.
Vir.l. 7.
Mart.
Rom.
Molá. &
alii.

licke

licke tymes, to be kept with great veneration of all *England,* vntill thefe later dayes of fchifmes and herefyes in our Kingdome.

THe fame day at *Towers in France* the depofition of *S. Alcuine,* Abbot and Confeffour, who borne in *Yorkeshire,* and fomtyme School-maifter of *Yorke,* went ouer into *France,* and became Maifter to the Emperour *Charles* the Great, by whofe help he founded the Vniuerfity of *Paris,* about the yeare of Chrift, eight hundred and foure, hauing himfelfe byn fcholler to our famous *S. Bede* in his youth. His notable labours and workes in Gods Church are yet memorable throughout the Chriftian world   He died at *Towers* in *France* about the yeare of Chrift 813. & was the firft that compofed the Maffe & Office of the bleffed Trinity, and of *S. Stephen* the Protomartyr, which being afterward approued by our Mother the holy Catholicke Church, is the fame that now is vfually faid in the Romã Miffal & Breuiary.

Trit. de Script. Eccl. l. 2. Vincent. in fpecul. lib. 23. Gazelin. Mola. & Wion hac die in fuis Martyrologijs.

G   The twentith Day.

AT *Hereford* the feftiuity of *S. Ethelbert* King of the *Eaftangles* and Martyr, who comming into *Mercia* to vifit King *Offa,* and to treate of a Marriage with his daughter, was through the malice of wicked *Quendred* wife

wife to *Offa*, miserably flayne at a towne now called *Sutton-wallis*, foure miles diftant from *Hereford*, partly for ambition, therby to inioy his Kingdome, and partly alfo for that he was a Chriftian. His body being prefently brought to *Hereford*, and there interred, it pleafedGod forthwith to fhew the innocecy of his caufe, by the wonderfull miracles wrought therat; Ouer which, King *Kenul-phus* afterward erected a goodly Church in his honour, placing there a Bifhops Sea, and which is now the Cathedrall Church of that Citty. He fuffered in the yeare of Chrift 793.

*Weft. an.*793. *Pol. Vir. lib.*4. *Cōtin. Vē. Bed. l.2.c.31, Molā.lo. Capgr.in Catal.SS. Britan. Girald, Cambr. & alij.*

A *The one and twentith Day*.

AT *Finchall* among the *Northumbers* the depofition of *S. Godricke* Eremite, who after ne had lead a folitary life, for threefcore yeares togeather, and twice on pilgrimage for deuotiō vifited our *Saniours* Sepulcner at *Hierufalem*, and the bleffed Apoftles bodyes at *Rome*, full of great fanctity of life & veneble old age, togeather with innumerable miracles, he finally repofed in our Lord, in the yeare of Chrift, one thoufand one hundred & feauenty. His body was buryed at *Finchall* in an Oratory which himfelfe had built. wherat, euen vntill the dayes of Queene

Matth, Weft. & Parif.an, 1170. *Guliel. Neubrig. l.2.cap. 20.Item in vita S. Roberti Abbat, Mart. Rom. & alij.*

Eli-

Elizabeth, many miracles were wrought.

THE fame day at *Conſtantinople* the depoſition of *Bleſſed Conſtantine* the *Great*,
who borne in our Iland of Great *Britany*,
according to ancient Traditions, was the
firſt Chriſtian Emperour, that reſtored peace
to the Church of God. He is by the Greekes
canonized for a Saint, and his feſtiuity appointed on this day: among whome alſo
many goodly Churches and altars, haue in
former ages, byn dedicated in his honour.
And in *North-wales* of our Iland; there is yet
remayning to be ſeene a fayre Church, cre-
ted and dedicated in his name.

Mænal.
Grecor.
hæc die.
Molan. in
addit. ad
Vſuard.

B *The two and twentith Day.*

AT *VVindeſore* the depoſition of holy K
Henry, the ſixt of that name, of *England*,
who being a moſt vertuous and innocent
Prince, was wrongfully depoſed by King
Edward the 4. & caſt into the tower of *London*,
where a little after he was moſt barbarouſly ſlayne by *Richard* Duke of *Gloceſter*, in
the yeare of Chriſt, one thouſand oure hundred threeſcore and eleuen. His body was
firſt burved in the Monaſtery of *Chertſey*,
where preſently it began to doe miracles,
which being ſeene, it was with great ſolemnity and veneration tranſlated to *VVindeſore*,
and

Pol. Vir.
l. 24. hiſt.
Angl,
Io. Sto. in
Annal.
Angl. in
Edou. 4.
Regiſtr.
Eccleſ.
Windeſ.

and there honourably interred in the Chappell of *S. Gregory*, wherat alſo it pleaſed God, in wittneſſe of his innocent life, to worke many miracles. Moreouer it *is* recorded, that his *Veluet hat* which he vſed to weare, being put on mens heads , that were troubled with the head-ake, were preſently cured. He builded the famous ſchoole of *Eaton*, and was the founder of the Kings Colledg in *Cambridge*. King *Henry* the ſeauenth dealt which *Pope Iulius* the ſecond about his Canonization, but by reaſon of both their deaths, the ſame was broken of.

C   *The three and twentith Day.*

AT *Rochefter* in *Kent* the depoſition of S. *VVilliam* Martyr , who borne in the towne of *Perth* in *Scotland*, and taking his pilgrimage towards *Hieruſale* on foote through *England*, was by his owne ſeruant ſlaine in the high way, a little frō the aforſaid Citty of *Rocheſter*; whoſe body being brought to the towne , it pleaſed God forthwith to worke many miracles therat in ſigne of his innocency, where the ſame was after interred, and kept with great veneration in the Cathedrall Church of *S. Andrew*, in the ſame Citty, vntill theſe our dayes. The ſtory of his martyrdōe & miracles, is writté at large by

Io. Capg. in Catal. SS. Ang. Thom. Monum. in eius vita. Molan. in addit. ad Vſuar.

Thomas Monmouth, who liued about the yeare of Christ, one thousand, one hundred and threescore.

D   *The foure & twentith* Day.

AT *Glastenbury* in *Somersetshire* the Commemoration of holy King *Edgar* Confessour, and first Monarch of England, whose glorious actes in Gods Church are famous to all posterity He builded and reedified seauen and fourty Monasteryes, that had byn destroyed by the incursions of other barbarous Nations, and endowed them with great maintenance; as also caused, by his intercession to the Sea Apostolicke, all the Clergy of his Realme to be reformed. In the houre of his Natiuity, it is recorded, that S. *Dunstan* heard a voyce of Angells singing, *Pax Anglorum Ecclesiæ*, &c. Peace to the Church of England. He died in all sanctity and holinesse of life, in the yeare of Christ, nyne hūdred threescore and fifteene: whose body was with all solemnity and veneration, honourably interred at *Glastenbury*; which being takē vp in the yeare, one thousand fifty and two (almost fourscore yeares after his death) by *Aldar* Abbot of that place, was found whole and vncorrupt, & being cut, fresh bloud issued therout, as if he had

Pol. Vir.
l. 6. histo.
Angl.
Matth.
West.
an. 975. et
1052.
Vincent.
in specul.
l. 25. c. 81.
Petr. in
Catal. l.
11. c. 65. et
alij. Wion
l. 4. ligni
vitæ.

byn

byn newly dead ; wherupon he was put
into a coftly fhrine of filuer, which himfelfe
had fomtime giuen to that Church, and
placed vpon the high altar, togeather with
the head of *S. Apollinaris,* and the reliques of
S. Vincent Martyrs, wherat miracles are recorded to haue byn wrought : And fo continued there vntill the tyme of King *Henry*
the eight, and decay of that Monaftery.

E   *The fiue & twentith* Day.

AT *Sherborne* in *Dorcetshire* the depofition
of *S. Adelme* Bifhop and Confeffour,
nephew to *Inas* King of the *Weftfaxons,* who
trauayling into *France* in his youth, after his
returne, became firft a monke of the Venerable Order of *S. Benedict* at *Malmefbury,* and
afterward being made Abbot of that Monaftery, went to *Rome* in company of King
Ceadwall, and was there created Bifhop of
Sherborne in *Dorcetshire* by Pope *Sergius,* and
fent backe to his bifhopricke, where after
great labours and many notable bookes
wrytten for the inftruction of men in Chriftian Religion, but efpecially one of Virginity, which he dedicated to the Nunnes
of *Barkenfteed,* and wherby many were moued to that holy kind of Religious life, he
finally repofed in our Lord, in the yeare of

Bed.l.4.
hift.c.19.
Weft. an.
794.Sur.
in eius
vita to.3.
Guliel.
Malmef.
de Pont.
Angl. in
Adelmo.
Mart.
Rom.
& alij.

Chriſt, ſeauen hundred and nyne. His body
was buryed at *Sherborne* firſt, but afterward
remooued to *Malmesbury*, where the ſame
was wont to be kept in Catholicke tymes
with great veneration.

F   *The ſix and twentith Day.*

A T *Canterbury* the depoſition of *S. Augu-*
ſtine Confeſſour and firſt Biſhop of that
Sea, who being ſent from *Rome* by S. *Gregory*
the *Great* to preach the Chriſtian faith to the
Engliſh nation, firſt conuerted King *Ethel-*
bert of *Kent*, and afterward by himſelfe and
others, the whole Nation, and ſo became
our Apoſtle. He died in the yeare of Chriſt,
ſix hundred, and was buryed at *Canterbury*,
where his feaſt was wont to be kept holy-
day with great ſolemnity, and ſo likewiſe
throughout the whole Dioceſſe.

T HE ſame day at *Glaſtenbury* in *Somerſet-*
ſhire the feſtiuity of the Saints *Fugatius*
and *Damianus* Confeſſours, who being ſent
into *Britany* by S. *Eleutherius* Pope (whoſe feaſt
is alſo this day celebrated) did baptize K.
Lucius with the greateſt part of his Kingdome, as alſo did inſtitute three Archbi-
ſhoprickes (to wit *London*, *Yorke*, and *Carleon*
in *VVales*) and twenty eight Biſhoprickes in
place of ſo many *Flaminies*, teaching and

in-

Margin notes:

Greg.l.5.
Regiſtr.
Epiſt. 53.
Bed.l.1.
cap.23. &
deinceps
Breuiar.
ſec. Vſum
Sarum.

Pont.
Virtot.
Gauf
Monum.
in hiſt.
Britan.
Pol. Vir.
Matth.
Weſt.
Ceſtrenſ.
& alij.

inftructing the people in all Christian
vertues and cerimonyes neceffary for that
new planted Catholicke Church. And
when they had thus laboured for many
yeares, full of moft venerable old age, and
fanctity of life, they both ended their bleffed dayes, about the yeare of Chrift, one
hundred fourfcore and eleuen, and are faid
to haue byn buryed at Gl ftenbury.

G   The feauen & twentith Day.

AT Geruaux in Yorkshire the depofition of
S. Bede Prieft, who being a monke of
the Order of S. Benedict in the Monaftery
of S. Peter and S. Paul, vpon the riuer-banke
of VVyre, in the Kingdome of the Northumbers, fo illuftrated Gods Church by his
wrytings, that not only in his life tyme, but
euer fynce he hath for the fame byn called
by the name of Venerable. He departed this
world in great fanctity and holineffe of life
about the yeare of Chrift, feauen hundred
threefcore & fix, and was buryed at Geruaux
in the Monaftery there, with this Epitaph.

Presbyter hic Beda requiefcit carne fepultus;
Dona Chrifte animam in cælis gaudere per æuum.
Daque i i fophia debriari fonte, cui iam
Sufpirauit orans intento femper amore.

Matth.
Weft. an.
734.
Contin.
eius hift.
l.1.cap.7.
& 8. Bar.
in annot.
ad Mart.
Rom. hac
die. Trit.
de vir.
Illuftr. l.
3. c. 155. et
l. 4. c. 21.

But

But his body being afterward tranflate
to *Durham*, and placed in the tombe togea
ther with *S. Cuthbert*, was there kept wit
great reuerence, euen vntill the dayes o
the late Queene *Elizabeth*. There is a ver
ancient Table hanging in the new Churc
of S. *Peter* at *Rome*, which my felfe haue feen
and read, wherin are regiftred thefe word
*In medio Ecclefia ante portā, qua dicitur Argentea, fi
lapide circulari, fepultum eft corpus Venerabilis Be
Presbyteri &c.* But it is not (I fuppofe) to l
vnderftood of this our *S. Bede* of Englan
(as many do) but rather of another of tl
fame name, though not fo anciēt as he, wh

*Tabulæ
Cænobij
S. Benig.
prope
Genuam.*

was a Mōke alfo of S. *Benedictes* Order, &vei
famous for learning, in the tyme of *Chan
the *Great*, with whome he liued; and aft
his death (which was in the yeare of Chrii
eight hundred and ninteene) his body fh
ning with miracles, was for a tyme tranfk
ted to the Monaffery of *S. Benignus*, nee
Genua in *Italy*, and perhaps afterwards i
Rome. But whofoeuer this was, it is not an
way manifeft, that our *S. Bede* was euer
Rome, eyther aliue or dead.

A *The eight & twentith Day.*

*

A T *Luxouiū* in *France* the Commemor
tion of *S. Ionas* Abbot and Confeffot

W

vho borne in *Scotland* of a noble parentage,
nd contemning the world in the flower
f his youth, went ouer into *France* and
hence into *Lombardy* to S. *Columbane* the
ireat, where he became a monke of the ve-
erable Order of S. *Benedict*, and S. *Colum-
anes* disciple, and was afterward made Ab-
ot of *Luxouium*, where in all kind of good
arning, sanctity of life, and other vertues,
e ended his blessed dayes, about the yeare
f Christ, six hundred and thirty. He wrote
he liues of S. *Columbane* aforsaid, S. *Eusta-
bius* and S. *Bertulph* Abbots, which are to be
eene at large in *surius*, though being anne-
ed to the third Tome of S. *Bedes* workes,
ire, by errour, attributed vnto him.

Arnol.
Wion l.
2.ligni
vitæ de
Script.
ord. Diui
Benedict.
Molan,
passim
in addit.
ad vsuar.

B The nine & twentith Day.

A T S. *Buriens* in *Corn-wall*, the Commemoration of S. *Burien* Virgin, who
being an Irish-woman of great nobility by
birth, came ouer into *England* and liued a
most vertuous and godly life for many
yeares in *Corn-wall*, where in very great
sanctimony and working of Miracles, she
finally gaue vp her soule to her heauenly
spouse. Her memory is very famous, euen
vntill this day in our Ilád of GreatBritany,
especially among the *Cornish-men*, where

there

*
Ex antiq.
Monum.
Cornu. et
Registr.
eiusdem
Eccl.ibid.

there is a towne and port of her name in the Cape or Fromont of *Cornwall*, commonly called S. *Buriens*: where also in tymes past hath byn a famous Church erected in her honour.

C　　*The thirtith Day.*

＊

De ea vid.
ven. Be∂.
l. 4. c. 23.
de gest.
Angl.
Huius
meminit
Arnold.
Wion in
Append.
ad l. 3. lig.
vitæ.

AT *Colchester* in *Essex* the Commemoration of S. *Hieu* Virgin, who borne of a noble bloud in the Kingdome of the *Northumbers*, & building there a goodly Monastery called *Heortheu* (of which the holy Virgin *Hilda* was first Abbesse) is said to haue byn the first woman in that Kingdome, that tooke vpon her the vow and habit of a Nunne, being veyled and consecrated therunto by S. *Aidan* Bishop of *Lindisferne*. And afterward cōming into the Prouince of the *Eastangles*, to the Citty called *Calcaria* (and now *Colchester*) in all sanctimony and holines of life, she finally there ended her blessed dayes, about the yeare of Christ, six hundred fifty and seauen.

D　　*The one & thirtith Day.*

AT *Euesham* in *VVorcester-shire* the festiuity of S. *VVolstan*, Nephew to two

Kinges

Kinges of *Mercia*, who being flaine in hatred of Chriftian Religion by one of
his owne Kinfmen , a great light from
heauen was feene for thirty dayes togeather to defcend and remayne ouer the
place, where he lay killed. By this miraculous token, his body being found out, was
firft buryed in the Monaftery of *Rependowne*
(now called *Ripon*) in *Torkeſhire* : and after
when many miracles were wrought therat,
it was tranflated to the Abbey of *Euesham*
(which holy S. *Egwyn* Biſhop of *Worcefter* had
founded not many yeares before) and there
with great folemnity and veneratiõ placed
in the Church of that Monaftery wherat
it pleafed God, in teftimony of his innocency, to ſhew wonderous things . He
was martyred vpon the vigill of
Pentecoft, about the yeare of
Chrift, eight hundred
fourty and nyne.

Matth.
Weſt.
*an.*849.
Io. Capg.
in Catal.
SS.Britã.
Author
Contin.
hiſt.Ven.
Bed. l. 2.
*cap.*31.

✽ ✽
✽

THE

THE
MONETH
OF IVNE.

E   *The first Day.*

Ex mo-
numentis
Monast.
Petri de
burgo, &
Regiftr.
Lichfield.

AT *Stone* in *Staffordshire* the Commemoration of the Saintes *Rufin* and *Vlfade* brothers &martyrs, fons to *VVulferus* a Pagā King of the *Mercians*; who for that they were made Christians, and had receyued baptifme at the hands of S. *Chad* Bifhop of *Lichfield*, were both by their owne Father flayne in hatred therof, as they were at prayer in S. *Chads* Oratory, about the yeare of Chrift, fix hundred threefcore & eight. Their bodyes were by their mother Queene *Ermenild* (afterward alfo a Saint) conueyed to *Stone*, and there kept with great veneration, where alfo in tyme, was erected a

goodly

goodly Church, togeather with a Priory, and dedicated in their honour. But the K. their Father soone after repéting him of the fact, with great sorrow and contrition came to S. Chad, and asking him forgiuenes, receyued the Christian faith : wherupon destroying all the Téples of the Idolatrous Gods in his Dominions, did in their places build Churches and Monasteryes ; and amõg the rest, he founded the goodly Abbey of *Medeshamsteed* (now called *Peterburrow*) dedicating the same vnto God and S. *Peter* the Apostle , and enriching it with many and large possessions.

F   *The second Day.*

AT *Dunfermelling* in *Scotland*, the Commemoration of Blessed *Malcolme*, the third King of that name, and husband to the famous S. *Margaret* Queene of *Scotland*, whose godly workes of piety &deuotiõ are famous all to posterity, especially to his successors, as well in that Kingdome, as to other Princes of bloud in Europe. He was so zealous in the loue of God, that he became more holy then any of his predecessors had byn before him , being wholy addicted to the repayring and erecting of Churches, Monasteryes, and Bishoprickes. Moreouer

K   he

Turgot.
Epiſc. S.
Andreæ
in eius
vita.
Hector
Deidona-
tus l. 12.
hiſt.Scot.
Molan.in
append.
ad vſuar
Rob.Buc.
in vita S.
Margar.
Reg.Sco.

he was accuſtomed, with his Religious Qu. S. *Margaret*, euery day to ſerue with his owne handes 300. poore people, with meate & drinke, he on the one ſide, and ſhe on the other : & was the firſt King of that Natiõ that created Earles in *Scotland.* Which Kingdome after he had gouerned in all vertuous and pious manner, for ſix and thirty yeares, cõming into England, was violently oppreſſed and ſlayne at *Anwicke* in the borders of *Scotland*, by *Robert Mowbray* Earle of *Northumberland*, togeather with his eldeſt ſonne *Edward*, to the great lamentation of his Countrey, and was buryed at *Dunfermelling*, in the yeare of Chriſt, one thouſand fourſcore and twelue.

G   The third Day.

*

Ex Ar-
chiuio
Eccl.
Arcenſ.
& inſcri-
ptione
ipſius Se-
pulchri.

AT *Arke* in *Apulia* in the Kingdome of *Naples*, the Commemoration of S. *Eleutherius* Confeſſour, who borne of a very good parentage in *England*, and taking his iorney to *Hieruſalem* for deuotion, returned thence backe by *Italy*, where for the loue of God he became an Eremite or pilgrime, leading a ſtrict and ſeuere kind of life, ſo far from his natiue Countrey ; at what tyme the plague infecting ſorely thoſe partes, full of great ſanctity, and holynes of life, he fi-

nally

nally rested in our Lord. His body is kept at the forsaid towne of *Arke* vntill this day, with due honour and veneration of the inhabitants, for the Miracles, that by his merits, it hath pleased God to worke therat, and there is visited as chiefe Patrone of the Village.

A   *The four th Day.*

AT *Bodmin* in *Corn-wall* the deposition of S. *Patrocke* Bishop & Côfessour, whose most godly life and vertues, haue byn very famous in former ages, throughout our whole Iland, but especially in *Corn-wall*, where his memory is fresh vntill this day, and where many altars and Oratories in Catholicke tymes, haue byn erected and dedicated in his honour. He liued about the yeare of Christ, eight hundred and fifty; & is said to haue byn the first bishop of *Corn-wall*, placing his Episcopall Sea at the fornamed towne of *Bodmin*, which Bishopricke was afterwards translated to S. *Germans* at *Cridington* (now called *Kirton*) in the same Prouince, & lastly to *Excester* in *Deuonshire* by King *Edward* the Côfessour, in the yeare of Christ, one thousand and fifty.

Matth. West. in hist. maiori ad an.905. Calend. sec. vsum Sarum hac die. Sto. in vita S. Edou. Conf.

B   *The fifth Day.*

Ve. Bed.
in Epit.
Sigebert
in Chron.
Marian.
Scot.l.2.
hist.an.
717. Tri.
de vir.
Illustr.
Mart.
Rom.
Ado,
Vsuard.
& alij.

AT *Dockum* in *VVest-frizland* the passiõ of S. *Boniface* Archbishop of *Mentz* and Apostle of *Germany*, who being an Englishman by birth, went ouer into *Germany*, & thece to *Rome*, where he was created the first Bishop of the forsaid Citty of *Mentz*, and sent thither to preach the Christian faith, which he did incessantly for sixteene yeares togeather, reducing many thousands from their Idolatry, to the true worship of Christ, building Churches & Monasteryes for the cõtinuation and propagation therof. And at last going into *Frizland* to preach to that people was there slayne by the enemyes of Christ, at the forenamed towne of *Dockum*, in the yeare of our Lord, seauen hundred fifty and foure. His body was afterward translated to *Mentz*, and there honourably placed in the Monastery of *Fulda*, which himselfe had founded.

Io.Molã.
i.1 addit.
ad Vsuar.
& in
Indic.
SS.Belgij

THE same day also, and same place, the passion of S. *Eboam*, & S. *Adlar* Bishops; S. *Vintruge*, S. *VValter*, and S. *Adelhere* Priests; S. *Hamunt*, and S. *Boso* Deacons; S. *VVaccare*, S. *Gunderhere*, S. *VVilhere*, S. *Hildebrand*, and S. *Adolph* Monkes, and others to the number of fifty, most of them Englishmen, who

were

were with the forsaid S. *Boniface* martyred in *Frizland* for preaching the Christiā faith. And as they were his fellowes in trauaile & labours of propagating the name of Christ: so were they worthy to be made partakers of his Martyrdome. Their bodyes are most of them kept at *Maestricht* vpon the Riuer of *Mosa*, with great veneration of the Inhabitants.

Sur.to.3. in Vita S. Bonifacij

C   *The sixt Day.*

IN the Monastery of *Blandine* neere *Gaunt* in *Flanders* the depositiō of S. *Gudwall* Bishop and Confessour, who borne of a noble and ancient Brittish bloud, and despising all worldly honours and preferments, built many Monasteryes in our Iland, and became Father to an hundred and fourscore mōkes, which he instructed in all kind of vertūe & good learning: & at last being made Bishop, he went ouer into *France* and *Flanders* to preach the Christian faith in those parts, where famous for sanctity of life and miracles, he finally reposed in our Lord, about the yeare of Christ, foure hūdred and three. His body was first buryed in the forsaid Monastery of *Blandine*, but being afterward brought into *England*, was thence againe in the second persecution of the *Danes*, tran-

10. Molā. in addit. ad Ysuar. hoc die. Sige-bert.in Chrō. an. Do. 958. Sur.to.3. Vit. SS, & alij.

flated to *Gaunt*, by *Arnulph* Earle of *Flanders*, and S. *Gerrard* Abbot, about the yeare of our Lord, nyne hundred and fifty.

D   *The feauenth Day.*

A T *Knaresburge* in *Yorkeshire* the depofition of S. *Robert* Abbot & Confeffour, who borne in the fame Prouince, became firft a mōke at *VVhitby*, and then at *Fountaines*, and laft of all was ordayned Abbot of *Knaresburge* of the Order of *Cifterce*; whofe moft holy life & cōuerfatiō, hath byn wittneffed by the manifold miracles wrought at his body after his death; out of which (in the time of King *Henry* the third)there diftilled a pretious fweet oyle, very foueraigne for many difeafes. He was wont in his life time to recite euery day an hundred and fifty pfalmes, in honour of Chrift and the bleffed Virgin *Mary*. He died in the yeare of our Lord, one thoufand one hundred and fifty, & was buryed in his owne Monaftery.

T H E fame day at *VVorcefter* the Tranflation of S. *VVolftan* Confeffour and Bifhop of the fame Sea, whofe wonderfull life and miracles haue byn famous throughout Englād. His body being takē vp on this day was found found & vncorrupted, togeather with his Pontificall veftments, wherin he

Sur. to. 3. Rom. Mart. & Molā. hac die. Matth. Parif. an. 1238. 1243. & 1272. de eius miraculis.

Matth. Parif. an. 1201. & 1218.

was

was buried, which was more thē an hūdred
yeares after his death ; and was very solemnely, and with great veneration set in
a more eminent place of his owne Cathedrall Church of *VVorcester*, in the yeare
of Chrift 1218. It is recorded , that the
said Church being afterward burned by
casuall fire , the tombe wherin his body
lay, was not so much as touched with the
flame.

Wion
hac die.
in suo
Martyr,
Malmes.
& Flor.
in hist.
Angl.

E   *The eight Day.*

AT *Yorke* the deposition of *S. VVilliam*
Confessour and Bishop of that Sea,
kinsman to *Stephen* King of *England*, who by
false slaunders being accused to *Pope Eugenius*
the third, was depoled frō his Bishopricke,
and one *Murdacke* set vp in his place, but after
againe restored by *Pope Anastasius* the fourth:
wherin with great signes of sanctity and
innocency of life, togeather with many
miracles, he finally ended his blessed dayes,
in the yeare of Chrift, one thousand one
hundred fifty and foure, and was buryed
at *Yorke*. It is recorded by *Polidor Virgil*, that
when he was restored againe to his Bishopricke, and comming towards *Yorke*, the
people flocked in so great number to con-
gratulate and welcome his returne, that

Pol. Vir.
lib. 12.
Guliel.
Neubrig.
l.1.cap.
17,& 27.
Molā. in
addit. ad
Vsuard.
Catal.
Epis.
Eboracēs.

passing ouer the Riuer beyond *Pont-fract*,
the throng and presse was so great, that the
bridge (being but of wood) brake, euen
iust, as the Bishop was ouer, and threw all
the rest into the water : which when the
holy man saw, he fell downe vpon his
knees, and besought our Lord to saue
them. Whose prayers were soone heard. For
though the streame was very strong and
violent, yet were they euery one preserued
from drowning.

Io. Trit.
l.3.cap.
288.de.
vir.Illust.
ord. D.
Benedict.
Wion in
Mart.
hac die.
et l.3.
lig. vitæ.

THe same day in the Diocesse of *Metz* in
the higher *Germany*, the deposition of *S.*
Disibode Bishop & Cofessour, who borne
in *Ireland*, and a monke of the Order of *S.*
Benedict, was ordayned Bishop of *Dublyn* in
the same Kingdome ; but going ouer into
Germany to preach the Christian faith, he
resigned that dignity, and became Abbot of
a Monastery there, which vntill this day is
called of his name *S.Disibodes*, in the forsaid
Diocesse of *Mentz*, where in great sanctity
of life and Miracles, he ended his blessed
dayes, about the yeare of Christ, seauen hundred.

F   *The ninth Day.*

†Colme.

IN *Scotland* the deposition of S. † *Columbe*
Abbot and Confessour, who borne in *Ire-*
land

land, and defcended of a noble parentage, forfooke the world, and all other earthly preferments, and became a monke in one of the ilands of *Orcades*, called *Hoy*, in a Monaftery there of the Order of S. *Benedict*, wherof at laft he being made abbot, was fo famous for fanctity and holines of life, that euen vntill this day his memory is frefh to the Chriftian world, efpecially in the Kingdomes of *England*, *Scotland* & *Ireland*, where there be many Churchs yet remayning, dedicated in his honour. He defceafed about the yeare of Chrift, fiue hundred fourfcore and fixteene: whofe body was afterward tranflated into *Ireland* to the towne of *Dune* in the Prouince of *Vlfter*, and there with great folemnity and veneration interred, togeather with the facred reliques of S. *Patricke* & S. *Brigit*. He by his preaching conuerted to the faith of Chrift, the *Pictes* that inhabited *Scotland*, and is called their Apoftle, working very many miracles among them to his dying day.

Bed.*l.3.c.*
4.&25.*et*
in Epit.
an.565.
Herm.
Contr.
in Chron.
an.596.
Mart.
Rom.
Baron.
tom.3.
Annal.et
ones alij.
hac die.

G   *The tenth Day.*

AT S. *Edmūdsbury* in *Suffolke* the Tranflatiõ of S. *Edmūd* King of the *Eaſtāgles* & martyr, who in the *Danish* incurfions, vnder the Captains *Hinguar* & *Hubba*, being firft whipped

ped, and then, bound to tree, and ſhot full of ſhaftes, was finally beheaded. All which torments he moſt conſtantly indured, euer calling vpon the name of Ieſus, vntill he had finiſhed his Martyrdome, which was in the yeare of Chriſt, eight hũdred threeſcore and ten .His principall feſtiuity is celebrated in our Catholicke Church of England, vpon the twentith of Nouember: but his body being taken vp afterward on this day, was with great ſolemnity tran-

Sur.to.6. in eius vita 20. Nou. Regiſtr. Monaſt. S.Edmũd. Burienſ.

ſlated from Hexam in Northumberland (where he was martyred) and placed in a goodly ſhrine, richly adorned with iewells and pretious ſtones in a Church erected in his honour in Suffolke, which of his name was euer ſince called S.Edmũdsbury, wherat it is recorded many miracles haue byn wrought. And after this againe, in the yeare, one thouſand & ten, the Danes inuading the Prouince of the Eaſtãgles, Alwyn the Biſhop of that Dioceſſe brought the body of S. Edmũd from Bury aforſaid to London: at the comming wherof in at Criplegate many miracles were wrought, where for the ſpace of three yeares it remayned in the Pariſh Church of S. Gregory neere vnto S. Paules, and then was tranſlated the ſecond tyme to Bury, in the yeare of Chriſt, one thouſand and thirteene.

The

THE same day in *Scotland*, the festiuity of S . *Margaret* Queene, wife to holy *Malcome*, King of that nation, & daughter to *Prince Edward*, surnamed the *Out-law*, Sonne of *Edmund Ironside* King of *England*, whose godly life and vertues, especially in deuotion and liberall almes to the poore, are yet famous both at home and abroad. She died in great sanctimony of life and miracles about the yeare of Christ, one thousand fourscore and twelue, vpon the sixteenth of *Nouember*: though her principall festiuity be celebrated vpon this day both in *England* and *Scotland*.

Abbo Floriacēs, in eius vita.Pet, in Catal. Osbert. de stoke in eius vita, Breuiar. sec. vsum Sarum. Mart. Rom. Molan. & alij hac die.

THE same day also at *Rochester* in *Kent*, the deposition of S. *Ithimar* Bishop and Confessour, who being a man of excellent learning and wisdome, succeeded S. *Paulinus* in that Sea, being consecrated therto, by *Honorius* Archbishop of *Canterbury*: which when he had gouerned most worthily for 17. yeares togeather, in great sanctity, and holines of life, he reposed in our Lord, about the yeare of Christ, six hundred threscore and eleuen, and was buried in S. *Andrewes* Church at *Rochester*.

Bed.l.3. c. 14.& 20. Herebert. Rosweyd. in fast. SS. hac. die. wion *l.3.ligni vitæ.*

A

A   The eleuenth Day.

*

AT *Lindisferne* in the Kingdome of the *Northumbers*, the Commemoration of S. *Edilwald* Prieſt & Confeſſour, who borne in our Iland of a noble parentage, ſucceeded S. *Cuthbert* for twelue yeares togeather, in leading an Eremiticall life in the Iland of *Farne*, commonly called *Holy-Iland*. He was indued with ſo rare & ſingular vertues, that his very name was famous in thoſe dayes, throughout *England* & *Scotland*. S. *Bede* recounteth that a certaine skynne wherwith S. *Edilwald* had ſtopped a hole in his Oratory did miracles after his death; as alſo how by his prayers, he ceaſed a ſtorme or tépeſt, that aroſe on the ſea, when certayne of his friéds, that came to viſit him in the Iland, returned homeward, which happened about the yeare of Chriſt, ſix hundred, fourſcore and nynteene; about which tyme alſo he died, & was buryed in S. *Peters* Church at *Lindisferne* in the raygne of King *Elfride* of Northumberland

Vĕ. *Beda*
in vita S.
Cuthber.
& *l.5.c.1.*
Hiſt.
Angl.

B   The tweluth Day.

AT *Bischopssen* in the higher *Germany* the Commemoration of S. *Agatha* Virgin, who being an English woman by birth, and leading a religious life in the Monastery of *VVimborne* in *Dorcetshire*, went ouer into *Germany* with S. *Lioba*, *S. Tecla* and others, whome S. *Boniface* (an Englishman in like manner, and Archbishop of *Mentz*) had sent for into those partes, to be Directrices in Monasticall discipline, of certaine Nunryes, which he there had newly founded; where vnder the forsaid *Lioba*, that was constituted Abbesse of the fornamed Monastery of *Bischopssen*, she liued & died in great sanctimony and holinesse of life, about the yeare of Christ, seauen hundred fifty and seauen, and was buryed in the same place.

*

Arnol. Wion in addit. ad Mart. Bened. l. 3. & in vita S. Liobæ.

C   The thirteenth Day.

IN *North-VVales* the Commemoration of S. *Elerius* Abbot and Confessour, who borne of a noble British parentage, and setting aside the vayne pleasures of the world, built with the goods of his owne inheritance a Monastery in the North-west

*

Io.Capg.
in Catal.
SS.Brita.
Item in
Act.S.
Wenef.3.
Nouēbr.
Wion.in
addit. ad
l.3.ligni
vit.

part of our Iland , now called North-wales, where he gathering togeather many deuout perfons , lead a Monaſticall life, directing them in all kind of vertue and diſcipline, vntill his dying day. He liued in the tyme of S. VVenefrid, about the yeare of Chriſt, fix hundred threſcore and foure; of whome ſhe receyued the holy veyle of Chaſtity, and was ordayned Abbeſſe of a Monaſtery which S. Beno her maifter and tutour had erected in her Fathers territory : as alſo wrote the whole ſtory of her life, which is yet extant in wryttē-hand to be read in diuers libraryes of England. The bone of one of his armes, is yet in the cuſtody of a Catholicke Gentleman of our Countrey, who preſerueth the fame with great deuotion and veneration , as beſeemeth ſo pretious a Relique.

D   The fourteenth Day.

Maurol.
in Mart.
hac die
Pet. in
Catal.l.5.
c.117.

IN Scotland the Tranſlation of S. Brandan Abbot & Confeſſour, borne in the fame Kingdome, whoſe godly life and doctrine, togeather with his manifold miracles, are yet famous throughout the Chriſtiā world, eſpecially in our Iland of Great-Britany. His principall feſtiuity , in our Catholicke Church of England, is celebrated vpon the

sixteenth day of *May*, where also we haue
made mention of him. There was a goodly
Church, as also a towne builded in his honour, in one of the Ilands of *Orcades*, which
vntill this day, is commonly called by the
name of S. *Brandans*. He died about the yeare
of Christ, fiue hundred and seauenty.

wiõ in suo
Mart.
hac etiam
die.

E   *The fifteenth Day.*

AT *VVilton* in *VViltshire* the deposition of
S. *Eadburge* Virgin, daughter to King
Edward the elder, who refusing all worldly
honours and preferments, tooke a Religious
habit in the Monastery of *VVilton*, and became a mirrour and rare example to the Nobility of England, where she so excelled in
all manner of vertue, but especially humility, that she euer thought herselfe the most
contemptiblest of all the Monastery: Which
thing how acceptable it was to God, it pleased him to manifest to the world, by the
manifold miracles he wrought by her, both
aliue & dead. She deceased about the yeare
of Christ, nyne hundred and fourteene, and
was buryed at *Wilton*.

Petr.
in Catal.
Vincent.
in specul.
Pol. Vir.
West.
an. 901.
Molan.
in addit.
ad vsuar.

THE same day at *Huis* in the Diocesse of
Liege, the Translation of S. *Menigold*
Martyr, who borne in England of a great
parentage, became first a Captaine in the

French

Molan.
in addit.
ad Vsua.
& in
Indicul.
SS.Belgij
hac die.

French and German warres, and after an Eremite; vnto whome *Arnulph* the Emperour gaue a little Territory neere to the riuer-banke of *Mosa*, where he built himselfe an Oratory for his priuate deuotiõ:& as he was one day going to Church, was slaine by certaine wicked souldiers in hatred of his sanctity, about the yeare of Christ, nyne hundred. His body was afterward on this day, with great solemnity, translated to *Huis*, where the same is yet kept with due honour & veneration of the Inhabitants.

Petr. de
Viel.S.
Th. Doc.
in eius
vita.
Renat.
Bened.
in vit.SS.
Galliæ.
Belforest.
in descri.
Armoric.

THE same day also in little *Britany* the deposition of S. *Maine* Abbot and Confessour, who borne in our Iland of *Great Britany*, and kinsmã to S. *Sampson*, went ouer with him into little *Britany*, to preach the Christian faith, where he first lead a Monasticall life at *Dole*, vnder the forsaid S. *Sãpson*, and afterward being made Abbot of a Monastery dedicated to S. *Iohn Baptist* in the same Countrey, after many yeares of labour and toyle taken in the seruice of Christ, and conuersion of many soules to him, famous for miracles, he finally rested in our Lord, about the yeare of Christ, fiue hundred and nynty. His body was buryed in the same Monastery, which at this day of his name is commonly called S. *Maines*, and there is kept with great honour and veneration.

F

F   *The sixteenth Day.*

AT *Chichester* in *Sussex*, the Translation of
S. *Richard* Confessour and Bishop of
that Sea, who hauing studied seaue yeares
in the Vniuersity of *Bologna* in *Italy*, and returning home, was first made Chancelour
of *Oxford* and the Bishop o: *Chichester*: which
Sea when he had gouerned for nyne yeares,
in great sanctity & holinesse of life, he died
at *Douer* in *Kent*, in the yeare of Christ, one
thousand two hundred fifty and three. His
body being brought to *Chichester*, was
afterward on this day taken vp, and put into
a goodly siluer shrine, and translated to a
more eminent place of that Cathedrali
Church, wherat so many miracles were
dayly wrought, that infinite people made
concourse thither from all partes of Englād.
This Translation was made in the yeare, one
thousand two hundred threescore and sixteene.

Matth.
West.
& Paris.
an.1253.
& 1276.
Sur.to.2.
die 3. Apr.
Ereuiar.
sec. vsum
Sarum.
hac die.

THE same day at *Hereford* the passion
of *S. Leofgar* Bishop and Martyr, who
being Chaplyn to Duke *Harold*, succeeded
Ethelstane in that Sea; where in all kind of
vertue, and good workes, exercising his Pa-
storall functiō, he was by K. *Griffin* of *VVales*,
that violently and vniustly assaulted that

Matth.
West.
ad ait.
Do.:056.

L   Citty

Citty, flayne, togeather with feauen of his
Chanons that denied him entrance into the
Church, which when the faid *Griffin* had
fpoyled & robbed of all the reliques, iewels,
and other ornaments that were portable,
he laftly fired both it, and the whole Citty, in the yeare of Chrift, one thoufand fifty
and fix.

G   The feauenteenth Day.

AT *Hecknam* in *Normandy* the depofition
of S. *Botulph* Abbot and Confeffour,
who borne in *Scotland* of a noble parentage,
and going ouer into *France*, became there a
monke, and afterward was made the firft
Abbot of a new Monaftery called *Hecknam*
in *Normandy*, which himfelfe had caufed to
be built at his owne charges, where in
great fanctity of life, he ended his bleffed
dayes, about the yeare of Chrift, fix hundred
fifty and foure. There is yet remayning a
faire parifh Church dedicated in his honour
without *Aldgate*, in the Citty of *London*; befides many other ancient monuméts of him
in the Realme of England. And among the
reft, there was a goodly ancient Church &
Monaftery of Blackefriers erected in his honour in *Lincolnshire*, neere to the fea fide,
which in proceffe of tyme growing to a
fayre

fayre Market-towne, was called therof *Botulphs-towne*, and now by the corruption of our language, is vulgarly knowne by the name of *Boſton* ; which ſaid Church and Monaſtery were both in the raigne of King *Edward* the firſt conſumed by fire, in the yeare, one thouſand two hundred fourſcore and ſeauen.

A   *The eighteenth Day* .

I N *Scotland* the Cōmemoratiō of *S. Dunſtan* Abbot & Confeſſour, borne in that Kingdome and deſcended there of a great parentage, who contemning the vanities of the world in the flower of his youth, tooke a Religious habit, and became firſt a monke of the *Venerable* Order of *S. Benedict* in *Scotland*, and afterward was ordained Abbot of the whole Monaſtery ; where in great ſanctity of life, famous for his learning and workes of piety, in a good old age, finally reſted in our Lord, about the yeare of Chriſt, ſix hundred and ſeauenty, and was buryed in *Scotland*. This man is different from the other *S. Dunſtan* of *England*, whoſe feſtiuall dayes are celebrated vpon the nineteenth of *May*, and ſeauenth of *September*.

*

Io. Leſl.l. 4. de reb. geſt.Scot. Wion in append. ad.l.3. ligni vit. & alij.

B   The ninteenth Day.

AT _Ely_ in _Cambridgshire_, the Commemoration of S. _Iohn_ Confeſſour and Biſhop of the ſame Sea, who being firſt a monke, and then Abbot of _Fountaines_ in _Yorkeshire_, was for his great vertue and holineſſe of life ordayned Biſhop of _Ely_; In which dignity he ſo gouerned himſelfe, eſpecially in humility and charity to the poore, that his memory was very famous, aſwell throughout _England_ and _Scotland_ at home, as in other Countreys abroad. And when he had ſate in that Sea for fiue yeares or therabout, famous for holineſſe of life, full of venerable old age, he departed to our Lord, in the yeare of Chriſt, one thouſand two hundred, twenty and fiue, in the raigne of King _Henry_ the third, and was buryed in his Cathedrall Church of _Ely_, before the Altar of S. _Andrew_.

C   The twentith Day.

AT _Glaſtenbury_ in _Somerſetshire_ the Tranſlation of S. _Edward_ King and Martyr, who through the deceipt of his ſtep-mother Queene _Alfred_, was ſlayne at _Corſe-Caſtle_ in

Dor-

Dorſetſhire, as he was on hunting. His body was firſt buryed at _VVarham_, and then at _Shaftesbury_, and laſtly on this day with great ſolenity tranſlated to _Glaſtenbury_ the tweluth yeare after his Martyrdome, and yeare of Chriſt, one thouſand and one. He was canonized for a Saint by _Pope Innocentius_ the fourth.

Breuiar.
ſec. vſum
Sarum et
Epiſt.
Innocēt.
_PP._4.

THE ſame day at _VVinockes-berge_ in Flanders the Tranſlatiō of _S. Oſwald_ King of _Northumberland_ and Martyr, who after many glorious battayles and combatts fought in defence principally of the Chriſtian faith, was at length ſlayne in hatred therof by _Pēda_ a _Pagā_ King of the _Mercians_ (or middle Engliſhmen) at a place in _Shropſhire_, called afterward of his name, _Oſwaldes-tree_; where now is built a fayre Market-towne, ſtill retayning that anciēt name, though ſomwhat corrupted in pronunciation, and commonly called _Oſwiſtry_. His body was firſt buryed at _Peterburrow_ in _Northamptonſhire_, and after in the Daniſh perſecution on this day tranſlated to _Berghen_ in _Flanders_, where it is kept with great veneration of the inhabitants. His principall feſtiuity was wont to be celebrated in our Cathoncke Church of _England_ vpon the fifth day of Auguſt, and in diuers places kept holy day.

Matth.
Weſt.
_ad an._
789.
Io. Molā.
in addit.
ad V ſua.
hac die.

D The one and twentith Day.

Albin.
Flaccus
in vita S.
willebr.
Molā. in
Indic.SS.
Belgij
hac die.

AT *Beuerwicke* in the Diocesse of *Harlē* in *South-Holland*, the passion of S. *Englemund* Martyr, borne of a noble parentage in *England*, who going ouer into *Holland* and *Frizeland*, for the propagation of Christian faith, was by *Radbodus* King of *Frisia*, a *Pagan* and enemy to Chri∫t, most cruelly put to death, about the yeare of our Lord, seauē hundred twenty and seauen. His body was kept in an Oratory at the forsaid towne of *Beuerwicke* with great veneration, euen vntill the *Hollanders* in this la∫t age, falling from the Obedience of the Catholicke Church and Sea of *Rome*, imbraced herefy.

E The two and twentith Day.

Gild.
Epi∫t. de
excid.
Britan.
Bed.l.1. c.
7.Gaufr.
Monum.
lib.5.Sur.
tom.3.
Mart.
Rom.

IN *Derswolds* wood, neere to the towne of S. *Albas* in *Hartfordshire*, the pa∫∫iō of S. *Albā*, high Steward of the *Britans*, and the fir∫t Martyr in our Iland of the *British* nation, who in the persecution of *Dioclesian* the Emperour, was beheaded for being made a Chri∫tian, and receiuing and succouring a Chri∫tian Prie∫t, named *Amphibale*, by whome he had byn baptized. He suffered

about

about the yeare of Chrift, three hundred and three ; and was afterward canonized for a Saint by *Pope Adrian* the firft.

THE fame day, & fame place, the paſſion of one of the ſouldiers, that led *S. Alban* to execution, who ſeing his conſtancy and patience in ſuffering for Chriſt, being therwith greatly moued, confeſſed forthwith his errour, and asked the bleſſed Martyr forgiueneſſe: which when the perſecutors beheld, they grieuouſly tormented him for the fame . He notwithſtanding, following S. *Alban* to his death, when his head was cut of, tooke & imbraced it in his armes, & therby was immediatly cured of all his woûds inflicted by the perſecutors. And therupon confeſſing Chriſt, was by the enemyes of truth finally beheaded, and ſo baptized in his owne bloud.

Bed. Gild. Gaufr. Pariſ. & alij citati ſupra.

THE fame day in like manner at S. *Omers* in *Artoys* in the Monaſtery of S. *Bertin*, the Tranſlation of S. *Ortrude* Virgin, borne in England of a noble bloud : whoſe body in the Daniſh perſecution was tranſlated from an ancient Monaſtery in our Iland, called *Andria*, to the forſaid Abbey of S. *Bertin*, and is there yet preſerued in a ſiluer ſhrine, with great veneration among other Reliques in the Sacriſtia or Veſtrey of that Church. She died about the yeare of Chriſt, ſix hundred ſeauenty and nyne.

Io. Molā. addit . ad Vſuar. et in Indic. SS. Belgij hac die.

L 4   F

F   *The three and twentith* Day.

†S. Au-
dry.

AT *Ely* in *Cambridgshire*, the depofition
of *S.* † *Edilrude* Virgin and Abbeffe,
daugnter to *Annas* King of the *Eaftangles*, and
wife to King *Egfrid* of *Northumberland* ,
who liuing with her husband twelue
yeares in perpetuall viginity, as *S. Bede* recordeth, at laft, with his confent , renounced the pleafure of this world and dignity
of a Queene, & became a nunne, firft in the
Monaftery of *Coldingham* in the fame Kingdome, vnder *S. Ebba* her aunt , and thence
being ordayned Abbeffe of the Monaftery
of *Ely,* where before fhe had founded a goodly Church in honour of S. *Peter* the Apoftle,
full of great fanctimony and holines of life,
fhe finally wét to her heauenly fpoufe, about
the yeare of Chrift, fix hundred and fourfcore. Her body was buryed in the fame
Monaftery, ouer which there was erected
a goodly Church, & dedicated to her name.
And being taken vp fixteene yeares after her
death by her fifter *S. Sexburge* then Abbeffe
of that place , was found wholy vncorrupt,
and as frefh, as if fhe had byn buryed but the
day before. *S. Bede* himfelfe made a fonnet
in meeter, in praife of this Virgin, which
yow may read in the fourth booke of his

Ven.Bed.
l.4.c.19.
& 20.
Item in
Chron. de
fex ætat.
Trit. de
vir.Ill ft.
Vincent.
in fpecul.
Sigebert.
in Chron
Mart.
Rom.
Molan,
& alij.
omnes
hac die.

Hiftory

Hiſtory of *England* and twentith Chapter. She is called by ſundry writers *Etheldride*;but in our owne language , moſt commonly knowne by the name of S. *Audry.*

G   *The foure & twentith* Day.

AT *Mechlyn* in *Brabant*, the paſſion of S. *Rumwald* Biſhop and Martyr, ſonne to a King of *Ireland* , who, after he was conſecrated Biſhop of *Dublyn* in that Countrey, went to *Rome* , and thence returning into Flanders, began to preach the Chriſtian faith in the Territory of *Mechlyn* , and there firſt planted the ſame, vnder Count *Ado* of that Prouince, of whome he was very honourably intertayned. And when hé had thus laboured, in reducing the ſtrayed ſheep, to the fold of his Maiſter Chriſt, for many yeares, he was at length, there ſlayne in hatred of the Chriſtian faith by two wicked ſouldiers, one wherof, the bleſſed Biſhop had ſom tymes reprehended for adúltery, about the yeare of Chriſt , ſeauen hundred, threeſcore & fifteene. His body remayneth ſtill at *Mechlyn,* and there is kept with great veneration in the Cathedrall Church , in a very ſumptuous ſiluer ſhrine , though his principall feaſt be celebrated throughout the Dioceſſe, vpon the firſt of Iuly , with a

Io.Molã. in Indic. SS.Belgij & in addit. ad Vſua. hac die.

double

double office as chiefe Patrone of that Citty.
He was canonized by Pope *Alexander* the 4.

A   *The fiue & twentith Day.*

A T *Verolamium*, now called *S. Albans*, in
Hartfordshire, the Paſſion of *S. Amphibale*
Prieſt and Martyr, who being a noble yong
man of *Britany*, & going to *Rome* with *Baſſianus*
Sonne to *Seuerus* Viceroy of the *Britans*,
was there by Pope *Zepherinus* inſtructed ſecretly in the Chriſtan faith, baptized, made Prieſt, and ſent backe into *Britany*,
there to preach vnto others, where he conuerted and baptized *S. Alban* then high Steward of the *Britans* for the Roman Emperour. And being at laſt accuſed for teaching
the doctrine of Chriſt, had, by the perſecutours, a hole made in his ſide ; and one
of his guttes being taken out of his belly, &
faſtened to a ſtake, was driuen about the
ſame, vntill all the reſt were pulled
out, and woone about the ſaid ſtake. And
when he was ready to giue vp the ghoſt,
two angells were ſeene to deſcend, & carry
his ſoule vp to heauen. There was a faỹre
Church dedicated in his honour in *VVincheſter*, where many miracles haue byn
wrought at his Reliques. And amõg others
it is recorded, that one that had byn dead

*Gild. de
excid.
Brit.
Matth.
Pariſ. &
Weſt.
paſsim.
Io. lidgat.
Monac.
Burieſ. in
eius Vita.
Gerard.
Liegh. in
rudim.
Inſigniũ.*

foure

foure dayes, was raifed againe to life. He
fuffered about the yeare of Chrift 304. being
aboue an hundred yeares of age.

THE fame day at *Egmond* in *Holland* the depofition of S. *Adalbert* Prieft and Confeffour, nephew to *Ofwald* King of *Northumberland*, and fonne to K. *Edilbald* of the *South
faxons*, who going ouer into the lower *Germany* with S. *VVillebrord* and his fellowes to
preach the Chriftian faith, conuerted infinite foules in *Holland*, and is therfore worthily called their Apoftle. *Count Theodore* of
that Prouince, built a goodly Monaftery
neere vnto *Harlem* in honour of him, whofe
fonne was afterward cured of a dangerous
feuer by the meritts of S. *Adalbert*. He died
about the yeare of Chrift 705.

THE fame day in like manner at *Dauentry*
in *Gelderland* the Tranflatiõ of *S. Lebuine*
Prieft and Confeffour, borne of a noble family in *England*: who going ouer alfo into
the *Low-Countreyes*, to preach and inftruct
the new-made Chriftiãs of thofe Prouinces,
after many labours & much fruite wrought
in that kind, he ended there his venerable
old dayes, about the yeare of Chrift, feauen
hundred, and threefcore. His body was
afterward on this day tranflated to *Dauentry*,
and there kept with great veneration, as
chiefe Patrone of that Citty and Dioceffe.

*Io. Molã.
in Indic.
SS. Belgij
Sur. to. 3.
Mart.
Rom.
& alij.
omnes
hac die.*

*Marcel.
in vita S.
Simibert.
Io. Molã.
in Indic.
SS. Belgij*

B

B   *The six and twentith Day.*

*
Io. Trit.
l.3.de vir.
Illuſtr.
cap. 339.
Arnol.
Wion in
append.
ad.l.3.
lig. vitæ.

AT *Benchor* in *Ireland* the Commemoration of *Nine hundred holy Monkes* Martyrs, who being oppreſſed by certaine Pagã Pirates, that landed in that Iland , were in hatred of Chriſtian Religion ſlayne, and their Monaſtery robbed and defaced, to the great lamentation of all *Ireland*; for that it was, in thoſe dayes, a common ſtore-houſe (as it were) of all good learning and vertue, out of which came the Apoſtles of diuers Prouinces of *France*, *Flanders* and *Germany*, who reduced them to the Chriſtian faith, and true worſhip of one God. Many Authors (of forrayne Nations eſpecially) do often tymes confound this Monaſtery of *Benchor* in *Ireland*, with that of *Bangor* in *Caernervanshire* of *North-wales* , thinking them to haue byn all one, wheras they were different, and ſituated in two ſeuerall Kingdomes.

C   *The ſeauen & twentith Day.*

AT *Cayon* in the Dioceſſe of *Towers* in *France*, the depoſition of S. *Iohn* Prieſt & Confeſſour, who being a noble *Brytan* by

birth

birth, and refuſing all worldly and temporall honors in his Countrey, went ouer into *France*, and there built himſelfe a little Oratory for his owne priuate deuotion in a ſolitary place neere vnto *Towers*, where he was very famous for ſanctity of life, working many miracles both aliue and dead. His body was buryed in the ſame Oratory after his deſceaſe, about the yeare of Chriſt, fiue hundred thirty and ſeauen. There is a ſtory recorded of a certaine *Bay tree*, that this S. *Iohn* had there ſomtymes planted; which when after many yeares, it withered with age, and was cut downe, being laid two yeares vnder a wall, and ſerued for a ſeate to ſit on, was againe put into the ground, and through his merits, ſprong and budded forth a freſh, to the admiration of all *France*.

Rom. Mart. hac die. Greg. Turon. l. de gloriæ Conf. c. 23 & in hiſt. 562.

THE ſame day at *Gaunt* in *Flanders* the Tranſlation of S. *Leuine* Biſhop and Martyr, an † *Iriſhman* by byrth, and diſciple to S. *Auguſtine* our Engliſh Apoſtle, who leauing his Biſhopricke (which was in *Scotland*) went ouer into *Flanders* with S. *Kilian* and his fellowes, where preaching the Chriſtiā faith to the infidels of thoſe partes, was by them apprehended, and had his tongue cut out of his mouth, which being by a miracle immediatly reſtored him againe, he was finally beheaded, about the

† *Scottiſhman.*

Breui.t. Gādauẽſ. & Ioan. Molan. in addit. ad Vſuard. hac die. & in Indic. SS. Belgij.

yeare

yeare of Chrift, feauen hundred and twelue. His body being firſt interred in a Village of the ſame Prouince, was afterward on this day with great ſolénity tranſlated to *Gaunt*, where being placed in the Cathedrall Church of that Citty, is there yet preſerued with great Veneration of the inhabitants.

D   *The eight & twentith Day.*

*Io.Leſt. l.
4.de geſt.
Scot.
Arnold.
Wion. in
append.
ad l.3 lig.
vitæ.*

IN *Scotland* the Commemoration of S. *Columbane* Monke and Confeſſour, who borne in the ſame Kingdome of an honourable family, contemned the world, and became a monke of the Venerable Order of S.*Benedict* in *Scotland*, where in great ſanctity of life, and other vertues therto agreable, he ended his bleſſed dayes, in the yeare of Chriſt, ſix hundred and fourty; where alſo his memory hath byn famous in tymes paſt, hauing had many Chappells & altars dedicated in his honour. This man is different from the other *S. Columbane* of *Ireland*, ſurnamed the *Great*, ſomtymes Abbot and founder of the Monaſtery of *Bobia* in *Lombardy*, whoſe feaſt is celebrated vpon the one & twentith day of *Nouember*.

E *The nine & twentith Day.*

*Mænal.
Græc. ex
Sym.
Metaph.
2. . Iunij.
Innocēt.
PP. Epiſ.
ad Decēt.
Eyſengr.
Cē. 1. p. 7.
Theodor.
Epiſt. ad
Tim. &
in Pſal.
116. & l.
9. de cu-
rand.
Græc.
affect.
Sophron.
ſerm . de
natal.
Apoſt.
A'lred .
Rieual.in
vita Edo.
Conf.
Mart .
Rom.*

AT *Rome* the Paſſion of the glorious Apoſtles S. *Peter* & S. *Paul*, who in the perſecution of *Nero* the Emperour, were on one, and the ſelfeſame day put to death; S. *Peter* being faſtened to a Croſſe with his head downward, and S. *Paul* beheaded. Of theſe two Apoſtles it is recorded by diuers very ancient wryters, that about the yeare of Chriſt, threſcore and ſeauen, they came both perſonally into our iland of great *Britany*, and there preached the Chriſtian faith, founded Churches, ordayned Prieſts and Deacons, and therfor may worthily be called our Apoſtles, of whome we haue receyued ſo great benefitts. There are very many Churches in our Countrey dedicated in their honour, as ſpeciall Patrons of our Iland. And in the tyme of King *Edward* the Confeſſor, S. *Peter* appearing to a very holy man, ſhewed him, that himſelfe had ſometymes preached in *Britany*, and conſequently the ſpeciall care he had of that Church and Countrey.

THE ſame day at *Lindisferne* in the Kingdome of the *Northumbers*, the Commemoration of S. *Ethelwyne* Biſhop and Confeſſour, who of a Monke of S. *Benedicts* Order

＊

Io. *Trit.*
l.4.c.156.
Wi̅ol.2.
lig. Vita.
in Catal.
Epiſ.
Lindiſ.

in *S. Columbes* Monaſtery in the Iland of *Hoy* in *Scotland*, was ordayned Biſhop of *Lindis-ferne*, where for many yeares hauing inſtru-cted his flocke, in all vertue, and good lear-ning, finally in great ſanctity of life, he re-poſed in our Lord, about the yeare of Chriſt, ſeauen hundred and nynty, and in the raigne of *Oſred* King of *Northumberland*..

F   The thirtith Day.

Bed.l.3.
hiſt.c.28.
& l.4.c.1
weſt. an.
645. &
653.
Ioan.
Molan.in
addit. ad
Vſuar.
14. Iulij.

AT *Canterbury* the depoſition of *S. Deus-dedit* Biſhop and Confeſſor, ſurnamed *Frithona*, who being an Engliſh Saxon by birth, ſucceeded *S. Honorius* in the Sea of *Can-terbury*, being conſecrated therto by *Ithimar* Biſhop of *Rocheſter* : wherin when he had ſpent nyne yeares, in continuall preaching and inſtructing his flocke, famous for lear-ning and ſanctity of life, he gaue vp his bleſſed ſoule to reſt, in the yeare of Chriſt, ſix hundred threeſcore and foure, and was bu-ryed in the Church of *S. Auguſtines* in *Canter-bury*, with his predeceſſors; at whoſe body in confirmation of the innocency of his life, it pleaſed God to worke many miracles.

THE
MONETH
OF IVLY.

G   *The first Day.*

T † *Carleon* vpon *Vske* in *South-wales*, the paſſion of the Saintes *Iulius* and *Aaron* Martyrs, who being two noble anciét Britans of the same Citty, were in the perſecution of the Roman Emperour *Dioclesian* with many others in our Britiſh primitiue Church, moſt cruelly put to death for the Confeſſion of Chriſt, about the yeare of our Lord, three hundred and foure. There was an ancient goodly Church erected & dedicated in their honour in the forſaid City of *Carleon*, where alſo their bodyes haue in tymes paſt byn kept with

† Cair-legion.

Gild. de excid. Britan. Ven. Bed. l. 1. hiſt cap. 7. Mart. Rom. hac die. cū Molā. Humf. Lhuide in fragm deſcript. Britan.

M   great

great veneration of the old *Britans* of *South-VVales.*

THE same day in little *Britany* the depofition of S. *Goluin* Bifhop and Confeffour, borne in our Iland of great *Britany* of very honourable parents, who going ouer into little *Britany*, and there leading an Eremiticall life, for many yeares, was at laft, againft his will, elected, and vpon obedience confecrated Bifhop, about the yeare of Chrift, fix hundred. In which function & dignity he excelled in all kind of fanctity and holines of life, working many miracles among the Frenchmen, both aliue and dead.

Rob. Cænalis de reb. Gall. l. 2. Perioch. G. Renat. Benedict. in Vit. SS. Gall. hac. die. wion. in addit. ad l. 3. lig. Vit.

A   *The fecond Day.*

AT *VVincheſter* in *Hampſhire* the depofition of S. *Swithin* Confeffour and Bifhop of that Sea, whofe rare life, togeather with his working of miracles, is very famous to all pofterity through the Chriftian world. Whenfoeuer he was to confecrate any new Church, though it were neuer fo far of; yet would he go thither on foote. It chanced on a Market-day at *VVincheſter* that a womã paffing ouer the bridg, with a basket of egges, where the holy man was fitting to fee the workmen labour, about mending of the bridge; and one of the faid labou-

Matth. Weſt. an. 861. Sur. to. 4 de Vit. SS. Molã in addit. ad Vſua. 2. et 15. Iulij.

rers offering to ieſt with the woman, and ſhe reſiſting, brake all her egges : which thing the good Biſhop ſeeing, and lamenting the womans loſſe, made the ſigne of the Croſſe ouer the ſaid broken egges, and immediatly they all became whole againe. He died about the yeare of Chriſt, eight hũdred threeſcore and two, and was buryed at VVincheſter.

THE ſame day at *Landaſſa* in *Clamorganſhire* of *VVales* the depoſition of S. *Oudocke* Conſeſſour and Biſhop of that Sea, who being deſcended of a noble bloud in *Britany*, was famous for holines of life and working of miracles, both aliue and dead. He was the third Biſhop of *Landaſſa*, and ſucceeded S. *Telean* in the ſame Sea, about the yeare of Chriſt, ſix hundred and thirty.

Catal. Epiſco. Landafenſ. hac die.

B *The third Day.*

AT *Canterbury* the Tranſlation of *S. Lanfranke* Conſeſſour, and Biſhop of the ſame Sea, who being Abbot of *Cane* in *Normandy*, was thence, at the ſuite of K. *VVilliam* the Conquerour, promoted to the Sea of *Canterbury*, where in great holines of life, he gouerned the ſame moſt laudably for nineteene yeares togeather, and at laſt deſceaſed the third yeare of the raigne of K.

Maurol. in Mart. hac die vnà cum vvion & alijs.

West.
an. Do.
1089.
Vincent.
in specul.
& alij.

† aliâs
Ireland

Io. Molā.
in Indic.
SS. Belgij
& in
addit.
ad Vsua.
hac die.

VVilliam Rufus, and yeare of Chrift, one thoufand fourfcore and nyne. Vpon this day his
body being taken vp afterward, was with
great folemnity tranflated to a more emiñet
place of the Church of Cāterbury, wherat, it is
recorded, many miracles haue byn wrought.

THE fame day at Ooftkerke in Flanders the
depofition of S. Guthagon Conſeffour,
Sonne to a king of † Scotland, who taking
vpon him a voluntary pouerty for the loue
of Chrift, went ouer into Flanders, and
there became a pilgrime or Eremite in the
territory of Tornay, where in great fanctity
& holineffe of life, he repofed in our Lord.
His body was afterward taken vp by Gerrard Bifhop of Tornay, and fet in a more eminent place of the Church of Ooftkerke, in the
yeare of Chrift, one thoufand fifty and
nyne, where the fame is kept with great honour and veneration of the inhabitants, and
is yet to be feene there through iron grates,
placed in a wall of the fame Church.

C   The fourth Day.

AT Canterbury the depofition of S. Odo
Conſeffour & Archbifhop of the fame
Sea: Who being a man of excellent learning
& wifdome, was firft made Bifhop of VVelles,
& after of Canterbury. In which dignity, in

gre at

great sanctity of life & spirit of prophesy, he ended his venerable old dayes, in the yeare of Christ, nyne hundred fifty and eight, and was buried at *Canterbury. Matthew* a Monke of *VVestminster* recounteth a dreadfull exáple of reuenge, taken vpon his successour in that Bishopricke, *Ealfsine*, who so soone as S. *Odo* was dead, and procuring himselfe to be elected in his roome by Symony, the very first day of his induction to that Sea, he most cótemptuously trode him vnder his feete in his graue. With which fact God being highly offended, soone after reuenged the same in the behalfe of S. *Odo.* For *Ealfsine* going to *Rome* for his Pall, perished most miserably, through hungar and cold, in the *Alpes* (which thing was fortould also by S. *Odo*) being forced before his death, to put those his feete in the warme dung of horses, with which he had so insolently troden vpon the others body in his graue.

Matth. West. an. 934. *&* 958. *Hereb. Rofweyd, in ast.SS. hac die. Molan.in addit. ad psuar..*

D   The fifth Day.

AT *Burton* vpon *Trent* in *Staffordshire* the festiuity of *S. Modwene* Virgin and Abbesse, daughter to *Nangthee* King of *Ireland*, who after infinite miracles wrought in that Kingdome, came into *England*, & there by the help of K. *Ethelnulfe*, whose sonne she by her prayers, had cured of a dangerous ficknesse, builded two famous Monalteryes, neere to the forrest of *Arden* in *VVarwickshire*, the one at *Polesbury*, the other by the forrest side; of which later she her selfe was Abbesse first,

Herebert.
Rof. in
fastis SS.
hac die.
Pol. Vir.
l. 5. hist.
Matth.
West.
an .857.
Sur. to. 5.
in vita S.
Ofithæ
Virg.

and then of another Monastery at the forfaid *Burton* in *Staffordshire*. And after this she went into *Scotland* to King *Conwall* her kinfman, and thence backe againe into *Ireland*, where in all kind of rare fanctimony of life and miracles, she finally ended her blessed dayes, about the yeare of Christ, eight hundred and feauenty, bequeathing her body to the forfaid Monastery of *Burton*, whither it was brought, and kept with great reuerence and veneration, euen vntill our dayes. Among her many miracles, one is recorded, that by her prayers, she raifed to life S. *Ofith*, being the but a girle, that had byn drowned in a riuer three dayes, as may be read in the Acts of S. *Ofithes* life.

THE fame day at *Canterbury* the Translation of S. *Anfelme* Confessour & Bishop of the fame Sea, whose rare learning, vertues, and labours in Gods Church, togeather with his miracles and fanctity of life, are yet famous to the Christian world. He died in the yeare of Christ, 1 1 0 9. and in the nynth yeare of K. *Henry* the first his raigne. His body was afterward on this day taken vp and tranflated to a more eminent place

Petr.
Gafelin.
Maurol.
& wion
in fuis
Mart.
hac die.
Petr. in
Catal. l.
6. c. 56.

of his Churh at *Canterbury*, with great folemnity and veneration, wherat, through his meritts, it hath pleafed God to worke many miracles.

E   *The fixt Day.*

AT Ely in *Cambridgshire* the depofition of S. *Sexburge* Queene and Abbeffe, wife to *Ercombert* K. of *Kent*, and daughter to *Annas* King of the *Eaftangles*, who after the death of her husband, gouerned his Kingdome for a while, and built a goodly Monaftery of *Nunnes* in the ile of *Sheppey* in *Kent*, & then became herfelfe a Religious woman in the Monaftery of *Ely*, wherof alfo (after the death of her fifter S. *Audry*, who had that dignity whilft fhe liued) fhe was made Abbeffe: and there in moft godly wife, finally gaue vp her foule to her heauenly fpoufe Chrift, about the yeare of our Lord, fix hundred fourfcore and nynteene; and was buryed in the fame place, neere to her faid fifter S. *Audry*. Whofe body being taken vp fcauen yeares after her death, was found whole and vncorrupt, which well declared the fanctimony, and holines of her life, whilft fhe liued.

*V en. Bed.
l. 4. c. 19.
Weft. an.
640.
Vincent.
in fpecul.
l. 15. c. 32.
Rob.
Buckl.
in eius
vita fol.
128.*

F   *The ſeauenth Day.*

Sur.to.6.
Staplet.
de trib.
Thomis.
Sander.
de ſchiſ.
Angl.
Breuiar.
ſec. vſum
Sarum.
hac die.

AT *Canterbury* the Tranſlation of *S. Tho-mas* Archbiſhop of the ſame Sea and Martyr, who being violently oppreſſed by King *Henry* the ſecond his ſeruantes, was, after many ſlaunders, calumniations and baniſhment ſuffered in defence of Eccleſiaſticall libertyes, ſlayne in the tyme of Euenſonge, in his Pontificall veſtments, before the high altar in his owne Church of *Canbury*, in the yeare of Chriſt, one thouſand one hundred threeſcore and ſeauenteene. His body being afterward on this day taken vp, and put into a coſtly ſiluer ſhrine, guilt, and ſet with pretious ſtones, was tranſlated to a more eminent place of the ſame Church, wherat it pleaſed God to worke infinite miracles. King *Henry* the eight at his breach with the Sea Apoſtolicke deſtroyed this goodly monument, and taking all the treaſure therof to his owne vſe, cauſed his body to be burned to aſhes & diſperſed in the ayre, in the yeare of Chriſt 1538.

Bed. l. 4.
c. 12. & 5.
cap. 19.

THE ſame day at *VVincheſter* in *Hampſhire* the depoſition of *S. Hedda* Confeſſour and Biſhop of that Sea, whoſe godly and innocent life was afterward confirmed by

the

the miracles wrought at his body in *VVinche-*
ster, where he died, and was buryed in the
yeare of Chrilt , leauen hundred and
fiue.

THE lame day allo at *Eyſt* in *Germany*,
the depolition of S. *VVillebald* Confel-
four and firſt Bilhop of that Sea , Sonne
to S . *Richard* King of the Englilh: who
going ouer to his vncle S . *Boniface* into
Germany , was by him ordayned Bilhop of *Eyſt* , where full of great holines
of life, he repoled in our Lord, in the yeare
of Chrilt , leauen hund red fourlcore and
one. His body is buryed in the Cathedrall
Church of that Citty, and there prelerued
with great veneration.

THE lame day in like manner at *Brige*
neere *Paris* in *France*,the depolitiõ of the
Saintes, *Edilburge* daughter to *Annas* King of
the *Eaſtangles*,and *Ercongote* daughter to King
Ercombert of *Kent*, who being both Abbelles
of the laid Monaltery of *Brige*, the one luc-
ceding the other , and dying both on one
day, in diuers yeares , delerued to haue their
memoryes celebrated togeather, on one and
the lelfe lame day , by our Mother the holy
Cath. Church. The former,*S. Edilburge*, died
about the yeare of Chrilt, lix hundred and
threelcore: and the other lome foure yeares
after,and were both buryed at *Brige* aforlaid.

Tritem.
de vir.
Illuſtr.

Democh,
l. 2.de
Sacrif.
Miſſæ.
& in
Catal.
Epiſco.
Eyſtenſ.
Mart.
Rom.
& alij.

Bed.l.3.c.
8. Trit.
de Vir.
Illuſtr.
Contin.
Ven.Bed.
Vincent.
in ſpecul.
& alij,

G   The eight Day.

Matth.
Well.
an.872.
Molan.
in Indic.
SS.Belgij
Gotzel.
Monach.
in eius
vita.

AT VVinchester in Hampshire the depositiō
of S. Grimbald Abbot and Confeffour,
whome King Alfred calling out of Frāce into
England, vfed in all his confultations for the
gouernment of his Kingdome. He refufed
the Archbifhoprickc of Canterbury, and chofe
rather to be Abbot of a newMonaftery,ere-
cted by the faid K. Alfred in the Citty of
VVinchefter, where in moft godly wife he
ended his bleffed dayes, in the yeare of
Chrift, feauen hundred and foure.

Io. Trit.
de vir.
Illuftr.
Rom.
Mart.
Molan.
Gafelin.
& Wion
hac die.

THE fame day at VVirtzburge in Franconia
the paffiō of S. Kilian Bifhop,togeather
with the Saints Colinā, Totnā & Eruvald mōkes
and Martyrs, who being borne in Ireland
all of very honourable families, and S. Kilian
fonne to the King of that Iland, went ouer
into Germany, where S. Kilian was ordayned
Bifhop of VVirtzburge, and preaching the
Chriftian faith in thofe partes, were all at
laft by the enemyes of truth, flayne for the
defence therof, vnder Gosbert King of Franconia, about the yeare of Chrift, fix hundred
nynty and feauen. Their Reliques are kept
vntill this day at VVirtzburge, with great veneration of the inhabitants.

A

A   *The ninth Day.*

AT *Barking* in *Essex* the depofition of *S.*
Edilburge Queene, who being wife to
Inas King of the *VVeſtſaxons*, both ſhe and her
husband conſented to enter into two Mo-
naſtery⁻s, and become religious : wherupon
the King himſelfe going to *Rome*, and there
taking vpon him the habit of a monke of
S. Benedicts Order, the Queene likewiſe entred into the Monaſtery of *Barking* aforſaid,
and receyued the holy veyle of Chaſtity,
where in all kind of ſanctimony of life, ſhe
finally ended her bleſſed dayes, about the
yeare of Chriſt, ſeauen hundred and fourty.
Of this name of *Edilburge*, there are three
Saintes of our Nation, to wit, *S. Edilburge*
daughter to *Annas* King of the *Eaſtangles*, and
Abbeſſe of Brige in *France* : *S. Edilburge*, ſiſter
to *S. Erconwald* Biſhop of *London*, and the firſt
Abbeſſe of this aforſaid Monaſtery of *Bar-*
king : and this *S. Edilburge* wherof we now
ſpeake, Queene of the *VVeſtſaxons*. All which
three being Engliſhwomen by byrth, liued
togeather within the ſpace of leſſe then an
hundred yeares.

Io. Trit.
de Vir.
Illuſtr.
Pol. Vir.
hiſt. l. 4.
Stephan.
Luſingā.
Corona
4. c. 21. &
Chron.
Britan.
fol. 155.
Wion
hac die.
in Mart.
Benedict.

B

B　　　The tenth Day.

†Hanno-
nia.

AT *Fisciacum* in † *Hennalt* the depofition of *S. Etto* Bifhop and Conteſſour, who being an Irifhman by byrth, and comming cut of that Kingdome with *S. Furſeus* and

Io. Molā.
in addit.
ad Vſua.
hac die, et
in Inaic.
SS. Belgij

his fellowes, went ouer into *France* and *Germany*, to preach the Chriſtiā faith, which he did with as great fruite and profit, as holineſſe of life, vntill his dying day: which happened about the yeare of Chriſt, fix hūdred fifty & fix. His body was afterward tranflated to *Letias* in the fame Prouince, and there is kept vntill this day with great honour and veneration of the inhabitants, for the manifold miracles, that it hath pleaſed God in figne of his fanctity to worke therat.

C　　　The eleuenth Day.

＊

IN *Scotland* the Commemoration of S. *Dronſton* Confeſſour, who borne in the fame Kingdome of the bloud Royall, and

Io. Leſl.
Roſ. Epiſ.
l. 4. hiſt.
Scot.

vncle to *Aidan* King of *Scotland*, contemned the vanities of the world in his youth, and entring into a Monaſtery there, tooke the Religious habit of S. *Benedict*. In which kind of life he so excelled in all humility and perfection, that his name was very famous throughout *Scotland* and *Ireland*, euen vntill his dying day, which happened full of sanctity of life and miracles, about the yeare of Chriſt, six hundred: where also in ancient *Catholicke* tymes, many Chappells and altars haue byn dedicated in his honour.

Wion l.4. ligni vit. Ioan. Maior in hiſt. l. 2. cap. 7.

D   *The tweluth Day.*

IN *Ireland* the Commemoration of *S. Luane* Abbot and Confeſſour, who being borne in the ſame Iland of a noble parétage, became there firſt a monke of the Order of S. *Benedict*, and afterward Abbot of the Monaſtery of *Benchor* in the ſame Kingdome, where he was very famous for ſanctity of life, in the tyme of S. *Malachy* Biſhop of *Connerthen* & Primate of all *Ireland*, with whome he liued many yeares, ending his venerable dayes in a good old age, about the yeare of Chriſt, one thouſand one hundred and fourty, and in the raigne of King *Stephen* of *England*.

✱

Arnold Wion in append. ad.l.3. lig. Vitæ. Item in Actis S. Malac. Epiſ. 5. Nouemb.

E

E   The thirteenth Day.

AT Canterbury the Tranflation of S. Mil-dred Virgin and Abbeffe, daughter to Merualdus King of the Mercians (or middle Englifhmen) who contemning the vanities of this life, became a religious woman in the Ile of Thanet in Kent , and afterward Abbeffe of that Monaftery: in which kind of life fhe fo excelled , efpecially in humility, that it pleafed God to worke many miracles at her body after her death : which being on this day tranflated to Cāterbury by s. Lafranke Archbifhop of that Sea, was, togeather with the venerable body of S. Edburge , moft honourably placed there in the Church of S. Gregory , in the yeare of Chrift, one thoufand fourfcore and fiue. There was alfo a famous Monaftery built in her honour in the Prouince of Kent, befides many goodly Churches erected and dedicated in her name in diuers places of England. Part of her Reliques were tranflated to Dauentry in Gelderland, and there kept vntill thefe our dayes, with great veneration of the people of Geldria. She died about the yeare of Chrift, fix hundred threefcore and foure.

Matth.
weft. an.
676. &
1011.
Pol. Vir.
l. 4. Io.
Molan.
in addit.
ad Vfua.
& in
Indic,
SS. Belgij

F

F   The fourteenth Day.

AT *Dauentry* in *Gelderland* the feftiuity of
S. *Marchelme* Prieft and Conteffour,
who being an Englifhman by birth, and
going ouer into the low-Countreyes as
companion to *S. Willebrord*, preached there
the faith of Chrift inceffantly, for more
then threefcore yeares togeather, wherby he
conuerted the greateft part of *Frizeland*, and
is called their Apoftle. And after infinite
labours and toyles taken in that holy enter-
prize, full of great fanctity and holines of
life, and in a good old age, he finally repofed
in our Lord, at a place in *Tranfyfleania* (to
wit beyond the Riuer of *Yfle*) called *Oldfeele*,
about the yeare of Chrift, feauen hundred
threefcore and two. His body was after
tranflated to *Dauentry*, where the fame was
honoured, and preferued euen vntill our
dayes, with great veneration of the Inhabitants.

Huebal.
Monac.
in vita.
S.Leb.
Mart.
Rom.
Molan.
in Indic.
SS.Belgij
hac die.

G   The fifteenth Day.

AT *VVinchefter* in *Hampshire* the Tranflation of S . *Swithin* Bifhop of the fame
Sea and Confeffour, whofe life was fo inno-

cent, and vertues fo rare, that it pleafed God by him to worke many miracles both aliue and dead. When he was ready to depart out of this world, he commanded (for humilityes fake) his body to be buryed in the Church-yard, wheron euery one might tread with their feet. But afterward when many and dayly miracles, were, by his merits, wrought at his graue, and the concourfe of people therto began to be great, he was on this day taken vp, and tranflated to a Church of his owne name, erected in *Winchefter*, commonly called S. *Swithins*, which now of late in hatred of his memory is by the Proteftants named the *Trinity*. This his tranflation happened about the yeare of Chrift, nyne hundred; which day was afterward by commaundement kept holy, throughout the Dioceffe of VVinchefter.

THE fame day at *Oldfeele* beyond the Riuer of *Yfle* in *Gelderland*, the depofition of S. *Plechelme* Bifhop and Confeffour, who borne in our Iland of Great Britany, and going to *Rome* with S. *VViro*, was ordayned Bifhop of an old towne in Scotland named *Candida-Cafa*, now called *VVhitherne*, & in his returne homward preached the Chriftian faith to the *Frifians*, where full of fanctity of life and miracles, he repofed in our Lord, about the yeare of Chrift, feauen hundred thirty and two. His body is yet preferued

at

[margin left column:]
Matth. Weft. an Do. 862. Sur.to.4 Io.Molā. in addit. ad Vfua. Matth. Parif. an. 970. & 854.

Ven. Bed. l.5.c.24. in fine. Io.Molā. in addit. ad Vfua. & in Indic. SS.Belgij

at the forfaid towne of *Oldfeele* with great veneration of the people therabout.

THE fame day alfo at *Pollesbury* in *VVar-wickeshire* the depofition of S. *Eadgith* Queene of *Northumberland*, and fifter to King *Ethelftane*, who was giuen in Matrimony to *Sithricke* Prince of the *Northumbers*, a Pagan, vpon condition he would become a Chriftian. Which he accepted of: but foone after renouncing both his Queene & faith, ended his life in a moft miferable fort. And fhe fetting afide the cares and troubles of this world, became a Religious woman, & receyued the holy veyle of chaftity in the Monaftery of *Polesbury* aforfaid : where in great fanctimony of life, fhe ended her bleffed dayes, about the yeare of Chrift 926.

Matth. Weft. 901.& 926. Wion in Mart. Benedict. hac die.

THE fame day in like máner at *VVerdt* in *Cleeueland*, the paffion of S. *Harrucke* Bifhop and Martyr, who being a Scottifhman by birth, and a monke of the Monaftery of *Imarbaricke* in *Scotland*, went ouer into the low Countreyes and *Germany* to propagate the Chriftian faith, where being ordayned Bifhop of *VVerdt*, was at laft put to death by the enemyes of Chrift, and fo ended a glorious Martyrdome, about the yeare of Chrift, eight hundred thirty and one.

Albert. Cranz in Metrop. l,1.c.29. . Lefl. l. . de geft. Scot.

MOreouer in *Suetia* the depofition of S. *Dauid* Confeffour, who being an Englifhmá by birth & an Abbot of the Venera-

Breuiar.
Sueticum
hac die.
Item.
in Chron.
Suet. &
Norueg.
de Gent.
Apostolis

ble Order of *Cluniacke*, went into *Suetia* to preach the faith of Christ to the infidels of that Coûtry, which he did for many yeares; and after aboundant fruite reaped in that haruest by his holy labours and indeauours, famous for sanctity of life, he finally rested in our Lord, about the yeare of Christ, one thousand and two.

A   The sixteenth Day.

AT *Salisbury* in *VViltshire* the Translation of *S. Osmund* Confessour and Bishop of the same Sea, whose life and doctrine hath much illustrated, as well the vniuersall, as our Catholicke Church of England. He was the first that compiled the *Sarū Breuiary*, and other Cerimonies of that Church, which were afterward receyued and vsed throughout the whole Realme. For which cause in ancient tymes, the Catholicke Bishops of *Salisbury* obtayned the Title of the *Popes* Maister of Cerimonyes, and had their places alwayes assigned them in the Popes Chappell & other solénityes at *Rome*, according to that dignity. His body was on this day solemnely translated to new *Salisbury* from a village a mile distant from the same, now called old *Salisbury*, where he died in the yeare of Christ, one thousand fourscore

Ranulph.
Cestr.n.in
eius Vita.
M.S.l.7.
cap.3.
Matth.
West.
passim in
histor.
& alij,
Calendar.
sec. vsum
Sarum.
hac die.

and

and ninteene, and there placed in the great
Minster or Cathedrall Church of that Citty,
in the middle of the Chappell of our Bleffed Lady , vnder a faire marble Monument,
wherat it pleafed God to worke miracles
through his merits. He wrote many learned
bookes, and among others, the life of *S. Adel-
mus* the firft Bifhop of *Sherborne* , yet extant
in diuers libraryes to be read. He was canonized for a Saint by Pope *Calixtus* the fecōd,
and his feaft in many places of England
hath on this day byn kept holy .

B   *The feauenteenth Day.*

AT *VVinchcombe* in *Glocefterſhire* the Paffion of *S. Kenelme* King of *Mercia* and
Martyr, who being but feauen yeares of age,
and committed vnto his fifter *Quendrede* for
his education, was, through her ambition
of defire to raigne , caufed fecretly to be
flayne by one of his guard, who caſt his
body into an obfcure place among bufhes
and thornes : which thing being firſt miraculoufly reueyled at *Rome* by an Angell, that
let fall a paper vpon *S. Peters* aultar, wherin
was wryttē in goldē letters the whole pro-
ceſſe and manner of his death, the Pope fent
prefently into *Englād* to other ChriftiāKings
to inquire and fearch out his body : and the

Matth.
Weſt.
an. 821.
Contin.
Ven. Bed.
l. 2. c. 31.
Vincent.
in fpecul.
l. 25. c. 3.
Matth.
Par if.
an. 1257.
Mart.
Rom.
Molā. &
Breuiar.
fec. vfum
Sarum.

same being at laſt found, and with a ſollemne proceſſion brought vnto the Church
of VVinchcombe aforſaid, it pleaſed God forthwith to worke many miracles in witneſſe
of his innocency. His ſiſter the Authour of
the foule fact was ſtroken blind, both her
eyes falling out vpon a Primer, wheron ſhe
was reading: which being ſtayned with the
bloud of her ſaid eyes, is yet kept in memory
of the miracle of Gods Iuſtice. His Martyrdome hapned about the yeare of Chriſt 821.

Matth.
Weſt.
an. 1214.
in hiſt.
Flor.
Britan.

THE ſame day at S. *Albans* in *Hartfordſhire*,
the depoſition of S. Iohn Confeſſour,
who being Abbot of the Monaſtery of the
Benedictines in that towne; was very famous
for ſanctity of life and miracles throughout
England, about the yeare of Chriſt, one
thouſand two hundred and fourteene.

Io. Molā.
in addit.
ad Vſua.
et in Ind.
SS. Belgij

ALſo the ſame day in the territory of
Namures the feſtiuity of S. *Fridegand*
Prieſt and Confeſſour, who being an Iriſh-
mā by birth, went ouer into the Low-Coū-
treyes with S. *Foillan* and his fellowes to
preach the Chriſtian faith, which he did
moſt feruently with great fruite of his holy
labour, till his dying day, which happened
about the yeare of Chriſt, ſix hundred and
fourty. His body was loſt in the troubles of
the late warres made by the French in the
Low-Countreyes, to the great lamentation of the Inhabitants of that place, who

for

for their fynnes were depriued of fo glorious a Patrone.

C   The eighteenth Day.

AT *Alisbury* in *Buckinghamshire* the depofition of *S. Edburge* virgin, daughter to
Reduuald King of the *Eaftangles*, who togeather with her fifter S. *Edith* became a Religious woman in a Monaftery at the forfaid
towne of *Alisbury* : where in great fanctimony of life, fhe ended her bleffed dayes, about
the yeare of Chrift, fix hundred and twenty.
Her body was afterward tranflated to a
towne of her owne name, called *Edburge-
towne*, which now more corruptly we cōmonly call *Edburton*, where the fame hath
byn preferued euen vntill our dayes, with
great honour and veneration, for the Miracles that haue byn wrought therat.

*Maurol.
in fuo
Mart.
hac die.
vnà cum
Wion &
Chron.
Britan,
fol.302.*

THE fame day at *Huis* in the Confines of
the higher *Germany*, the Tranflation of
S. *Odilia* one of the eleuen thoufand Brittifh
Virgins, martyred with S. *Vrfula*, whofe
name & body being reueyled by her felfe to
a holy religious man in *Paris*, called *Ioannes de
Eppa*, was found out, and vpon this day by
Siffred Archbifhop of *Cullen* with great fo-
lemnity tranflated to th forfaid towne of
Huis, where the fame was very honourably

*Io.Molā.
in addit.
ad Vfua.
et in Ind.
SS.Belgij*

placed in the Church of the Religious men there of the Order of the *Holy-Croſſe* , and is preſerued yet in the ſame place with great veneration of the Inhabitants.

D   The ninteenth Day.

Io.   Leſſ.
Roſ.E ſi .
de geſt.
Scot.l. 4.
Wion in
append.
ad.l.3.
lig. vitæ.

IN *Scotland* the Commemoration of *S. Diman* Conſeſſour , who deſcended of an honourable linnage in the ſame Kingdome, contemned the world , and entring into a Monaſtery, became a Religious man of the Venerable Order of S. *Benedict* in *Scotland,* vnder the care and gouernment of S. *Sigenius* Abbot, whoſe ſcholler and diſciple he was: where in all kind of ſingular humility, and other ſanctity of life, in a venerable old age, he finally repoſed in our Lord, about the yeare of Chriſt, ſix hundred and ſeauenty.

E   The twentith Day.

Matth.
Weſt.
an. 904.

AT *VVilton* in *Wiltſhire* , the Commemoratiō of *S. Ethelwide* Queene, wife to K. *Alfred* of the *VVeſt ſaxons;* who after the death of her husband , built a goodly Monaſtery in the forſaid towne of *Wilton* for religious women , endowing it with great

rentes

rentes and reuenewes: among whome also
herselfe entring, tooke their habit and holy
veyle of Chastity, and became one of the
number; where in all kind of singular humility, vertue, and other sanctimony of
life, she ended her blessed dayes, about the
yeare of Christ, nyne hundred and foure,
and was buryed in the same place.

Chron.
Britan.
fol.196.
Wió l. 4
lig. Vitæ.

F   The one & twentith Day.

AT Strasburgh in the higher Germany, the
deposition of S. Arbogastus Confessour
and Bishop of that Sea, who being an
Irishman by birth, and a monke of the
Order of S. Benedict, went ouer into France
and Germany, where he became an Ermite for
diuers yeares in the forrest of Alfatia, and
afterward was ordained Bishop of Strasburgh:
which Sea, when he had gouerned for
twelue yeares, in great sanctity of life, and
other vertues, he departed this world, and
reposed in our Lord, in the yeare of Christ,
six hundred fifty and eight. Among many
of his miracles, one is recorded, that by
his prayers he recalled to life Sigebert Sonne
to King Dagobert of France, that by misfor-
tune had byn slayne by a wild boare.

Cratepol.
de Epif.
German.
Ant.
Democh.
de Sacrif.
Missæ.
to.2.c.35.
Wion l. 2.
lig. Vit.
in Catal.
Episco.
Argent.

G   *The two and twentith* Day.

AT *VVinchester* in *Hampshire* the Commemoration of *Bl. VVilfreae* Queene and
Abbesse, wife to holy King *Edgar*, and Mother to *S. Edith* Virgin, who being from a
child brought vp among the Religious
woman in the Monastery of *VVinchester*, and
afterward married to King *Edgar*, reiecting the vanities of the world after her
husbands death, entred againe into the said
Monastery, and became Abbesse of the same;
where in all kind of sanctimony and exemplar good life, she gaue vp her soule to her
heauenly spouse, about the yeare of Christ,
nyne hundred fourscore and auen : In
which place also her body was interred, and
there kept with great veneration , euen
vntill our dayes.

Pol *Vir.*
lib. 6
Ranulph.
Cestr.
in hist.
Angl.
Item in
Actis
S. Edithæ
Virg.

A   *The three and twentith* Day.

AT *London* the Commemoration of *S.*
Vodine Martyr and Archbishop of the
same Sea in our British Primitiue Church,
who being a man of singular sanctity of life,
reproued King *Vortiger* of *Britany*, for putting away his lawfull wife, and taking ano-

ther

ther woman , whofe Father was a great enemy to the Chriftiá faith:wherfore King *Hingift* of Kent,the faid womás Father, incéfed with rage againft the holy Bifhop, caufed him forthwith to be flayne (like another *S. Iohn Baptift* ,) togeather with many other Britifh Priefts and religious men,and fo he receyued a crowne of Martyrdome, about the yeare of Chrift , foure hundred and fifty.

Gul. Malmef. hiftor. ex antiq. Monum. Britan. & Sto. Ibidem.

B *The foure & twentith Day.*

AT *VVinocks-berghen* in Flanders , the tranflation of *S.Lewyne* Virgin & Martyr, who defcending of a very honourable parentage in our Iland of *Great-Britany,* was in the tyme of *S. Theodore* Archbifhop of *Canterbury,* flayne for the confeffió of Chrift, in the yeare of our Lord , fix hundred fourfcore and feauen. Her body was kept with great veneration in an old Monaftery of *S. Andrew,*neere *Seaford- hauen* in *Suffex*, vntill the tyme of the fecond *Danish* and *Norman* incurfions,& then on tnis day was tráflated to *Berghen* aforfaid , and there placed in the Cloifter ofs. *Winocke,* in the yeare of Chrift, one thoufand fifty and eight, wherat many miracles haue byn wrought. In the laft vaftation of *Flanders* by the French , the faid

Io.Molá. in addit. ad V fua. hac die,et in Indic. SS.Belgij Antiq. Britan. Monum.

glorious body was loft, to the great lamentation of all *Flanders*, but efpecially of the Inhabitants of *Berghen*, who by that meanes where depriued of fo great a treafure .

C *The fiue & twentith* Day

*

IN *Gothland* the Commemoration of the Saintes *VViaman*, *Vnaman*, and *Suraman*, brethren and martyrs, nephewes to *S*. *Sigfride* of *Yorke* and Apoftle of *Gothia*, who going out of *England* into that Countrey with their faid vncle *S. Sigfrid* for the Conuerfion therof, were, by the enemies of Chrift, flayne in hatred of Chriftian Religion. Their bodyes were throwne into a riuer, and their heads being put into a veffell, & a great ftone háged therat, were caft into a poole neere vnto the place of their Martyrdome, where on a tyme *S. Sigfride* walking and deploring their deathes, on a fuddaine there appeared three miraculous lightes vpon the water, that compaffed the veffell wherin their faid heads were, which he feeing, prefently leaped into the poole, & imbracing thē wept & faid : *Vindicet Deus*. Wherto one anfwered, *Vindicatum erit*, Another replyed, *In quem* ? The third added, *In filios filiorum &c*. This happened about the yeare of Chrift, one thoufand.

Io. Mag. in hift. Gothorū l.17.c.20. Olaus Magnus etiam in addit. ad Ioan.

D

D The *fix and twentith* Day.

AT *Derremond* in *Flanders* the feftiuity
of S. *Chriftian* Virgin, who defcended
of the bloud Royall of our Kings of *England*, had an angell fent from heauen (as
writeth *Molanus*) to inftruct her in the
Chriftian faith: by whofe admonition, to
efchue the dangerous allurements of the
world, fhe firft ftole fecretly into *Scotland*, and
thence into *Flanders*, and there after a priuate & moft faintly life, full of miracles, fhe
gaue vp her bleffed foule to reft with her
heauenly fpoufe, about the yeare of Chrift,
one thoufand fourfcore and twelue, and in
the raigne of K. *VVilliam Rufus* of *England*. Her
principall celebrity is kept at the forfaid
towne of *Derremond*, vpon the feauenth day
of *September*, when her body was taken vp
and tranflated to a more eminent place of
the fame Church, where it is yet preferued
with great veneration of the Inhabitants,
as Patroneffe of that Village.

*Io. Molã.
in addit.
ad Vfua.
hac die, et
in Indic.
SS. Belgij*

E The *feauen & twentith* Day.

AT *Glaftenbury* in *Sommerfetfhire* the
feftiuity of S. *Iofeph* of *Arimathia*, who

going

going out of *Iury* (after he had buryed Chriſt) with S. *Mary Magdalen* and her company, to *Marſelles* in *France*, came thence into *Great - Britany* , with his owne ſonne *Ipſeph* , and ten other diſciples , where he obtained of *King Aruiragus,* a little Iland in *Somerſetsĥire* , called in the Britiſh tongue *Ins-witrin* (now *Glaſtenbury*;) & there leading a ſolitary life with his ſaid fellowes , at laſt he côuerted to the Chriſtian faith *Marius* & *Coillus*, ſonne and nephew to *King Aruiragus,* and then full of moſt venerable old yeares, he died , about the yeare of Chriſt, fourſcore and two. There was afterward a goodly Monaſtery erected in that place of the Order of S. *Benedict* , which was the greateſt in all *England*, and ſo remayned vntill the tyme of King *Henry* the 8 . when by his commandement the ſame was deſtroyed by *Sir VVilliam Goald* Iuſtice of Peace, to the lamentation of all Chriſtendome. His feaſt was wont to be celebrated on this day in many places of our Realme, euen yntill the raigne of the late Queene *Elizabeth.*

T H E ſame day at *Lincolne* the paſſion of S. *Hugh* Martyr, who being a Child of ten yeares old , was by the Iewes of that Citty in contêpt of Chriſt & Chriſtian Religion, nayled on a croſſe , & ſo deſerued to be crowned with the ſame death , that our bleſſed Sauiour ſuffered for the Redêptiô of

makind

Jo. Capg.
in Catal.
SS. Brit.
Pol. Vir.
L.1. Camd.
in deſcrip.
Britan.
pag. 162.
Nicol.
Harpesf.
in hiſt.
Eccleſ.
fol. 30

mankind. The perfidious Iewes, when he was dead, buryed his body in an obfcure place, which the earth miraculoufly caft vp: and then they threw him into a well, who being there alfo by a miracle found out by his owne Mother, the Chanons of the fame Citty, with great veneration carried the fame in proceffio to the Cathedrall Church or Minfter, and there interred his holy Reliques, in the yeare of Chrift, one thoufand two hundred fifty and fiue, and in the raigne of King *Henry* the third of England.

Io. Capg. in Catal. SS. Ang. Matth. Weft. & Parif. an. 1255.

F   *The eight & twentith Day.*

AT *Dole* in little *Britany* the depofition of S. *Sampfon* Bifhop and Confeffour, who borne in our Ilád of a Royall Britifh bloud, was firft created Archbifhop of *Carleon* vpon the riuer of *Vfke*, and Metropolitan among the old *Britans* of VVales, now commonly called *Carline*; and being inflamed with defyre of helping his neighbour-Countreyes for their Conuerfion, went ouer into *France*, and there was conftituted Bifhop of *Dole* in little *Britany* by King *Childebert* of *France*: where after he had conuerted many thoufands to the faith of Chrift, famous for miracles, he finally ended his venerable dayes,

*Sigeb. in Chron. an.*565. *Petr.in Catal.l.*6. *Vincent. infpecul. lib.*20. *Tritem. de vir. illuftr. Mart. Rom. Molan.* & a ij hac die.

and

and repofed in our Lord, about the yeare of Chrift, fix hundred and foure. His body was buryed at *Dole*, and there in ancient times wont to be kept with great veneration and reuerence of the Inhabitants.

G   *The nine & twentith Day.*

AT *Troys* in *France* the depofition of S. *Lupus* Bifhop and Conteffour, who about the yeare of Chrift, foure hundred and foutty, togeather with S. *German* Bifhop of *Auxier*, came ouer into our Iland of *Great - Britany*, to expell the *Pelagian* herefy, and to reeftablifh the Catholicke and Roman faith, which was among them before, and then began to be extinguifhed by the doctrine of *Pelagius* the Britan. At what time alfo is recorded a famous & miraculous victory achicued by the prayers of thefe two Saintes, againft thofe heretickes, by only crying and founding out the word *Alleluia*, wherwith the faid Pelagians were driuen away and difcomfited. And for this fingular benefit, that our Countrey hath receyued by this feruant of Chrift, it feemeth not amiffe, that his memory fhould be recorded among the ancient Saintes of our Nation (though he were a Frenchman by birth) and his feftiuity celebrated by vs, for the increafe of

Mart.
Rom.
Molan.
& alij
omnes
hac die.
Bed. l. 1.
hift. Eccl
c. 17. 18.
19. 20. &
21.
Gild.
Sapien.
in eius
vita.
Greg.
Turon.
de glor.
Conf.

deuo-

deuotion in our Iland, that was once made worthy of fo glorious a Patrone and Protectour.

THE fame day at *Lichfield* in *Staffordshire*, the Commemoration of Bleſſed *Owen* Confeſſour, who being a man of great eſteeme and birth, and high Steward to Queene *Edildride* of the Eaſtangles, renounced the world, and became a monke, firſt in the Monaſtery of *Leſting* in the Kingdome of the *Northumbers*, vnder *S. Chad*, that then was Abbot therof, and after at *Lichfield:* where being made worthy by God, to heare the voyce of Angells one day deſcending vpon *S. Chads* Oratory to call him to heauē, in great ſanctity and holines of life, he finally repoſed in our Lord, about the yeare of Chriſt, ſix hundred and fourſcore.

Ven. Bed. l.4. hiſt. Angl. cap.3.

A   *The thirtith* Day.

IN *Northumberland* the depoſition of S. *Lefrone* Virgin and Martyr, who being Abbeſſe of a Monaſtery in the ſame Kingdome, was in the ſecond Daniſh perſecution togeather with many holy men and women, ſlaine in contēpt of the Chriſtiā faith. For the furious Danes ſurprizing all the Monaſteries that ſtood in their wayes, put moſt of the Religious perſons, eyther to ſword

Matth. Weſt. an. 1011. *Arnol.* W*ion in Mart. Benedict. hac die*

or

or fire. And among others, cōming to this Monaſtery, wheroi S. *Leſrone* was Abbeſſe, aiter that they had moſt barbarouſly and by violence abuſed the ſacred Virgins, they tithed the whole Monaſtery, putting nyne to death, and leauing the tentn to ſhiit for herſelfe: which vnheard-of-cruelty, the perfidious Danes ſhewed towards many religious perſons in our Coútrey, at their arrinall, and incurſions, about the yeare of Chriſt, one thouſand and eleuen.

THe ſame day at *Canterbury* the depoſition of S. *Tacwyne* Confeſſour, and Archbiſhop of the ſame Sea, who being a man of excellent learning and wiſdome, was, of a monke of the Monaſtery of *Brewton*, promoted to the Archbiſhopricke of *Canterbury*, and ſucceeded S. *Brituald* in that office: where in all kind of holy conuerſation, and ſanctity of life, he ended his bleſſed dayes, about the yeare of Chriſt, ſeauen hundred and fourty, and in the raigne of King *Edbert* of *Kent*. His body was buryed in the Cathedrall Church of Canterbury, where it yet remayneth in th eold *Cloiſter*.

Bed.l.5.c. 24. Ioan. Tritem. l.4.c.69. Pol. Vir. lib.6. wion l.2. lig. vitæ.

F   *The one and thirtith Day.*

AT *Hunſtocke* in *Corn-wall* the depoſition of S. *Neoth* Prieſt and Confeſſour, who

leading

leading a solitary life in the *VVest-part* of England, was famous for sanctity of life & miracles, both aliue and dead. He was very familiar with king *Alfred* of the *VVestsaxons*, by whose counsell and exhortation, the said King founded the famous Vniuersity of *Oxford*. With this man also there liued at the same tyme, another venerable holy man (and as it were his companion) called S. *Guier*, vnto both which there haue byn many Chappells and altars, in Catholicke tymes past, dedicated with in the Realme of England. And in *Huntingtonshire* in particular, there is yet remayning a faire towne and Church, sometyme erected in memory of *S. Neoth*, which vntill this day retayneth that ancient name, and is commonly called *S. Neots*. He died about the yeare of Christ, eight hundred threescore and eleuen.

* *
*

THE

Matth.
West.
an .871.et
878.
Molam.
in addit.
ad Vsua.
& alij
omnes
hac die.

THE
MONETH
OF AVGVST.

C   *The first Day.*

Sur.to.4
in eius
vita.
Tritem.
de vir.
Illustr.
Pol.Vir.
lib. 6.
histor.
Mart.
Rom.
Molan.
& alij
omnes
hac die.

T VVinchester in *Hampshire* the depoſition of S. *Ethelwold* Biſhop and Confeſſour, who being firſt a Monke of *Glaſtenbury* Monaſtery, vnder S. *Dunſtan,* was afterward made Ab- bot of *Abington*, & thence promoted to the Biſhopricke of *VVincheſter:* which when he had gouerned for one and twenty yeares togeather, in great ſanctity of life & working of Miracles, he reſted in our Lord, in the yeare of Chriſt 984. & was buryed in his owne Cathedral Church of *VVincheſter:* at whoſe body it hath pleaſed God to worke many miracles. It is recorded of this

holy

holy Bishop, that in tyme of a great dearth, he brake all the plate belonging to his Church, and gaue it to the poore, saying: *That the Church in good tyme might be againe proui-ded of Ornaments necessary, but the poore that perished for want of food, could not be recouered.*

THE same day at *Gaunt* in *Flanders* the Translation of *S. VVenlocke* Abbot and Confessour, who descended of the ancient Royall bloud of *Britany*, became Father to many Monkes in an old Monastery in the lesser *Britany*, called *Tauracum*, where in all kind of most holy life, he ended his blessed dayes. His body was afterward on this day with great solemnity translated to *Gaunt*, about the yeare of Christ, one thousand and fifty, and is there vntill this day preserued with great honour and veneration.

Sur. in vita. S. Ethbini 19. Octo. Io. Mola. in addit. ad Vsua. hac die.

D   *The second Day.*

AT *Durham* in the Bishopricke, the Commemoration of *S. Alrike* Eremite and Confessour, who leading a solitary life in the forrest of *Carliele* for many yeares to-geather, was of such admirable sanctity and holinesse of life, that his memory, euen vntill our dayes, hath byn famous through-out the whole Iland of *Britany*. S. *Godricke* an Eremite also liuing in those partes at the

*

Matth. Parif. in Chron. ad an. 1107. & 1170.

fame tyme, and being present at his death, saw his soule ascend into heauen, as it were in a Sphericall forme of a burning wynd. His body was with great veneration interred at *Durham* by the Clergy of that Church, about the yeare of Chrift, one thoufand one hundred and feauen, in which yeare he died.

E   *The third Day.*

*

Io.Lefl.
Epifco.
Roffenf.l.
4.de geft.
Scot.
Wion in
append.
ad l. 3.
lig. vitæ.

IN *Scotland* the Commemoration of *S. Domitius* Confeffour, who defcended of a worthy lynage in the Kingdome of *Ireland*, became there a Monke of the holy Order of S. *Benedict*, vnder the famous Abbot S. Columbe, whofe fcholler and difciple he was, where in all kind of good learning, vertue, & other fanctity of life, he ended his venerable old dayes, about the yeare of Chrift, fix hundred threefcore and eleuen. His memory hath, in tymes paft, byn very famous throughout the Iland of *Great-Britany*, efpecially in *Scotland*, where he liued and died.

F   *The fourth Day.*

AT *Furne* in *Flanders* in the Dioceſſe of *Ipres*, the Tranſlation of part of the glorious body of S. *VValburge* Virgin and Abbeſſe, daughter to *S. Richard* King of the Engliſh, who being ſent for into *Germany* by *S. Boniface* her vncle, Archbiſhop of *Mentz*, was by him ordained Abbeſſe of a monaſtery there, which he had newly founded, called *Heydentine*, where in all kind of ſanctimony of life, ſhe gaue vp her ſoule to her heauenly ſpouſe, in the yeare of Chriſt, ſeauen hundred threeſcore and ſixteene. The reſt of her body remayneth at *Eyſt*, whither it was before tranſlated; wherout, vntill this day, diſtilleth a precious oyle, very ſoueraigne for many diſeaſes. Her principall feſtiuity was wont to be celebrated in our Catholicke Church of *England*, vpon the one and twentith day of Iune, according to the vſe of *Sarum*; and in Germany vpon the firſt of May.

Marcel. in vit. S. Simib. c. 14. Mol. in addit. ad Vſua. e: iu Ind. SS. Belgij Wion. *hac die in Mart. Benedict.*

G   *The fifth Day.*

AT *Oſwiſtree* in *Shropshire* the Paſſion of S. *Oſwald* King of the *Northumbers* and

Martyr , who after he had brought the *Angles, Scots* , and *Pictes* vnto his subiection, was so zealous in the new planted faith of Chrift , that for defence therof principally he was flayne by *Penda* the Pagan King of *Mercia* , at the forfaid towne of *Ofiftree,* in the yeare of Chrift , fix hundred thirty and fiue. *S. Bede* recounteth , that on a day as he fate at dinner with *S. Aidan* Bifhop of *Lindisferne,* there was a filuer difh brought before him full of daynties , which when he faw , he caufed prefently to be broké in little peeces, and giuen to the poore attending at his gate for almes, togeather with the meate that was therin , faying , *They had more need therof then himfelfe.* The Bifhop fitting by , and delighted with fuch rare piety in a King, tooke him by the right hand, and faid: *This hand, I pray God, may neuer confume.* And fo faith *S. Bede,* it fell out : for that his arme and hand being cut of at his death, remayned till his dayes whole and incorrupt , being kept in a filuer cafe, in *S. Peters* Church at *Bambrough* . He finifhed the Cathedrall Church of S. *Peter* at *Yorke ,* which was before begun by his predeceffour King *Edwyn.* His body was firft buryed at *Peterburrow,* and part therof tráflated afterward to *VVinockes-Berghen* in *Flanders,* where the fame was preferued with great Veneration.

Bed. in Epit. & l.3.c.6. 9. 10. & 11. Io. Maior Hiftor. Scot. l.2. cap.11. Mart. Rom. & alij omnes. hac die.

A

A   *The sixt Day.*

AT VVincheſter in *Hampshire* the depoſitiõ of Bleſſed *Henry* Confeſſour and Biſhop of the ſame Sea, who being a Frenchman by birth, and brother to King *Stephen* of *England*, became firſt a monke of the Order of *S. Benedict*, and after Abbot of *Glaſtenbury*, and laſt of all Biſhop of *VVincheſter*, and Legat Apoſtolicall of *England*. In which dignity he behaued himſelf with ſo great humility and loue of the common people, for more then fourty yeares togeather, that his name was famous throughout all *England* & *France*. He died in great ſanctity of life, and ſpirit of Propheſy, in the yeare of Chriſt, one thouſand one hundred ſeauenty and one, about foure monethes before the Martyrdome of *S. Thomas* of *Canterbury*.

THE ſame day at *Fone* in *France* the Commemoration of S. *Alexander* Confeſſour, who deſcended of the bloud-Royall of *Scotland*, ſtole ſecretly thence for the loue of Chriſt in baſe attyre, and went into *France*, where he became a Lay-brother in a Monaſtery of Ciſtercian monkes at *Fone*, labouring in the baſeſt offices of the houſe, vnknowne till his dying day: Which being then reueyled to the *Prior* of the Monaſtery vpon obe-

Pol. Vir. lib. 11. *&* 12. *Matth. Weſt. & Pariſ. ad ann. citat.* Wiõ *l.* 2. *in Catal, Epiſco. winton.*

*

Rob. Buckl. in vita S. Mechtil. Virg. L. M. de vit. SS. Mulierũ. Angl.

dience,

dience, it pleafed God to teftify his wor-
thines by a Miracle after his death, which
was thus. A Monke of the fame Monaftery,
that had a fore vlcer in his breft, and now
growne to a fiftula, came to the faid *Alexan-*
ders tombe, and there prayed. Vnto whome
Alexãder appearing brighter then the funne
with two Crownes, one on his head, and
another in his hand; the Monke demaunded
what that double Crowne meant? He anfwered and faid: The Crowne in his hand
is for the temporall Crowne, which I forfooke for Chriftes loue (for he fhould haue
byn King of *Scotland,* being next heyre thervnto by fucceffion, as the Story relateth:)
The other on my head, is that which I
haue receyued common with other Saintes.
And that yow may be affured of the verity
of this vifion, you fhal now be cured of your
infirmity. And hauing thus fpoken, and the
other immediatly healed, he vanifhed away.
He died about the yeare of Chrift, one thoufand and two hundred.

B　　　*The feauenth Day.*

*　A T *VVeftminfter* by *London* the Commemoration of S. *Maude* Queene, daughter to S. *Margaret* and holy King *Malcolme* of
Scotland, & wife to K. *Henry* the firft of *England,*

w hofe

whose admirable and rare vertues, togeather with her singular & exemplar life, hath
byn a patterne euer synce to all Princesses in
Europe; especially her exceeding Charity
towards the poore, whome she disdayned
not, though neuer so foule leapers, but rather imbraced them with all delight , yea
washed their soares and vlcers, neuer so
loathsome and filthy : For whome she built
also a goodly hospitall in the suburbes of
London called S. *Giles*; as also founded the
Priory of Christes-Church within *Ald-gate*
of the same Citty . Her body was with all
veneration buryed at *VVestminster* in the
yeare of Christ, one thousand one hundred
and eighteene, which yeare she desceased.
In whose praise these distiches following
were composed .

Prospera non lætam fecere , non aspera tristem ,
  Aspera risus ei, prospera terror erant.
Non decor effecit fragilem , non Sceptra superbam,
  Sola potens humilis , sola pudica decens.

She was in her tender yeares brought vp in
the Monasteries of Religious womē at *VVin-*
chester and *Rumsey* , in all exercise of vertue
and learning. She built a faire stone-bridge
ouer the riuer of *Lue* at *Stratford-vpon-Bow* , as
also gaue diuers goodly mannours and lands
to the Abbey of *Barking* in *Essex*, for mayn-
tayning of the same.

Matth.
West.
et Parif.
an. 1118.
& 1105.
Item in
Actu S.
Marg.
Matris
apud
Sur. to 3.
10. Iunij

C   *The eight Day.*

Eyfengr.
Cent 2.
part.3
dift.4.Io.
de Kirk-
ftat in
Monaft.
Tabulæ.
Glafcon.

AT *Glaftenbury*-Abbey in *Somerfetshire* the Commemoration of S. *Fagane* Confeſſour, and Scholler to S. *Ioſeph* of *Arimathia*, with whome when he had led a ſolitary life for many yeares in the Iland of *Auallonia*, now called *Glaftenbury*, and being by S. *Ioſeph* throughly inſtructed in the Chriſtian faith and other vertues, became himſelfe a preacher therof and S. *Ioſephs* ſucceſſour in his Oratory, where the famous Monaftery of *Glaftenbury* was afterward built: Where alſo in great ſanctity & holines of life he finally repoſed in our Lord, about the yeare of Chriſt, one hundred and twelue; and was one of the firſt Confeſſours of our Britiſh Nation.

D   *The ninth Day.*

Matth.
Weft.
an.1254.
& Parif.
eodem an.
Pol. Vir.
l.16.in
fine.

AT *Ely* in *Cambridgshire* the depoſition of S. *Hugh* Biſhop and Confeſſour, who being firſt a Monke and then Abbot of the Monaftery of S. *Edmundsbury* in *Suffolke*, was thence promoted to the Biſhopricke of *Ely*, where in all kind of moſt commendable vertues, eſpecially in humility and abſti-

nence

nence, hauing gouerned that Sea fiue and twēty years, he happily ended his venerable dayes, about the yeare of Chriſt, one thouſand two hundred fifty and foure. His body was very honourably interred in the Cathedrall Church of *Ely*, within the Chancell, which himſelfe had newly built from the ground, conſecrating the ſame in preſence of King *Henry* the third . and his ſonne Prince *Edward*, in the yeare 1235. and was there kept vntill our dayes with great honour and veneration of the people . He alſo built the Biſhops Pallace at *Ely*, beſydes many other publicke works of Charity, which he perfourmed whilſt he liued.

Wion in
Mart.
Benedict.
hac die.

E   *The tenth Day.*

AT *Leſmor* in *Ireland* the Commemoration of S. *Malcus* Biſhop and Confeſſour, who borne in *England*, and a Monke of the Monaſtery of *VVincheſter* in *Hampſhire*, and of a moſt vertuous conuerſatiō, was elected & conſecrated Biſhop of *Leſmor* in *Ireland*. In which Paſtorall office, in great ſanctity of life & working of Miracles, he finally ended his bleſſed dayes, about the yeare of Chriſt, one thouſand one hundred twenty & fiue. He is alſo much praiſed by S. *Bernard*, that liued at the ſame tyme; who wryting the

*

Io. Molā.
in appēd.
ad Mart.
Vſua . &
Ber. in
vita S.
Malach.
Epiſ.

life

life of *S. Malachy*, Bishop and Primate of *Ireland*, among other thinges, he faith of *S. Malcus* : *That the wisdome of God was in him.* &c.

F   The eleuenth Day.

*

AT *Chichester* in *Sussex* the Commemoration of *bl. Gilbert* Confessour & Bishop of the same Sea , whose integrity of life and vertuous conuersation , hath made him famous to posterity. He was a Father of the fatherlesse (faith the Story of his life) a comforter of mourners , a defender of widdowes, a relieuer of the poore, a helper of the distressed, and a diligent visitour of the sicke. And thus heaping vp heauenly treasure by the excercise of these and other like vertues, and by his continuall teaching and instructing the people , like a true Pastour of Christs flocke, full of venerable old age, he finally reposed in our Lord, in the yeare of Christ, one thousand three hundred and fiue , & was buryed in his owne Cathedrall Church. At whose body *Matthew* of *VVestminster* recordeth diuers Miracles to haue byn wrought. He raised the foundations of our Blessed Ladyes Chappell at *Chichester*, but death preuenting his pious endeauour, the same was finished by another.

Matth.
West.
in hist.
Angl.
ad an.
Citat.
Regiſtr.
Ciceſtren.
Catal.
Epiſ.
Ciceſtreſ.

G

G   *The twelfth Day.*

AT *Stafford* in the fame Shire, the Commemoration of *S. Bertelme* Confeſſour, who deſcended of a noble Britiſh lynage in our Iland, contemned the puddle and vanityes of the world in the flower of his youth, and became an Ermite for the loue of God, leading a moſt ſtrict & ſeuere kind of life, in the woods neere *Stafford* aforſaid: where in very great ſanctity and holines of life, he ended his bleſſed dayes, & finally repoſed in our Lord. His body was afterward brought to *Stafford*, and being there interred, was wont, in ancient tymes, to be kept with great veneration of the people of that Prouince.

Regiſt. Eccle. Stafford. & monument. antiq. eiuſdem Prouin.

*

A   *The thirteenth Day.*

IN *Frizeland* the Commemoration of S. *VVigbert* Prieſt and Martyr, who being an Engliſh-man by birth, deſcended of an honourable ſtocke, lead firſt a ſolitary life in *Ireland*, and thence returning into *England*, went ouer into *Frizeland* to preach the Chriſtian faith to the Pagans of that Countrey, which when he had done for two yeares,

*

without

Ven.Bed.
l.5.c. 10.
& 11.
Marcel.
in vita S.
Simibert.
Molan.
in Indic,
SS.Belgij

without any great profit, returned againe, and gaue himfelfe to his former Eremiticall kind of life. But being fent thither the fecond tyme with S.VVillebrord & his fellowes, was by Radbodus King of the Frizians put to a moft cruell death, for perfuading the people to breake downe a certaine Image of Iupiter, which the faid King had fet vp to worfhip and offer facrifice vnto, about the yeare of Chrift, fix hundred fourfcore and fourteene. This man is different from the other S. VVigbert, whofe feaft is alfo celebrated vpon this day by the Roman Martyrologe, vnder the name and title of a Confeffour.

B   The fourteenth Day.

Io.Molā.
in addit.
ad Vfua.
et in Ind.
SS.Belgij
Io. Trit.
de vir.
Illuftr. l.
3. c. 147.
Wion in
Mart.
Benedict.

AT Elft in Gelderland the Tranflation of S.VVerenfrid Prieft & Confeffour, who being a Monke of the monaftery of Rippon in Yorkeshire, went out of England into Fláders and Germany to preach the Chriftian faith, where he conuerted the whole Countrey of Geldria, and became their Apoftle, labouring inceffantly, by teaching and inftructing them in the true way of life, vntill his dying day. His body was afterward with great folemnity and veneration, on this day tranflated to the forfaid towne of Elft, wher-

at

at infinite miracles haue byn wrought, especially in curing the difeafe of the *Goute.* He died about the yeare of Chrift, feauen hundred and fiue; and is honoured of the Inhabitantes of *Elft,* as principall Apoftle and Patrone of that Prouince.

C   The fifteenth Day.

IN the Monaftery of *Cateby,* the Commemoration of *S. Margaret* Prioreffe, who borne at *Abington* in *Barkeshire,* and fifter to S. *Edmund* Archbifhop of *Canterbury,* was by him ordayned Prioreffe of the forfaid Monaftery of *Cateby* : whofe moft vertuous life and conuerfation, full of fanctimony and miracles, deferued to be famous euen vntill our dayes throughout *Englād.* She died about the yeare of Chrift, one thoufand two hundred fifty and feauen, and was buryed in the fame place. At whofe body it hath pleafed God, in teftimony of her holines, & increafe of deuotion in our Iland of *Great-Britany,* to worke miracles,

Matth. Weft. in hift. ad an. 1257.

D   The fixteenth Day.

AT *Douer* in *Kent* the Commemoration of S. *Thomas* Monke & Martyr, who by

cer-

certain *French* Pirates, that láded there in the night, was moſt barbarouſly ſlayne in defence of the goods of the Church & Monaſtery committed to his charge, about the yeare of Chriſt, one thouſand two hundred fourſcore and fifteene, and raigne of King *Edward* the firſt of England. His body was with great ſolemnity and veneration interred in the Church of *Douer*, wherat it is recorded that miracles haue byn wrought, in ſigne of his innocency.

Matth.
Weſt.
an. 1295.
Pol. Vir.
lib. 17.
Hiſtor
Sto. in
vita.
Edou. 1.

E   *The ſeauenteenth Day.*

AT *Hartford* in the ſame Shire, the feſtiuity of *S. Thomas* Archdeacon of *Northumberland* and Confeſſour, who hauing byn a diſciple of *S. Edmund* Archbiſhop of *Canterbury*, was of ſo great ſanctity and holineſſe of life, that it pleaſed God to manifeſt the ſame after his death, by the manifold miracles wrought at his body. He died in the yeare of Chriſt, one thouſand two hundred fifty and three, and was buryed in a little Chappell of the *Carmelites* at *Hartford.* And for that there are three other Saintes of this name, of the Engliſh nation, this man is cōmonly called, for diſtinctions ſake, by the name of *S. Thomas* of *Northumberland.*

Matth.
Weſt.
& Pariſ.
an. 1253.

The

THE same day at *Egmond* in *North Holland* in the Dioceffe or *Harlem* the depofition of S. *Ieron* Prieft and Martyr, who borne in *Scotland* of a Noble bloud, went ouer into *Holland* to preach the Chriftian faith to the people of that Coûtrey: which whê he had done moft painfully for many years togeather with great fruite and profit of his holy labours, was at laft flayne in hatred therof by the *Danes* and *Normans*, that made incurfions into thofe partes, about the yeare of Chrift, eight hundred and fifty. His body was with great veneration brought to the Monaftery of *Egmond*, and there placed neere to the venerable Reliques of S. *Adalbert* their Apoftle, both which are now deftroyed and caft out of the Church, in thefe our vnhappy dayes, togeather with all other facred Reliques and images, in thofe partes, to the lamentation of the Chriftian world.

Io. Molã. in addit. ad Vſua. e in Ind. SS. Belgij Petr. Crater. de Epiſco. German. Wion & a ij.

F   *The eighteenth Day.*

AT *Rome* the depofition of S. *Helen* Empreffe mother to *Conftantine* the *Great*, who borne at *Colchefter* in *Effex* (as ancient Records teftifie) and daughter to Prince *Coelus* of *Britany*, was for her great zeale in Chriftian Religion, made worthy both of an earthly & heauély crowne. She defceafed

Niceph. l. 8. Eufeb. in vit. Conftant. Socrat. l. 2. cap. 12.

at *Rome*, about the yeare of Chriſt, three hundred twenty and ſix, being of the age of fourſcore yeares. Her body was afterward tranſlated to *Rhemes* in France, and there is kept with great veneration. The Greeke Church doth celebrate her feaſt vpon the one and twentith day of May, togeather with her ſonne *Conſtantine*. She going to *Hieruſalem* found out the Croſſe, wheron our Sauiour was nayled, and ſuffered his paſſion for the Redemption of man-kind, and repayred that Citty ſore ruined through the warres of the Roman Emperours, adorning the ſame with many goodly Churches and monumētes. She alſo builded the walles of the Citty of *London* & *Colcheſter* in *England*, togeather with a goodly Church in the Towne of *Bedford*, which being turned into a Monaſtery, was called of her name *Helenſlow*, but afterward quite deſtroyed and ouerthrowne by the Incurſions of the *Danes*, about the yeare of Chriſt, eight hundred threeſcore and eight.

G　*The ninteenth Day.*

*　IN *South-wales* the Commemoration of S. *Clintanke* K. of *Brecknocke* and Martyr, who being a very zealous and godly Prince, as he was one day on hunting, was ſlayne by a

Pagan

Pagan fouldiar, partly in hatred of Chriftian Religion, and partly alfo for that a noble Virgin fhould fay, fhe would neuer marry any man except the faid King, who was fo zealons a Chriftian. There was afterward a goodly Church erected in his honour, neere to a Riuer in *South-wales*, where he was flayne, and where with great veneration his holy body was interred, at which it pleafed God in figne of his innocency to worke many miracles.

Io. Capg. in Catal. SS. Brit.

A   *The twentith Day.*

IN *Northumberland* the paffion of S. *Ofwine* King of the ✝*Deires* & Martyr, who for that he was a moft zealous Chriftian, was impioufly flayne by *Ofway* the Pagan King of the *Bernicians*, about the yeare of Chrift, fix hundred fifty and one. His body being throwne into an obfcure place, & after miraculoufly found out, was with great veneration brought vnto *Tinmouth,* and there placed in an ancient Church erected in honour of our bleffed Lady. S. *Aidan* liuing at the fame tyme, and Bifhop of *Lindisferne*, had a reuelation of his death, euen at the inftant of his paffion, who when he preached to the people, was wont oftentymes to fay of him: *This Nation of ours is not worthy to haue fo*

✝ now *Yorkshire*

Bed. in Epit. & Hiftor. l. 3. c. 14. Weft. an. 645. & 941. Molan. in addit. ad Vfua.

     good

good a Ruler or Gouernour. &c.

B   The one & twentith Day.

*
Regiſ.
Eccleſ.
S. Andr.
in Calab.
& Oſciu
cius im-
preſſ.
Romæ.

IN *Calabria* in *Italy* the Commemoration of S. *Richard* Biſhop and Conſeſſour, who deſcended or a worthy parentage in England, and going to the Court or *Rome*, was there made Prieſt, and at length, for his vertue and learning, ordayned Biſhop of a place in *Calabria* called S. *Andrews*: where in great ſanctity and holines, or life togeather with exceeding vigilancy ouer his flocke committed to his charge, he finally repoſed in our Lord. His body was interred in his ſaid Cathedrall Church of S. *Andrew*, and there is yet preſerued with great deuotion and veneration of the Inhabitantes, for the frequent Miracles that haue byn wrought therat. He is Patrone of that Dioceſſe, and his feaſt is there celebrated with a double Office, wherin he hath three proper leſſons, conteyning the whole Story of his life.

C   The two and twentith Day.

*

IN *Bedfordſhire* the Commemoration of S. *Arnulph* Conſeſſour, who deſcended of a noble Britiſh lynage in our Iland, for the

loue

loue of God, contemned the world, and became an Eremite, leading a most strict and seuere kind of life in the County or Prouince of *Bedford* : where in great sanctity and holinesse he also ended his blessed dayes. His body was buryed in the same shire at a place called afterward of his name *S. Arnulphs-bury* , where for a long tyme it was honoured , for the miracles it pleased God to worke therat.

Ex antiq. monum. Prouinc. Bedford.

D   *The three and twentith Day.*

AT *Meneuia,* now called S. *Dauids* in *Penbrookeshire* of VVales the Commemoration of *S. Iustinian* Monke and Martyr, who being a noble Britan, and building a Monastery with his owne inheritance, in the Iland of *Ramsey* in *Penbrookeshire* aforsaid, and hauing there gathered many monkes togeather vnder Monasticall discipline, was in the said iland, by the diuells instigation , in hatred of his sanctity, slayne by three of the brethren of his said Monastery, who were all presently stroken with a filthy leprosy by diuine Iustice, in reuenge of so odious a fact, about the yeare of Christ, foure hundred fourscore and six. His body was withall veneratiō & honour brought to the Church of *Meneuia,* where the same was by

*

Io. Capg. in Catal. SS. Brit.

S. Dauid himſelfe then Biſhop therof, ſolemnely interred, and wherat it pleaſed
God to worke many miracles.

E *The foure & twentith* Day.

Matth.
Pariſ.
in hiſt.
Maiori.
ad an. D.
1257. &
deinceps.

IN *Cateby-Monaſtery* the Commemoration
of S. *Alice* Prioreſſe, and ſiſter to S. *Edmund*
Archbiſhop of *Canterbury* , who borne at
Abington in *Barkeſhire* & a woman of admirable ſpirit and vertue, was after the death of
her ſiſter S. *Margaret*, made Prioreſſe of the
Monaſtery of *Cateby*,where in very great humility and holineſſe of life , ſhe ended her
bleſſed dayes, about the yeare of Chriſt, one
thouſand two hundred and ſeauenty. Her
body was buryed in the ſame Monaſtery
neere to the body of her forſaid ſiſter S. *Mar-*
garet, wherat in token of her ſanctimony
of life, whilſt ſhe liued , it pleaſed God to
worke miracles after her death.

F *The fiue & twentith* Day

AT *Colaingham* in *Norhamſhire* , in the
Marches of *Scotland*, the paſſion of S.
Ebba Abbeſſe and Martyr , deſcended of the
bloud royall of the Kings of *Northüberlãd*, togeather with all her *Siſters* in the Monaſtery

who

who in the firſt *Daniſh* Incurſions, vnder the
Captayns *Hinguar* & *Hubba*, cut of their noſes
and vpper lippes, to deforme themſelues,
therby to auoyd the barbarous luſt of the
Pagan perſecutours; who ſeeing them ſo
mangled and defaced, commaunded their
Monaſtery to be fiered, and ſo they all
ended their courſe of Martyrdome. She
was afterward canonized for a Saint, about
the yeare of Chriſt, eight hundred and fourſcore. This woman is different from the
other of the ſame Name, who was the
foundreſſe and firſt Abbeſſe of this Monaſtery of *Coldingham*, and no Martyr, for that
the *Danes* were not in her tyme yet come
into England, nor almoſt two hundred
yeares after. Her Commemoration we haue
put downe before, vpon the ſecond day of
Aprill.

T**HE** ſame day at *Monte-Flaſcone* in *Tuſcany*
the depoſition of *S. Thomas* Confeſſour
and Biſhop of *Hereford*, who going to *Rome*
to Pope *Martyn* the ſecond, about the affaires
of his Church, died in his way homward
at the forſaid Towne of *Monte - Flaſcone*,
where his fleſh being ſeparated from his
bones, was there honourably interred in
the Church of *S. Seuerine*; but his ſacred
Reliques were brought to *Hereford*, and
there placed in a faire marble Tombe in his
owne Cathedrall Church, with great ſo-

Chron.
Britan.
*fol.*609.
Weſt.
an. 870.
Pol. Vir.
lib. 4.
Arnold.
Wion.
lib. 4.
lig. vitæ.
Baron.
tom. 10.
Annal.
in defenſ.
earumdē.

Catal.
Epiſ.
Herefor.
Regiſt.
eiuſdem
Eccle.
Pol. Vir.
*l.*17.*Hiſt.*
Angl.

lemnity and veneration, the fecond day of
October, in the yeare of Chrift, one thoufand two hundred fourfcore and feauen. He
was afterward Canonized for a Saint by
Pope *Iohn* the two and twentith.

G   *The fix and twentith* Day.

*

Rich.
Parochus
Iffelb.
in eius
vi aabud
Io.Capg.
in Cat.SS.
Ang.
Mola. in
append.
ad Vfua.

AT *Iffelbey* in *Lincolnshire* the Commemo-
tion of *S. Pandayne* Virgin, who defcended of a noble parentage in our Iland of
Great-Britany, was of fuch admirable vertue, and aufterity of life, that in figne
therof it pleafed God to worke many miracles at her body after her death, which was
kept for a long tyme with great veneration
of the Countrey-pleople, at the forfaid
towne of *iffelbey*. She died about the yeare of
Chrift, nyne hundred and foure. The ftory
of her life is wrytten at large, by *Richard* Paftour of the Church of *Iffelbey*, wherof there
is mentiõ made in the Catalogue of Englifh
Saints, gathered by *Iohn Capgraue* a learned
man of our Nation, who liu d in the tyme
of King *Richard* the fecond, and lead an
Eremiticall life in the Prouince of *Kent*.

A

A   *The seauen & twentith Day.*

IN *Glocestershire* the Commemoration of
S. *Decaman* Eremite and Martyr , who
borne of a very noble Britiſh parentage in
South-wales, and brought vp in the Chriſtian
faith from his youth , ſtoe ſecretly away
from his friends, and with a fagot of wood,
inſteed of a boat , miraculouſly paſſed ouer
the riuer of *Seuerne* , and came into *Glocefter-*
shire, where leading an Eremiticall auſtere
life, was at length ſlaine by a Pagan ſoul'-
dier, in hatred of Chriſtian Religion: whoſe
head being cut of from his body , himſelfe
tooke vp from the ground, and carried to a
fountayne , wherat he was wont to waſh
it. At which place there was afterward a
Goodly Church erected in his honour,
about the yeare of Chriſt , ſeauen hundred
and ſix, where his body was wont to be
kept with great veneration of the Inhabitants: as alſo another dedicated vnto him
in the Towne of *VVells* in *Somerſetshire,*
which at this day is there ſtanding to be
ſeene.

Io. Capg.
in Catal.
SS. Ang.

B

B   *The eight & twentith Day.*

AT *Brackley* in *Northamptonshire,* the Commemoration of *S.Rumbald* Confeſſour, Sonne to a Britiſh King of our Iland , who as ſoone as he was borne into the world and baptized, did miraculouſly ſpeake and fortell diuers wonderfull thinges ; and profeſſing himſelfe a Chriſtian , preſently yielded vp the ghoſt. His body was with great veneration buryed at the forſaid towne of *Brackley*, wherat, it is recorded, diuers miracles haue byn wrought.

THE ſame day at *Cullen* in the higher *Germany* , the Commemoration of *S. Agnes* Virgin and Martyr, who being a noble Britan by birth, and one of the number of the *Eleuen thouſand Virgins* martyred with *S.Vrſula,* was for defence of her chaſtity there put to death with the reſt of her fellowes, about the yeare of Chriſt, three hundred fourſcore and three , herſelfe afterward miraculouſly reuealing her name : for which cauſe her body is peculiarly honoured of the Inhabitants of *Cullen.*

C

C   The nine & twentith Day.

AT *London* the depofition of S. *Sebbe* King of the *Eaftfaxons* and Confeffour, who after he had gouerned that Kingdome thirty yeares in great peace and tranquillity, became a Monke in the Monaftery of S. *Peter* and S. *Paul* at *London*, diftributing the greateft part of his goods to the poore before his entrance, where within a few yeares after, in great fanctity of life, he peaceably refted in our Lord, about the yeare of Chrift, fix hundred threefcore and fifteene. His body was buried in the Church of *S.Paul* in *London*, in a coftly marble Coffin, where it was kept vntill our dayes with great veneration of the Cittizens, for the miracles that are recorded to haue byn wrought therat.

Ven.Bed. l.4.c. 11. Mart. Rom. hac die. Sto. in. Annol. Angl. de Regib. Eaftfax.

THE fame day at *Dorchefter* in *Oxfordshire*, the Tranflation of *S.Edwold* Confeffour and Eremite, brother to S. *Edmund* King & Martyr, who refufing the Kingdome of the *Eaftangles*, gaue himfelfe, for loue of Chrift, to a folitary life; In which when he had liued many yeares in all fanctity and holines, at laft ended his bleffed dayes at *Dorchefter*, where his body being interred about the yeare of Chrift, eight hundred threefcore

Gul. Malmefb. lib. de Pontif. & Reg. Angl. an. 871.

and

and eleuen, was afterward, on this day, taken vp and tranſlated to a more eminent place of the ſame Church, where before it was laid.

D   *The thirtith Day.*

IN *France* in the Dioceſſe of *Meldune* the depoſition of S. *Fiaker* Confeſſour, Sonne to *Eugenius* the fourth of that name, King of *Scotland*, who forſaking all worldly dignities and delightes, went ouer into *France* with his ſiſter S. *Syra*, and became a Religious man, by the help and directions of S. *Pharao* Biſhop of *Meldune* : where in very great ſanctity and holineſſe of life he ended his bleſſed dayes, about the yeare of Chriſt, ſix hundred and thirty. In the Citty of S. *Omers* in *Artoys*, there is a Chappell or Oratory dedicated vnto S. *Fiaker* within the Pariſh Church of S. *Margaret* in the ſame Towne, where his feaſt is kept on this day with great ſolemnity, and veneration, by the Sodality or Confraternity that is there inſtituted in his honour. Where alſo is graunted Plenary Indulgence to all that rightly viſit his Chappell on this day, and fullfill the other circumſtances conteyned in the Bull of *Graunt*, by Pope *Clement* the

eight

Io.Leſl.
Epiſ.
Roſſ.de
reb.Sco.
lib. 4.
Hect.
Boet.l. 9.
Bellefor.
in Ann.
Francorū
*L.*1.c.36.
Mola. &
omnes
hac die.

eight, dated in the yeare of Chrift one thoufand fiue hundred nynty and feauen.

E   *The one and thirtith* Day.

AT *Lindisferne* in the Kingdome of the
Northumbers the depofition of *S. Aidan*
Confeffour, and Bifhop of the fame Sea,
whofe foule *S. Cuthbert*, being then but a
Sheepheard, faw carried vp to heauen by
two angells, and was therby conuerted to
a Religious life, about the yeare of Chrift,
fix hundred fifty and one.

Bed. l. 3. c. 3. 5. & 14 Et in vita S. Cuthber.

THE fame day at *VVimborne* in *Dorcetshire*
the depofition of S. *Cuthberge* Abbeffe
fiffer to King *Inas* of the *VVeftfaxons*, who
building a Monaftery of her owne charges
at *VVimborne*, entred her felfe therin, tooke
a Religious habit, and became Abbeffe of
the fame. Where in all kind of vertuous exercife, and Monafticall difcipline, togeather
with working of many miracles, fhe finally
gaue vp her foule to her heauenly fpoufe,
about the yeare of Chrift, feauen hundred
twenty and feauen,

Matth. Weft. an. 719. 727. & 901. Breviar. Sarum & Molan. hac die.

ALfo the fame day at *Fulkstone* in *Kent* the
Tranflation of S. *Eanfwide* Abbeffe
daughter to *Eadbald* King of *Kent*, who defpifing all worldly and temporall honours
                                    ftudied

Io.Molā.
hac die
Chron.
Brit. fol.
264.
Rob·
Buckl.
in eius
vita
pag. 119.

ſtudied how to attaine to Celeſtiall. And entring into a monaſtery at *Fulkſtoe* aforſaid, was afterward made Abbeſſe therof; where in great ſanctimony and holineſſe of life ſhe died, about the yeare of Chriſt, ſix hundred and fourty. Her body was afterward on this day taken vp, and tranſlated to a more eminent place of the ſame Church, wherat it pleaſed God to worke miracles

**
*

THE

THE
MONETH
OF SEPTEMBER.

F *The first Day.*

 T *VVinchester* in *Hampshire* the Commemoration of S. *Elphege* the first of that name , Confeſſour and Biſhop of the ſame Sea, whoſe godly life and do-ctrine , togeather with the ſpirit of propheſy, hath byn very famous in ancient tymes throughout England. He was the firſt that perſuaded S. *Dunſtan* to lead a Monaſticall life, as alſo ordayned him and *S. Ethelwold* Prieſtes. And when the ſaid *Dunſtan* was expelled the Court by King *Ethelred,* he came to this holy man *Elphege,* of whome he was very gratefully receyued and cóforted. And

Matth.
Weſt.
an. Do.
934. &
947. in
hiſtor.
Angl.
maiori.

*

finally

finally full of venerable old age, replenished
with sanctity of life & miracles, he peaceably rested in our Lord, about the yeare of
Christ, nyne hundred fourty and six, and
was buried at *VVinchefter*. This man is different from the other S. *Elphege* or the same
name, who was Bishop of *Canterbury*, and
martyred by the *Danes* in the yeare 1012.

G   The second Day.

Tritem.
de Vir.
Illuftr.
Bed.l.5.c.
16. & 22.
Sixt. Se-
nenf. in
biblioth.
lib. 4.
Molan.in
Append.
ad Vfua.

IN *Scotland* the Commemoration of *S.*
Adaman Abbot and Confeffour, a man of
wonderfull vertue and aufterity of life, who
being made Abbot of *S. Columbes* Monaftery
in the Iland of *Hoy* by *Scotland*, gouerned the
same in great sanctity and holines, toge-
ther with obferuance of Monaftica l difcipline vntill his dying day. He was one of
the firft, that by his doctrine and exhorta-
tions brought the *Scottishmen*, as also a great
part of the *Britans*, to the Catholicke obferua-
tio of the feaft of *Eafter*, who before follow-
ed the errour of the *Quartadecimans* in kee-
ping therof. He wrote in like manner a
learned Treatife of the same fubiect; as also
another worke yet extant, intituled, *De Locis*
Sanctis, and flourished about the yeare of
Christ, fix hundred and feauenty.

A

A   The third Day.

AT *Foßis* in the Territory of *Namures*, the Tranflation of *S*. *Foillan* Bifhop and Martyr, Sonne to King *Philtan* of Ireland, who going to *Rome*, was there created Bifhop by Pope *Martin* the firft, and fent thence to preach the Chriftian faith in *France* and *Flanders*; which when he had done for many yeares with very great labour & profit in that kind, he was at length flayne, togeather with three of his fellows at a place in *Namures*, called *Silua Carbonaria*, or *Colliers-wood* : which thing being reueyled to his brother *S*. *Vltan*, and *S*. *Gertrude* Abbeffe of *Niuell* in *Brabant*, his body was fought for, and being found out, was on this day afterward folemnly tranflated to the Monaftery of *Foßis*. and there is yet preferued with great veneration. He fuffered about the yeare of Chrift, fix hundred and threefcore.

Molan.
in addit.
ad Vfuar.
et in Ind.
SS. Belgij
Wion in
Mart.
Benedict.
hac die.

B   The fourth Day.

AT *Durham* in the *Bishopricke*, the Tranflation of S. *Cuthbert* Bifhop and Confeffour, who firft leading a folitary life in the Iland of *Farne* (now called *Cochet*) be-

Bed. l. 4.
c. 27. 28.
29. & 30.
Weſt.
an. 696.
875.878.
995.
Alan.
Copus in
dialog.
dial. 3.
cap. 19.
Abbo
Floriac.
in Prolo.
ad vit. S.
Edmundi
Breuiar.
ſec. vſum
Sarum.

Democh.
l. 2. de
Miſſa.
contr.
Caluinū
c. 37.
Eyſengr.
cent. 2. p.
4. d 7.
Molan.
Mart.
Rom.

came afterward a Monke, and then Abbot of the Monaſtery of Mailros in Northumberland, and laſt of all was promoted to the Biſhop-ricke of Lindisferne; the which he reſigned after ſome yeares againe, & became an Ere-mite. Whoſe great holines of life hath byn manifeſted by the wonderfull miracles wrought by him, both aliue and dead. He deſceaſed in the yeare of Chriſt 687. His bo-dy being afterward on this day takenvp, & foūd altogeather whole and vncorrupt, was with great ſolēnity trāſlated to the Cathe-drall Church of Durham, & there kept with great veneration: whither alſo many thou-ſandes went on pilgrimage, euen vntill the dayes of King Henry the eight.

THE ſame day at Treuers in the higher Germany, the Paſſion of S. Marcellus Bi-ſhop and Martyr, who being a noble Britan by byrth, and gathering togeather the diſ-perſed Chriſtians in our Countrey, that were conuerted to Chriſt by S. Ioſeph of Arimathia and his fellowes, in our Primi-tiue Britiſh Church, did by his preaching and doctrine ſo mooue King Lucius, that he ſent forth with to Rome to Pope Eleutherius to treate about his Conuerſion to Chriſtian faith. He afterward went ouer into Germany to preach, in like manner, the faith of Chriſt to that people, where, as he was exe-cuting the office of a good Paſtour, he was

finally

finally martyred at *Treuers*, about the yeare of our Lord, one hundred and fourscore; & was the first of our British Nation, that suffered death for Christ, out of the Iland of Great Britany,

C   *The fifth Day.*

AT *Alt-Munster* in *Germany*, the Commemoration of S. *Altho* Abbot and Confessour, who borne in *Scotland*, and descended of a noble parentage in that Kingdome, went ouer into *Germany*, in that Primitiue Church, and there became Abbot of a new Monastery, erected by S. *Boniface* (an Englishman) Archbishop of *Mentz*, and Apostle of that Countrey. Which Monastery was afterward of this mans name, commonly called *Altho-Monastery*, and now by continuance or tyme, more abruptly is tearmed *Alt-Munster*. He died in great sanctity and holines of life, about the yeare of Christ, seauen hundred and threescore, and was buryed in the same place.

Metrop. Salisbur. & Wion in append. lib.3. lig. vitæ.

D   *The sixt Day.*

IN *Cumberland* the Commemoration of S. *Bega* Virgin, who descended of a very

noble parentage in *Ireland*, and being inſtructed in the Chriſtian faith, came ouer into
our Iland of *Great-Britany*, and there led a
moſt vertuous life in the forſaid Prouince
of *Cumberland*: where in very great ſanctimony of life, and working of miracles, ſhe finally gaue vp her ſoule to h er heauenly
ſpouſe. There hath byn in ancient Catho-
lick tymes a goodly Church and Monaſtery erected in her honour in *Cumberland*,
where her body was wont to be kept with
great reuerence and veneration of the Inhabitantes of that Shire; which place, in
thoſe dayes, was a famous pilgrimage, eſpecially for the people of the Northerne partes
of England.

Chron.
Brit. fol.
650.
Wion.
in appēd.
ad l.7.
lig. vitæ.

E   *The ſeauenth Day.*

A T *Canterbury* the Tranſlation of *S.*
Dunſtan Biſhop and Confeſſour, who
being firſt Abbot of *Glaſtenbury*, then Biſhop
of *Worceſter*, and after of *London*, was laſt of
all created Archbiſhop of *Canterbury*, and
Primate of England: whoſe moſt holy life
and miracles, are yet famous throughout
the Chriſtian world. The Diuell appearing
to him on a time in the likneſſe of a yong
& beautifull woman, tempting him to vn-
cleaneſſe, he tooke vp a paire of pinchers,

Sur. to.5.
Malmeſ.
in hiſt.
Angl.
Petr.
in Catal.
lib. 8.
Pol. Vir.
lib. 7.

that

that then lay by him, and caught the foule beast by the vpper lippe, and so holding him fast, and leading him vp and downe his chamber, after diuers interrogatories, draue him away. He died in great sanctity of life, in the yeare of Christ, nyne hundred fourscore and eight. His body was on this day taken vp, and with great solemnity, set in a more eminent place of the Cathedrall Church of *Canterbury*, wherat it hath pleased God to worke many miracles.

F   *The eight Day.*

AT *Lyming* in *Kent* the Commemoration of Blessed *Ethelburge* Queene, wife to holy *Edwyn* the first Christian King of *Northumberland*, and daughter to K. *Ethelbert* of *Kent*, who after the martyrdome of her Lord and husband, fled out of *Northumberland*, and came backe to her Countrey of *Kent*, where forsaking the pompe and vanities of the world, she built herselfe a little Monastery at the forsaid towne of *Lyming*, and there receyuing the holy veyle of Chastity, was consecrated to God by the handes of *S. Honorius* Archbishop of *Canterbury*: where in very great holines of life seruing her heauenly spouse, she became mother to many holy

*

De ea habetur mentio in vit. Edwin.Reg. North. & in vit. Ethelb. & Eadb. Regum Cant. R. Buckl. in vit. S. Ethelb. Abbatiss. Bark. fol. 122.

Q 3   Vir-

Virgins and widdowes, that did imitate
her religious purpofe and profeſſion. And
fo continuing in that godly vocation, for
many yeares, full of all vertue and ſanͨti-
mony of life, ſhe finally went to her heauenly ſpouſe, about the yeare of Chriſt, ſix
hundred fourty and ſeauen.

G   The ninth Day.

Mart.
Rom.
Vſuard
Gaſel.
Wion
& alij.
omnes
hac die.

IN Scotland the depoſition of S. Queran Abbot and Confeſſour, who deſcended of a
noble family in that Kingdome, contemned the vanities of the world, and entring
into a Monaſtery, became a Monke of the
Venerable Order of S. Benedict, & afterward
Abbot of the ſame; whoſe ſingular life and
miracles haue byn manifeſted aboundantly
to the world, both at home and abroad.

Hereb.
Roſweyd.
in Faſt.
SS. Rob.
Buckl.
in eius
vital. M.
S. de vit.
SS. Mul.
Angl.

THE ſame day at Barking in Eſſex the depoſitiō of S. VVulfhild Virgin & Abbeſſe,
daughter to VVulfhelme an Earle among the
VVeſtſaxons, who being borne after eighteene
yeares barreneſſe of her mother, was in her
very infancy conſecrated to God, and cōmitted for her education to the Religious
Virgins in the Nunry of VVincheſter; but
comming to riper yeares, ſhe built herſelfe
a Monaſtery at Horton, and was by holy K.
Edgar confirmed Abbeſſe therof, as alſo of

the

the Monaſtery of *Barking*, which the ſaid
King had newly reeditied and repayred,
being ſorely ruined through the incurſions
of the *Danes*; from whence being ſoone after
expulſed, with all her company, by the ambition of Queene *Alſtrude*, was after 20.
yeares baniſhment reſtored againe by the
forſaid Queene, ſhe being admoniſhed therto by S. *Ethelburge* ſometyme Abbeſſe therof,
who had appeared vnto her in a viſion,
when ſhe lay ſicke, complayning of the in-
iuſtice of the faĉt; and there in very great
ſanĉtimony of life, ſhe ended her bleſſed
dayes, about the yeare of Chriſt, nyne hundred fourſcore and fiue, and was buryed at
Barking: whoſe body being taken vp thirty
yeares after her death, was found, togeather with all her cloathes, as whole and
ſound, as if ſhe had byn buryed but a few
dayes before.

A   *The tenth Day.*

IN the Territory of *Ruremond* in *Gelderland*
the Depoſition of S. *Otger* Deacon and
Confeſſour, who being a Monke in the
North of *England* where he was borne, and
going to *Rome* in company of S. *VViro* and
Plechelme, returned thence into the low
Countreyes, and was moſt honourably re-

Io.Molā.
in addit.
ad V sua.
et in Ind.
SS.Belgij
Wion
in Mart.
Benedict.
hac die.

ceyued of Duke Pepin of Brabant, who gaue
him a certaine Territory and place of habi-
tation in his dominions , where he might
preach and plant the Christian faith:which
when he had done for many yeares , with
great feruour of spirit, to the gayning of
many thousand soules in those partes ; in
great sanctity and holines of life , he receyued the reward of his labours by reposing
in our Lord, about the yeare of Christ, seauen hundred thirty and one. A great part
of his body remayneth yet in the Cathedrall Church of Ruremond , and is there kept
with great veneration of the Inhabitants of
that Diocesse.

B   *The eleuenth Day.*

Io.Lest.
Epis.
Ross.l. 4.
de gest.
Scot.
Wion in
append.
ad lib. 3.
lig. vit.

IN *Ireland* the Commemoration of S. *Ba-*
ther Abbot and Confessour, scholler to S.
Columbe the Great of that Kingdome , who
comming into *Scotland* with him to preach
the Christian faith to the *Pictes* , who then
inhabited that Countrey : and being a most
vertuous and innocent man of life , was by
him made Abbot of a Monastery in the same
Countrey, which he had newly erected . In
which office and dignity he so behaued
himselfe, especially in the reformation of
monasticall discipline, that his name hath

ſynce byn famous throughout the King-domes of *Ireland* and *Scotland*. He deſceaſed in great ſanctity and holines of life, about the yeare of Chriſt, fiue hundred fourſcore and eleuen.

C   *The tweluth Day.*

AT *Fulkeſtone* in *Kent* the depoſition of S. *Eanſwide* Virgin & Abbeſſe daughter to *Eadbald* King of *Kent*, who forſaking all worldly conuerſation and delights, obtay-ned of her Father a ſolitary place in his kingdome to ſerue her ſpouſe Chriſt, which being graunted her at *Fulkeſtone* aforſaid, ſhe there built her ſelfe a little Oratory for a tyme, and then gathering togeather many other noble Virgins, imbraced a monaſti-call life, and became Abbeſſe of the reſt, her Oratory being couerted into a Nūry; where in all kind of ſanctimony of life and pious conuerſation, glorious for miracles, ſhe fi-nally repoſed in our Lord, about the yeare of Chriſt, ſix hundred and fourty.

Rob. Buckl. in eius vital.M. S. Angl. pag. 119. ex antiq. Monum. Cantiæ.

THE ſame day at *VVimborne* in *Dorcetſhire* the Commemoration of S. *Quemburge* Virgin, ſiſter to *Inas* King of the *VVeſtſaxons*, who vnder the Gouerment of S. *Cuthberge* her ſiſter and Abbeſſe, receaued the holy veyle of chaſtity in the Monaſtery aforſaid:

*
Matth. Weſt. in hiſt. Maiori. ad an. 727.

where

where in very great vertue, humility, and other pious excercifes, fhe ended her happy dayes, about the yeare of Chrift, feauen hundred twenty and feauen.

D   *The thirteenth Day.*

Fælix in Martyr. hac die. Eius vita habetur tom. 7. Suurij. ex M. S. Codic.

AT *VVefter-woort* in *Gelderland*, the Depofition of S.*VVerenfrid* Prieft & Confeffour, who being an Englifhmã by byrth, and defcended of an honourable family, became firft a Monke in the Monaftery of *Rippon* in *Yorkeshire*, and thence went ouer into the *Low-Countreyes* & *Germany* to preach the Chriftian faith, where he conuerted the whole Prouince of *Geldria*, and fo became their Apoftle. He died on this day at the forfaid Towne of *VVefter-woort*, about the yeare of Chrift, feauen hundred and fiue: and was afterward folemnely tranflated to *Elft*, where his body hath byn kept with great veneration of the Inhabitants, for the manifold miracles that haue byn wrought therat, efpecially in curing the goute.

E   *The fourteenth Day.*

AT *Arpine* in the Kingdome of *Naples* the Commemoration of S . *Bernard*

Con-

Confeſſour, who being an Engliſhman by birth, and going to Ieruſalem on pilgrimage (togeather with S. *Gerard* his companiō) to viſit our Sauiours ſepulcher, in his returne backe fell ſicke in *Italy*, where after a ſhort ſpace, in all ſignes of ſanctity and holines of life, he repoſed in our Lord. His body being obſcurely buryed, was many yeares after miraculouſly reuealed to the Archprieſt of that place, who with a ſollemne proceſſion, brought the ſame vnto *Arpine*, and placed it very decently in the Church, where it is at this day kept with great veneration and honour of the Inhabitants, as their chiefe Patrone, for the manifold miracles, that euē in theſe our times are wrought therat, eſpecially in curing of Ruptures: wherby the ſame place is now becōe a famous pilgrimage, for ſuch as are grieued with that infirmity. His life and miracles are recounted more at large in the Records of the Church of *Arpine*; of whome alſo there is a proper prayer with a *Hymne*, or *Sequentia*, wherin briefly is declared the whole ſtory of his life : both which are commonly read in the Maſſe and Office of his feſtiuall day.

Ex Reg. Eccleſ. Arpineſ. & Arch. Lſcript. ipſius Sepulch.

F   The fifteenth Day.

IN the Monaſtery of *Dormundcaſter* in *Nor-thamptonſhire* two miles from *Peterburrow*, the Commemoration of Bleſſed *Chinneburge* Queene, daughter to *Penda* King of the *Mercians*, and wife to *Alfred* King of *Northumberland*, who with the conſent of her husband (he alſo hauing left the world, and retyred himſelfe to a Monaſticall life in the Abbey of *Mailros*) became a Religious woman in the forſaid Monaſtery of *Dormūdcaſter*, where in all kind of ſanctimony of life, and pious conuerſation, ſhe ended her bleſſed dayes, about the yeare of Chriſt, ſix hundred threeſcore and ten. This forſaid Monaſtery being afterward called of her name *Chinneburgcaſter* was in the yeare 1010. quite ouerthrowne by the *Danes* ; ſo as there is little or no memory therof left at this day, in our Iland of *Great-Britany*.

Chron. Brit. fol. 398. Wion l.4. lig. vit. Rob. Buckl. in eius vita l.M. S.fol.171.

G   The ſixteenth Day.

IN *Scotland* the depoſition of S. *Ninian* Biſhop and Confeſſour, who deſcended of a noble Britiſh bloud, was ordained Biſhop of a place called S. *Martins*, amōg the *South-Pictes* in the Marches of *Scotland*, whome he conuerted to the Chriſtian faith, and became their Apoſtle. He after died in *Scotland*, about the yeare of Chriſt, fiue hundred and twelue; whoſe body being buryed in the forſaid Church of S. *Martin*, was there kept with great honour and veneration euen vntill the dayes of K. *Henry* the eight. In whoſe honour alſo many goodly Churches and altars, haue in former Catholicke tymes byn erected and dedicated, in the Kingdome of *Scotland*.

THE ſame day at *VVilton*, in the Church of S. *Dionyſe*, the depoſition of S. *Edith* Virgin and Abbeſſe, daughter to holy *Edgar* King of *England*, who deſpiſing all worldly and temporall perfermentes became a Religious woman in the Monaſtery of *VVilton*, vnder the care and gouernment of her owne mother *VVilfrede*, after whoſe deſceaſe, ſhe was made Abbeſſe of the ſame place: where in all ſanctimony of life, ſhe gaue vp her ſoule to her heauenly ſpouſe, in the yeare of Chriſt, nyne hundred fourſcore and foure. There are many goodly Churches and monumentes of her name yet to be ſeene in diuers places of *England*: & one particularly at a Towne called *Church-Eaton* in *Staffordſhire*, where there is a little well-ſpring of water, very ſoueraigne for many diſeaſes, comonly called by the name of S. *Ediths* well.

Vē. Bed. *l.3.c.4.* *Io. Molā.* *in addit.* *ad Vſua* *& alij* *omnes* *hac die.*

Sur.to.5. *Cont.* *Vē. Bed.* *l.2. Pol.* *Vir.l.6.* *Vincent.* *in ſpecul.* *Matth.* *Weſt.* *an.961.*

A

A   The ſeauenteenth Day.

Mart.
Rom.
Bed.Ado.
Vſuar.
& alij
omnes
hac die.

IN *South-wales*, the paſſion of the Sayntes *Stephen* and *Socrates* Martyrs, who being two noble ancient Britans by byrth, and conuerted to the faith of Chriſt in our Primitiue Church, by the preaching of S. *Amphibale* Prieſt and Martyr, were in hatred tnerof, put to death in our Iland, in the perſecution of *Dioclefian* the Emperour, by moſt exquiſite tormentes, togeather with many others for the ſame cauſe, about the yeare of Chriſt, three húdred & foure. There are diuers Churches yet remayning in Wales that in ancient tymes haue byn dedicated in their honour: among whome alſo, their memory is yet famous vntill this day, eſpecially in *Monmouthshire*, and the Southerne partes adioyning.

B   The eighteenth Day.

AT *Berghen* in *Flanders*, the Tranſlation of S. *VVinocke* Abbot and Confeſſour, who deſcended of a noble Britiſh bloud, and going ouer into the Low Countreyes to S. *Bertin* Abbot of the Monaſtery of *Sitheu* (now called *S.Bertins*) in the Citty of S. *Omers*,

was

was by him ordayned Abbot of an ancient Monaſtery named *VVoromholt*, called afterward of his name S. *VVinockes*; where in all kind of ſanctity of life & Regular diſcipline, famous for miracles, he repoſed in our Lord. His body was afterward on this day tranſlated to the forſaid towne of *Berghen*, by *Baldwyn* Earle of *Flanders*, about the yeare of Chriſt, nyne hundred ; and there is yet conſerued with great veneration of the Inhabitants, for the manifold miracles which it hath pleaſed God to worke therat.

Mola. in addit. ad Vſuard. et in Ind. SS. Belgij Meyerus in Anna. Flandr. & alij.

C   *The ninteenth Day.*

AT *Canterbury* the depoſition of S. *Theodore* Archbiſhop of that Sea and Conſeſſour, who borne at *Tharſis* in *Cilicia* of a noble parentage, became firſt a Monke of the Venerable Order of S. *Benedict*, and afterward was ordayned Archbiſhop of *Canterbury*, and ſent thither from *Rome* by Pope *Vitalianus*. He celebrated two Prouinciall Synods in our Iland, the one at *Hartford*, the other at *Hedtfeld*, concerning the Reformation of the Clergy of *England*. And when he had in all vertuous and Saintlike behauiour gouerned the forſaid Sea of *Canterbury* for two and twenty yeares, in moſt godly wiſe, he finally repoſed in our Lord, about the

Bed. l. 5. cap. 8. & in Epit. Tritem. de vir. Illuſtr. Mart. Rom. & alij omnes hac die.

yeare

yeare of Chrift, fix hundred and nynty, and
was buryed at *Canterbury*, with a famous
Epitaph in heroicall verfe: fome part wherof yow may read in *S. Bede*, fetdowne in the
fifth Booke and eight Chapter of his Hiftory of England.

D   *The twentith Day.*

IN *Scotlãd* the Cõmemoratiõ of *S. Cybthacke*
Prieft & Cõfeffour, who being an *Irishman*
by birth , and Nephew to *S. Columbe* the
Great of that Nation, defpifed all worldly
preferments , and came ouer into *Scotland*
with his faid *Vncle*, to preach the Chriftian
faith to the *Pictes* who then inhabited part
of that Kingdome. And at laft entring into a Monaftery , became a Monke of *S. Benedictes* Venerable Order in the Iland of *Hoy*
vnder the care of the forfaid *S. Columbe*, who
had newly founded the fame, and was then
Abbot therof: where famous for fanctity of
life and miracles throughout the whole
Kingdome , there ended his bleffed dayes in
reft, about yeare of Chrift , fix hundred and
foure.

E   *The one & twentith Day.*

IN *Ireland* the Commemoration of *S. Edil-hun* Con essour, who being an English-man by byrth, of great learning and vertue, and brother to another *Edilhun* of the same name, then Bishop of *Lindisferne*, in the Kingdome of the *Northumbers*, went ouer into *Ireland*, to lead a more quiet kind of life, remote from the world ; where after he had passed a few yeares, in very great holines and sanctity, he gaue vp his soule to rest, about the yeare of Christ, six hundred fifty and fiue. He had for companion in this his peregrination into *Ireland*, a noble yong man named *Egbert*, with whome liuing in a Monastery there, called in the Irish tongue *Rathmelsig*, whilst the plague infected sorely that Countrey, he had a vision of his owne departure out of this life, and of the escape of his fellow *Egbert*; to whome, when he had related the whole, in all quietnes of spirit he gaue vp the ghost.

*Vé. Bed.
l.3.c.27.
Histor.
Eccles.
Gent.
Angl.*

F   *The two and twentith Day.*

AT *Lindissa* in the Kingdome of the *Nor-thumbers*, the Commemoration of *S.*

R   Hig-

Higbald Abbot and Confeſſour, whoſe integrity of life and conuerſation hath byn iamous, in tymes paſt, throughout the whole Iland of *Great-Britany*. He was Abbot of an ancient Monaſtery in the forſaid Kingdome of *Northumberland*, in the tyme of *VVulhere* King of the *Mercians*; and ended his happy dayes about the yeare of Chriſt, ſix hundred fourſcore & fiue. He went into *Ireland* a little before his death to viſit the holy Abbot *Egbert*, who at that tyme was there very famous for the great opinion of his ſanctity and holines of life : with whome he had very many ſpirituall conferences, and amóg other thinges, diſcourſing of the death of S. *Chad* Biſhop of *Lichfield* (being a little before deſceaſed) holy *Egbert* related to haue ſeene his ſoule carried vp to heauen, by the hands of Angells, that deſcended thence to accompany the ſame.

Vé. Bed:
l.4.c.3.
Io:Mold.
in appéd.
ad Vſua.
lit. H.

G　*The three and twentith Day.*

AT *Kale* in *France* the Commemoration of Bleſſed *Hereſwide* Queene, neece to S. *Edwyn* King of *Northumberland* and Martyr, ſiſter to S. *Hlida*, and wife to King *Ethelwold* of the *Eaſt-angles*, who after the death of her Lord and husband, forſaking all worldly pleaſures, friends, and other prefermentes

＊
Bed. l.4.
Hiſtor.
cap. 23.
Wion
lib. 4.
lig. vita.

what

whatſoeuer, went ouer into *France*,& there
taking a Religious habit, receyued therwith
the holy veyle of Chaſtity in the forſaid
Monaſtery or *Kale*, where in very great humility and ſanctimony of life, ſhe ſpent the
reſt of her dayes in prayer and contemplation of heauenly things, and finally gaue vp
her bleſſed ſoule to her heauély ſpouſe, about
the yeare of Chriſt, ſix hundred fourſcore
and ten.

A *The foure & twentith* Day.

AT *Eyſt* in the higher *Germany*, the
Tranſlation of S. *VVinibald* Abbot and
Confeſſour, Sonne to S. *Richard* King of
the Engliſh; who going ouer into *Flanders* &
Germany with S. *VVillebrord* and his fellowes
to preach the Chriſtiã faith to thoſe people,
founded a Monaſtery in the Prouince of
Franconia, called *Heydelmaine*, and became
himſelfe Abbot therof, which when he had
gouerned for ten yeares, in gteat ſanctity &
holines of life, he happily repoſed in our
Lord, about the yeare of Chriſt, ſeauen hundred and threeſcore. His body was afterward on this day, ſolemnely tranſlated to
the forſaid Citty of *Eyſt*, and there placed in
the Cathedrall Church, togeather with the
Venerable body of his brother S. *Willebald*,

*Author
eius vitæ
apud
Sur.to.7.
Wion
hac die in
Mart.
Benedict.*

where the fame is preſerued with great veneration of the Inhabitants.

B   The fiue & twentith Day

Ve. Bed.
l. 5. c. 22.
& l. de
ſex
Aetat.
Tritem.
de vir.
Illuſtr.
Molā. in
addit. ad
Vſuard.
Regiſtr.
Eccleſ.
Ligon.

AT *Langres* in *France* the Depoſition of S. *Ceolfrid* Confeſſour, and Abbot of the ancient Monaſtery of S. *Peter* and S. *Paul*, vpon the Riuer banke of *VVyre*, in the Kingdome of the *Northumbers*, now called *VVyremouth*, and Maiſter to our famous S. *Bede*, who going to *Rome* to obtayne Priuiledges for his ſaid Monaſtery, died in his iorney homward at *Langres*, in the yeare of Chriſt, ſeauen hundred & ſeauenteene : and there being moſt honourably interred in the Cathedrall Church of that Citty, his body is kept vntill this day with great veneration. There is a Letter of this holy mans yet extant in S. *Bedes* Hiſtory, which he wrote to *Naitonus* King of the *Picts* or *Redſhankes*, about the true obſeruation of the feaſt of Eaſter; as alſo for the Reformation of his Clergy. To whome in like manner (ſaith the Story) he ſent cunning Carpenters & workemen, to build him a Church, after the faſhion of thoſe in *Northumberland*.

C

C   _The six and twentith Day._

AT _VVestminster_ by _Londö_ the depositiö of _S. VVulsy_ Abbot and Confessour, who being a man of great vertue and innocency of life, was by _S. Dunstan_ created the first Abbot of _VVestminster_, where in all kind of exemplar good life, full of sanctity and miracles, he ended his blessed dayes, about the yeare of Christ, nyne hundred and threescore. His body was buryed in the same Monastery, and there was wont to be kept with great veneration of the Cittizens of _London_.

THE same day in _Scotland_ the Commemoration of _S. Iotaneus_ Monke and Confessour, who borne in _Ireland_, and descended of a worthy parentage in that Kingdome, came thence into _Scotland_ in company of _S. Columbe_ the great of that Nation, whose disciple he was, and afterward his coadiutour in preaching the Christian faith to the _Pictes_. After whose Conuersion, full of sanctity and miracles, he gaue vp his soule to rest, about the yeare of Christ, nue hundred and fourscore.

Matth.
West.
_ad an. D._
_958._
Wion in
append.
ad lib. 3.
lig. vit.

*

Hect.
Boet.
de rebus
gest.
Scot. &
Io. Lesl.
Episco.
Ross.l. 4.
Ibidem.

D　*The ſeauen & twentith Day.*

*
Bed. l. 3.
cap. 18.
Pol. Vir.
lib. 4.
hiſtor.
Matth.
Weſt.
an. 636. et
652. &
Wion.
lib. 4.
lig. vit.
Regiſtr.
Cantab.

AT *Knobhersburge* in the Prouince of the *Eaſtangles*, the Commemoration of S. *Sigebert* king of the ſame Prouince and Martyr, who inflamed with the loue of God, left the adminiſtration of his Kingdome to his Coſyn *Egricke*, and tooke a Religious habit in a monaſtery which himſelfe had newly erected called *Knobhersburge* ; but a little after *Penda* the Pagan King of *Mercia*, inuading his dominions, he was by his Subiectes drawne, by force, out of his Monaſtery, into the field, where vnarmed, hauing only a little rod in his hand, was ſlayne, togeather with his Coſyn *Egricke*, by the forſaid *Penda*, in the yeare of Chriſt, ſix hundred fifty and two, and the ſeauenteenth of his raigne ; and was afterward declared a Martyr. It is recorded by diuers Hiſtoriographers that he firſt founded the Vniuerſity of *Cambridge* in his owne Prouince, for the education and inſtruction of youth in all kind of good learning and liberall ſciences.

E *The eight & twentith Day.*

AT *Fulda* in the higher *Germany* the deposition of S. *Lioba* Virgin and Abbesse, who being first a Religious woman in the Monastery of *Wimborne* in *Dorcetshire*, was called thence, togeather with S. *Tecla*, S. *Agatha* and diuers others, into *Germany*, by S. *Boniface* an Englishman, and Archbishop of *Mentz*, and there made Abbesse of a new Monastery, which he had erected at a place called *Bifcopffen*; where after she had led a most Saintly life, full of miracles, she went at last to her heauenly spouse, about the yeare of Chrift, seauen hundred fifty and seauen, and was buryed at *Fulda*, where her body is yet kept, togeather with the venerable body of S. *Boniface*, with great veneration of that Countrey round about.

Rudolph. B. Rena. difcip. in eius vita. Mart. Rom. Molan. & alij.

F *The nine & twentith Day.*

IN *Scotland* the Commemoration of S. *Cogan* Abbot and Confessour, who borne in the same Kingdome of a very honourable parentage, became there a Monke of the Vene-

*

rable

Io. Leſſ.
Epiſ.
Roſſ.l. 4
biſt.Scot.
in fine.
Wion
inappēd.
lib.3. lig.
vitæ.

rable Order of S. *Benedict*, and after Abbot
of the whole Monaſtery; whoſe name being
famous throughout our whole Iland of
Great-Britany for ſanctity of life and learning, he gaue vp his ſoule to reſt in our
Lord, about the yeare of Chriſt 700. &
threeſcore. At whoſe body it pleaſed God,
in côfirmatiô of his holines to worke many
miracles. In which Kingdome alſo, there
haue byn in tymes paſt many Chappells
and altars dedicated in his honour, but
now all vtterly ruined by the vnfortunate change of Religion in that Countrey, to the lamentation of the Chriſtian
world.

G   *The thirtith* Day.

Bed. l. 2.
cap.18.
19. & l.3.
cap.20.
Sur.to.5.
Mart.
Rom.
Molan.
& alij
omnes
hac die.

AT *Canterbury* the Depoſition *S. Ho-*
norius Archbiſhop of the ſame Sea
and Confeſſour, who comming from
Rome into *England* with S . *Auguſtine* our
Apoſtle, ſucceeded him afterward in his
Office, and was the fifth Archbiſhop
of *Canterbury* . Which Sea, when he had
gouerned in all kind of ſanctity and holy
example of vertuous life, full of Venerable old age, he repoſed happily in our
Lord, in the yeare of Chriſt, ſix hun-

dred

dred fifty and three, and was buryed in
the Cathedrall Church of that Citty
with his predeceffours : where his body
was kept , euen vntill our dayes
with great honor and veneration,due to fo glorious
a Confeffour.

* *
*

THE

THE
MONETH
OF OCTOBER.

A   *The first Day.*

Matth.
Parif.an.
1247. *&*
*an.*1248.
& 1271.
Defcrip.
Ciuitat.
Parmef.
in Italia.
Regifir.
Ecclef.
D. Pauli
Londinē.

T *London* the depofition of S. *Roger* Confeffour and Bifhop of the fame Sea, whofe admirable vertues, and fanctity of life, wittneffe the Miracles that haue byn wrought at his body. He died at *Stepney* a mile from *London*, in a houfe belonging to that Bifhops Sea, in the yeare of Chrift, one thoufand two hundred and fourty: whofe body being brought to *London*, was with all honour and veneration, interred in the Cathedrall Church of *S. Paul* the Apoftle, in a faire tombe by the North-wall, a little aboue the Quire, with

this

this Epithaph, which is there yet remaying to be read.

Ecclesiæ quondam Præsul præsentis , in anno
M. bis C. quater X. iacet his Rogerus humatus.
Huius erat manibus Domino locus iste dicatus.
Christe suis precibus veniam des, tolle reatus.
The people of *Parma* in *Italy* haue chosen him for one of the chiefe Patrons of their Citty , by reason of a meruaylous victory they obtayned against *Fredericke* the Empeperour, by the prayers of S. *Roger* , whose body at that tyme shined with miracles in *England.*

T H E same day at *Oostkerke* in Flanders the Translation of *S. Guibagon* Confessour, Sonne to the King of *Scotland,* who taking vpon him a voluntary pouerty , for the loue of God, went ouer into *Flanders,* and there became a pilgrime or Eremite; where in great sanctity of life he finally reposed in our Lord. *Nicolas* Bishop of *Tornay* , on this day , caused his body to be reuerently eleuated, and placed more decently in the forsaid Church of *Oostkerke* , in the yeare of Christ, one thousand foure hundred fourty and foure , where the same is yet preserued with great veneration: whose feast in like manner in there on this day celebrated with great solemnity by the Inhabitantes round about.

Mola. in addit. ad Vsuard. et in Ind. SS.Belgij

M Oreouer the fame day at *Condy* in *Hennalt*, the depofition of *S. VVafnulph* Confeffour, who defcended of a noble bloud in the Kingdome of *Ireland*, and brother to S. *Etto* of that Nation, did, for the loue of Chrift, forfake his Countrey and friends, and went ouer into France, to lead a folitary and ftrict kind of life, where in great fanctity and holines, famous for miracles, he ended his bleffed dayes, in the Prouince of *Hennalt*, whofe body being yet preferued at the forfaid towne of *Condy*, is there honoured with great veneration of the Inhabitants.

Molan.
in addit.
ad Vfua.
et in Ind.
SS.Belgij

B   *The fecond Day.*

A T *Hereford* the Tranflation of S. *Thomas* Bifhop and Confeffour, who being firft Chancelour of the Vniuerfity of *Oxford*, & the of the whole Realme of Englad, was finally ordayned Bifhop of *Hereford*; which Sea, whe he had gouerned moft laudably for many yeares, he tooke his iorney to *Rome*, to Pope *Martin* the fecond, and died in his way homward at *Mote-Flafcone* in the Dukedome of *Florence*, in the yeare of Chrift, one thoufand two hundred fourfcore and feaue: whofe facred Reliques being brought into *England*, were with great veneration, on this

Pol.Vir.
lib. 17.
Mart.
Rom.
Molan.
Breuiar.
fec Vfum
Sarum.
Sur.to.5.
hac die.
& alij.

day

day placed in the Cathedrall Church of *Hereford*. His miracles are Regiftred in the fame Church to the number of foure hundred twenty & fiue: Amóg which, it is recorded, that by his prayers were raifed from death to life threfcore feuerall perfons, one and twenty leapers healed, and three and twenty blynd and dumme men to haue receyued their fight & fpeach.

C   *The third Day.*

IN *VVeftphalia* the Paffion of the Saintes *Ewaldi*, brethren and Martyrs, commonly called *Albus* and *Niger*, who being Priefts and Monkes of the Monaftery of *Rippon* in *Yorkeshire*, went ouer into *Ireland*, where liuing for diuers yeares in great aufterity of life, at laft returned, and went into *Frizeland* to preach the Chriftian faith to that Nation, which they did for a long tyme, with great labour and profit, till comming into *VVeftphaliæ*, they were flayne by the old Pagan Saxons, for the Confeffion of Chrift, about the yeare of our Lord, fix hundred fourfcore and fifteene. Their bodyes were afterward miraculoufly found in the riuer of *Rhene*, & moft honourably layd in the Church of S. *Cunibert* at *Cullen*, by Duke *Pepin* of *France*, about the yeare of Chrift 1074. and there

Bed. l. 5. cap. 11. Sigeb. in Chron. an. 693. Mart. Rom. Molan. & alij omnes hac die.

are kept with great veneration of the Cittizens of that place.

D   *The fourth Day.*

IN *Northumberland* the Paſſion of *S. Edwyn*
King and Martyr, who being the firſt
Chriſtian Prince of that Prouince, and
conuerted to the faith of Chriſt by the
preaching of *S. Paulinus* Biſhop of *Yorke*,
was afterward ſlayne in hatred therof, by
the impious *Cadwalline* King of the *Britans*, &
Penda King of the *Mercians*, in the yeare of
Chriſt, ſix hundred thirty and foure, and in
the ſeauenteenth of his raigne. There was
an ancient fayre Church ſomtyme erected
and dedicated in his honour in the Citty of
London, by *New-gate* Market, which there remayned vntill it was diſſolued in this laſt
age by King *Henry* the eight, togeather with
many other like goodly Monuments of
Catholicke piety in our Kingdome.

Ve. Bed.
in Epit.
& hiſt.
l.2.c.16.
17.&20.
& l.3.c.9
Weſt.
an.617.
625. 626.
634.
& alij.

E   *The fifth Day.*

*

IN *Scotland* the Commemoration of S. *Con-*
ſtalline Abbot and Confeſſour, whoſe rare
vertues and learning haue in tymes paſt byn
famous, not only throughout his owne

countrey

countrey, but in others alſo. He waſ firſt a Monke of the Venerable Order of S. *Bene-dict*, and then made Abbot of an ancient Monaſtery in the Iland of *Iona* belonging to *Scotland*, where in great ſanctity of life and other vertues, eſpecially in the Reforma-tion of Monaſticall diſcipline, he ended his bleſſed dayes, about the yeare of *Cnriſt*, fiue hundred and threeſcore.

Io. Leſſ. Epiſco. Roſſ.l. 4, hiſt.Scot. Wion in append. ad lib. 3. lig, vitæ.

F   *The ſixt Day.*

IN *Northuberland* the feſtiuity of S. *Twy* Dea-con and Confeſſour, ſcholler and diſciple to S. *Cuthbert* of *Durham*, whoſe great holines of life, hath in ancient Catholicke tymes byn famous in our Iland, eſpecially among the *Northumvers*. He died, as may be gathered out of antiquity, about the yeare of Chriſt, ſeauen hundred and foure.

Hereb. Roſw. in Tab. de faſt.SS. hæc die.

THE ſame day in *Scotland* the Comme-moration of S. *Comine* Abbot and Con-feſſour, who deſcended of a noble bloud in the ſame Kingdome, and diſciple to S. *Columbe* the *Great*, in a Monaſtery in the Iland of *Hoy*, was for his great learning and vertue, made Abbot, by him, of another Monaſtery in the ſame Prouince; whoſe godly life and miracles, haue in former tymes byn famous, both at home & abroad.

*

Io. Leſſ. Epiſco. Roſſ.l. 4. hiſt.Scot. Wion in Append. ad lib. 3. lig.vitæ.

He

He died about the yeare of Chriſt 600.

G   *The ſeauenth* Day.

†aliàs
O .ay .

AT *Chich* in *Eſſex* the Paſſion of S.† *Oſith*
Queene and Martyr, daughter to the
King of the *Eaſtangles*, and wife to *Suthred*
the laſt King of the *Eaſtſaxons*, who with the
conſent of her husband, forſooke the world,
and receyued the holy veyle of Chaſtity in
the Monaſtery of *Alisbury* ; but afterward
building another of her owne , in a Village

Io. Capg.
in Catal.
SS. Angl.
Pol. Vir.
l. 5. hiſt.
Sur. to. 5.
hac die.
Hereb. in
faſt SS.
Wion.
lib. 4.
lig. vitæ.

called *Chich*, in the Prouince of the *Eaſtſaxons*,
and gathering togeather many noble Virgins, became herſelfe Abbeſſe therof, vntill
the *Danes* inuading that Kingdome ; and
comming vnto her ſaid Monaſtery, cut of
her head in hatred of Chriſtian Religion.
The which ſhe taking vp from the ground,
carried three furlōges, to a Church of S. *Peter*
& S. *Paul*, where cōming to the Church dore
imbrewed in her owne innocent bloud, ſhe
fell downe, and ſo ended the courſe of her
martyrdome , about the yeare of Chriſt,
eight hundred and ſeauenty . In the place
alſo where ſhe was beheaded there preſently
ſprong vp a miraculous fountayne of water,
very ſoueraigne for many diſeaſes, which
euen vntill this day is greatly eſteemed by
the Inhabitantes neere about. Her body was

firſt

firſt buryed at *Alisbury* in *Buckinghamſhire*; but afterward, by a voyce from heauen it was commaunded to be tranſlated to the forſaid Monaſtery of *Chich*, now commonly called *S. Oſiths* of her name, ſituated not far from the ſea ſide, wherat it pleaſed God to worke many miracles,

THe ſame day at *Lincolne* the Tranſlation of *S. Hugh* Confeſſour and Biſhop of the ſame Sea; whoſe body after fourſcore yeares that it had byn buryed, was on this day taken vp, and being found altogeather vncorrupt, with a great quantity of cleere and ſweet oyle in the Tombe where it lay, was put into a coſtly ſhrine of ſiluer, guilt and richly adorned with precious ſtones, and ſet in a more eminent place of the ſame Church or Minſter at *Lincolne*, in the raigne of King *Edward* the firſt, and yeare of Chriſt 1282. where it hath euer ſynce byn kept vntill theſe our later dayes, with great reuerence and veneration, for the miracles that haue byn wrought therat.

Sur. to. 6. Weſt. an. 1297. Petr. Sutor in vit. Cart. Regiſtr. Eccleſ. Lincoln.

A ## *The eight Day.*

AT *VValciodore* in the Territory of *Liege* the Tranſlation of *S. Eloquius* Prieſt and Confeſſour, who borne in *Ireland* of a noble parétage, & cóming into *England*, went thece

into the low-Countreys with S. *Etto*, & his
fellowes to preach the Chriſtian faith;
where after much fruite reapt in gayning
of ſoules to God, in great ſanctity of life and
working of miracles, finally repoſed in our
Lord, about the yeare of Chriſt, ſix hundred fifty and one. His body was afterward
on this day tranſlated to the Monaſtery of
VValciodore aforſaid, where the ſame is kept
with great veneration of the Inhabitants.

THE ſame day in *Brecknockſhire* of *VVales*
the depoſition of S. *Keyna* Virgin,
daughter to *Braghan* King of *Brecknocke*, and
great Aunt to S. *Dauid* Biſh. of *Meneuia*, who
being in her infancy conſecrated to God,
left her Countrey and came ouer the Riuer
of *Seuerne* into *England*, and there liued a moſt
auſtere life in a ſolitary wood full of ſer-
pents, into which no man durſt enter for
feare of death: But by her prayers they were
all turned into ſtones, ſtill retayning the
ſhape of ſerpets. And after that ſhe had liued
many yeares therin, without humane aſſiſtance, ſhe returned againe to her friends
and Countrey, and built herſelfe a little
Cottage vpon a hill, where in continuall
prayer and abſtinence, clad in havrcloth ſhe
ſerued her Lord & Sauiour vntill her dying
day. And being ready to depart out of this
world, an Angell came downe from heauen, and put vpon her a white garment

wrought

Io. Molā.
in addit.
ad V ſua
et in Ind.
SS. Belgij

Rob.
Buckl.
l. mart.
ſcrip. de
vit. SS.
Mulier.
Angl.
Pag. 91.

wrought with gould, bidding her to be in readineſſe to enter into tne Kingdome of her Celeſtiall ſpouſe. She departed to our Lord vpon this day, about tne yeare of Chriſt, foure hundred and nynty, and was buryed in the ſame Prouince, where her memory hath byn famous euen vntill our dayes. She is called in the Britiſh tongue *Kem-vayre*, that is to ſay, *Keyne* the Virgin.

B *The ninth Day.*

AT *Lincolne* the depoſition of *Bl. Robert* ſurnamed *Groſſa-teſta*, Con ſſour and Biſhop o' the ſame Sea, whoſe great ſanctity of life and vertues, ioyned with learning, eſpecially in the Hebrew, Greeke, and Latyn tongues, hath byn very famous in the Church of Chriſt. Among other workes, he tranſlated the feſtamentes of the twelue Patriarkes out of Greeke into Latin, as alſo wrote very learned Comentaryes vpon the Pſalter, yet extant to be ſeene in wrytten hand in diuers Libraryes of *Europe*. He was borne in *Suffolke*, and in his youth trauayled into France, where applying his ſtudyes, he attayned to great knowledge in Philoſophy and Diuinity, and at his returne backe was promoted firſt to the Arch deaconry of *Li*

Matth.
Weſt.
& Pariſ.
an. 1253.
& 1251.
Sixt.
Seneuſ.in
Biblioth.
lib. 4.
Io. Trit.
de vir.
Illuſtr.
Regiſtr.
Eccleſ.
Lincoln.

eefter, and afterward to the Bifhopricke of *Lincolne*, which when he had gouerned moft laudably for eighteene yeares, he repofed happily in our Lord, in the yeare of Chrift, one thoufand two hundred fifty and three. His body was moft folemnly interred in a goodly marble Tombe in the fouth Ile of his owne Cathedrall Church of *Lincolne*, and there was wont to be kept with great reuerence and veneration, euen vntill the dayes of King *Henry* the eight.

THE fame day in the County of *Hennalt* in the Diocefle of *Cambray*, the feftiuity of *S. Giflen* Confeffour, who being an Irifhman by birth, went to *Athens* in *Greece*, where he became firft a Monke of the Order of S. S. *Bafil*, and thence returning by *Rome*, came backe into the Lower-Germany, and there built himfelfe an Oratory in a Village three myles diftant from *Montz* in *Hennalt*, teaching and inftructing the people of thofe partes in the Chriftian faith with great fruite and feruour of fpirit vntill his dying day, which happened about the yeare of Chrift, fix hundred & fourty. His body is kept in a Monaftery of his owne name in the forfaid Territory of *Hennalt*, cōmōly called S. *Giflens*, where it is honoured vntill this day with great veneration of the Inhabitants round about.

Ioan.
Maior
l. 2. hift.
Scot. c. 7.
Io. Molā.
in addit.
ad V fua.
et in Ind.
SS. Belgij

C

C   The tenth Day.

AT *Rochester* in *Kent* the Deposition of S. *Pauline* Bishop and Confessour, who comming into England with S. *Augustine* and his fellowes, conuerted the Kingdome of the *Northumbers*, togeather with *Edwyn* King of that Prouince, and so became their Apostle. He was ordayned the first Archbishop of *Yorke*; but being thence expulsed after King *Edwyns* death, he came backe againe into *Kent*, and there gouerned the Sea of *Rochester*, being then voyd : where in great sanctity of life, he finally reposed in our Lord, about the yeare Christ, six hundred fourty and fiue. His body was with all solemnity buryed in the Cathedrall Church of S. *Andrew* in *Rochester*, and there kept with great veneration.

THE same day at *Birlington* in *Yorkeshire* the deposition of S. *Iohn* Confessour, Prior of the Monastery of Chanons-Regular, whose godly life, full of sanctity, hath byn manifested sufficiently by the miracles he wrought both aliue and dead. He desceased in the yeare of Christ, one thousand three hundred threescore and nynteene, and was buryed at *Birlington*.

Ve̅. Bed. in Epit. & lib.1. Histor. cap.29.et l.2. c. 9. 10.11. & 12. Sur.to.5. & alij.

Io.Mola̅. in addit. ad Vsuar.

D   The eleuenth Day.

Bed. l. 4.
cap. 7. 8.
9. & 10.
Tritem
de v.
Ill. ftr.
Molm.
& alij.

AT Barking in Effex, the depofition of S. Edilourge Abbelle, fifter to S. Erconwald Bifhop of Lodon, who by him was cõftituted Gouerneffe of a new Monaftery that himfelfe had built, by the forfaid towne of Barking vpon the Riuer of Thames, where in all kind of fanctimony of life and Monafticall difcipline, fhe gaue vp her foule to her heauenly fpoufe, in the yeare of Chrift, fix hundred threefore and fixteene

Mart.
Rom.
Molm.
Petr.
in Catal.
l 11. cap.
vlt.

THE fame day in Scotland the depofition of S. Canicke Abbot & Cõfeffour, whofe godly life and miracles, haue byn famous throughout the Chriftian world, but efpecially in Scotland, where he was borne, liued, and died about the yeare of Chrift, eight hundred.

E   The tweluth Day.

AT Rippon in Yorkeshire the depofition of S. VVilfride Conteffour and Archbifhop of Yorke, who being twice expulfed his Bifhopricke by Egfrid King of the Northumbers, went and preached to the Southfaxons, where he conuerted the Ile of VVight,

and

and firſt planted the Chriſtian faith in that place. And when he had thus laboured for many yeares in his baniſhment to the gayning of infinite ſoules to God, being at laſt reſtored to his Biſhopricke, in all ſanctity of life and miracles, he finally reſted in our Lord, vpon the yeare of Chriſt, ſeauen hundred and eleuen; and was buryed in S. Peters Church at *Rippon* aforſaid, which himſelfe had built, on the ſouth ſide of the high Altar. Ouer whoſe tombe was engrauen this ancient Epitaph following.

Vè. Bed. *l.3. c. 28.* *& l.4.c* *12.& 13.* *& l.5.* *cap. 20.* *Mart.* *Rom.* *Molan.* *Sur.to.5.* *& omnes* *hac die.*

VVilfridus hic magnus requieſcit corpore Præſul,
Hanc Domino qui Aulam, ducius pietatis amore
Fecit, & eximio ſacrauit nomine PETRI,
Cui claues cæli Chriſtus dedit arbiter Orbis,
Atque auro ac Tyrio deuotus veſtijt oſtro.
Quin etiam ſublime Crucis radiante metallo,
Hic poſuit tropheum, nec non & quattuor auro
Scribi Euangely præcepit in ordine libros,
Ac thecam è rutilo his condignam condidit auro.
Paſchalis qui etiam ſolemnia tempora curſus,
Catholci ad iuſtum correxit dogma Canonis,
Quem ſtatuere Patres, dubioque errore remoto,
Certa ſuæ Genti oſtendit moderamina ritus.
Inq́ locis iſtis Monachorum examina crebra
Colligit, ac monitus cauit quæ regula Patrum
Sedulus inſtituit, multiſque domiq́ue foriſque
Iactatus nimium per tempora longa periclis.
Quindecies ternos poſtquam egit Epiſcopus annos,

Tranſijt

Tranſijt, & gaudens cæleſtia regna petiuit :
Dona I E S V, *yt grex Paſtoris calle ſequatur.*

F   *The thirteenth Day.*

AT *VVeſtminſter* by *London* the Tranſlation of *S. Edward* King and Confeſſour, whoſe body in the nynth yeare of King *Henry* the ſecond, was by S. *Thomas* of *Canterbury* taken vp, and put into a coſtly ſhryne of ſiluer, guilt with gold, made by K. *VVilliam* the *Conquerour*, and placed in the great Church of *VVeſtminſter*. In which alſo, euen vntill our dayes, was wont to be kept a Ring of gold, with great veneration, which *S. Edward* himſelfe had ſomtyme giuen to *S. Iohn* Euangeliſt, asking him an almes in the habit of a poore man, and was afterward brought vnto the ſaid King from *Hieruſalem*, by a certaine Pilgrime, as ſent vnto him for a token by *S. Iohn.* This day was afterward commaunded to be kept holyday throughout *England,* as is yet to be ſeene, aſwell by a Councell celebrated at *Oxford* in the yeare of Chriſt 1222. as alſo by the letters of Pope *Innocentius* the 4. regiſtred in the Roman Vaticane.

THE ſame day at *Vienna* in *Auſtria* the depoſition of *S. Colman* Martyr and ſomtyme Biſhop of *Lindisferne* in the Kingdome

of

(marginal notes:)
Pol.Vir.
lib. 8.
Matth.
Pariſ.
an. 1066.
& 1163.
Sur. &
Mart.
Rom.
5.Ian.
Regiſt.
Vati.
Romæ.

of the *Northumbers*, who being borne in *Ireland* of a noble Scottiſh bloud, after he had preached inceſſantly to the Engliſh *Saxons*, and among others conuerted *Penda* the Pagan King of *Mercia* to the faith of Chriſt, went ouer into the higher *Germany* to inſtruct that Nation alſo, where comming at laſt into *Auſtria*, was for defence therof, ſlayne by the barbarous people of that Prouince, about the yeare of Chriſt 675. His body was brought to *Vienna*, and is there yet preſerued with great veneration of that Citty.

Mart. Rom. Breuiar. Saltz. Hect. Boet. Leſl. de geſt. Sco. in Fer- quardo Rege.

G   *The fourteenth Day.*

AT *VVirtzburgh* in *Franconia*, the Tranſlation of S. *Burchard* Confeſſour and Biſhop of the ſame Sea, who being an Engliſhman by birth, & brother to S. *Swithin* Biſhop of *VVincheſter*, went ouer into *France* and thence into *Germany* to S. *Boniface*, with whome he wēt to *Rome*, & was there orday- ned Biſhop of *VVirtzburgh* by Pope *Zacharias*, and ſent backe to his Sea. And after that he had laboured inceſſantly for fourty yeares togeather in Chriſtes vineyard, teaching & preaching the Chriſtian faith, full of ſanctity and miracles, he gaue vp his ſoule to reſt, in the yeare of Chriſt, ſeauen hundred fourſcore and eleuen. His body was after-

Egilwar. in eius vita. Sur. tom. 5. Tritem. de vir. Illuſtr. Molan. Mart. Rom. & alij.

ward

ward on this day tranflated to the Monaftery of *S. Andrew* in that Citty, by *Hugh* Bifhop
of *VVirtzburgh*, and there is kept with great
Veneration.

A   *The fifteenth Day.*

AT *VVorcefter* the Tranflation of S.
Ofwald Bifhop & Confeffour, nephew
to S. *Odo* Archbifhop of *Canterbury* , who
being firft a *Chanon* of *VVinchefter*, was thence
promoted to the Bifhopricke of *VVorcefter*
and laftly to *Yorke* : Whofe godly life and
miracles are yet famous through the Chriftian world. He died in the yeare of Chrift,
nyne hundred fourfcore and twelue ; and
was afterward on this day tranflated to
VVorcefter, whofe feaft was wont to be kept
with great celebrity in Catholicke tyme, as
well in that Church, as throughout the reft
of England befides.

THe fame day alfo at *Ochnofort* in the
higher *Germany*, the depofitiõ of S. *Tecla*
Virgin and abbeffe, who being an Englifh-
woman by byrth, & fent for out of *VVim-
borne-Monaftery* in *Dorcetfhire* into *Germany* by
S. *Boniface* Bifhop of *Mentz*, togeather with
S. *Lioba* and S. *Agatha*, was there made Abbeffe of a Nunry called *Ochnofort*, which
the faid S. *Boniface* had newly erected, where

Sur.to.5.
Pol.Vir.
lib.7.
Weft.
an.959.et
960.
Molan.
& alij.

Sur. in
Vita. S.
Bonifac.
Tritem.
de Vir.
Illuftr.
Mart.
Rom.
& alij.

in

in great fanctimony & holines of life she ended her blessed dayes, about the yeare of Christ, seauen hundred and fifty.

B   The sixteentl Day.

AT *Mentz* in the higher *Germany* the deposition of *S. Lullus* Contessour, and Archbishop of that Sea, who descended of a noble parentage in *England*, & hearing of the fame of *S. Boniface* his Countreyman, went ouer vnto him into *Germany*, of whome he was first made Priest, and then Suffragan vnder him in the same Sea whilst he liued, and his successour after his death. Which when he had gouerned for two and thirty yeares, full of sanctity of life, he happily reposed in our Lord, about the yeare of Christ, seauen hundred fourscore and eight.

Breviar. Mogunt & Sur. tom. 5. Tri em. de vir-Illustr. Vincent. in spec. Molan. Mart. Rom.

THE same day at *Arbon* also in *Germany* the deposition of *S. Gallus* Abbot ond Confessour, whose life and doctrine haue in tymes past byn very famous in many places throughout *Europe*. He was borne in Ireland of a noble parentage, and disciple to S. *Columbane* the Great of that Nation ; and died in *Germany* about the yeare of Christ, six hundred and fourty, and was buryed at *Arbon* aforsaid.

Mart. Rom. Vsuard. hac die. Sur. to. 5. Lest. de gest. Sco. l. 4. in Chenetto Rege.

C

C   The feauenteenth Day.

AT VVye in *Kent* the Paſſiõ of the Saintes *Ethelbrit* and *Ethelred* Brothers and Martyrs, who being nephewes to *Eadbald* King of *Kent*, were ſlayne in hatred of Chriſtian Religion, about the yeare of Chriſt 664. Whoſe bodyes being caſt into an obſcure place, a miraculous light from heauen was ſeene to ſhine ouer them, and to deteċt the indecency of their buriall. Wherfore being therby found out, they were brought to the Monaſtery of *VVye* with great ſolemnity, wherat many miracles were forthwith wrought. And in the raigne of King *Edgar* of *England*, S. *Oſwald* Biſhop of *VVorceſter* cauſed them to be remooued to *Ramſey*, where alſo in ſigne of their innocency, it pleaſed God in like manner to worke many miracles. There was a goodly Church ereċted in *Kent*, and dedicated in their honour, by S. *Ermenburge* Queene of the *Mercians*, about the yeare of Chriſt, ſix hundred threeſcore and nyneteene .

THE ſame day at *Ely* in Cambridgſhire the Tranſlation of the Venerable body of S. † *Ediltrude* Virgin and Abbeſſe, daughter to *Annas* King of the *Eaſtangles*, and wife to *Egfrid* King of the *Northumbers*, who liuing

with

Matth.
Weſt.
an. 654.
Pol.Vir.
l.4.hiſt.
Cont.
Bed.l.2.
cap. 31.
Herebert.
in Tab.
faſt. SS.
hac die.

†Audry.

with her husband twelue yeares in perpetuall Virginity , with his confent became a Religious woman, and receyued the holy veyle of Chaftity in the Monaftery of *Coldingham*, vnder *S. Ebba* her Aunt, and afterward was made Abbeffe of the Nunry of *Ely*, where in all fanctimony of life fhe went to her heauenly fpoufe, about the yeare of Chrift, fix hundred & fourfcore , & was buryed in the fame Monaftery. But her fame increafing by the Miracles wrought at her body , the fame was taken vp fixteene yeares after her death by her owne fifter S. *Sexburge* then Abbeffe of that place, and being found frefh and wholy vncorrupt , was tranflated to a goodly Church newly erected there in her honour, where it was wont to be kept, euen vntill our dayes , with great veneration.

Bed. l. 4. cap. 19. Item de fex ætat. Tritem. de vir. Illuftr. Vincent. in fpec. Sigeb. in Chron.

D *The eighteenth Day.*

AT *Naffoin* in the Territory of *Liege* in the lower *Germany* , the Paffion of S. *Mono* Eremite and Martyr , who defcended of a noble parentage in *Scotland*, forfooke the world , and went ouer into *Flanders* and *Germany*, and there became an Eremite in the Foreft of *Arden*, leading a moft ftrict and feuere kind of life for many yeares togeather,

M of. und. apud Sur. to. 7 Molan. in addit. ad Vfu. et in Indic. SS. Belgij

ther, where being finally flayne by certaine Pagan theeues in hatred of his Religion, he happily attayned to the palme of Martyrdome, His body is buryed in the forfaid Vil age of *Naſſoin* belonging to the Abbey of S. *Hubert*, in a Church which himſelfe had there ſomtyme built, and is kept with great veneration of the Inhabitants of that place.

E   The nineteenth Day.

Pol.Vir.
l.r. hiſt.
Ereuiar.
ſec. Yſum
Sarum.
Mart.
Rom.
hac die.
Nicol.
Sand.l.2.
def.b.ſ.
Angl.
Vita eius
M. S.
Rob.
Buckl.

AT *Oxford* the Depoſitiō of S. *Frideſwide* Virgin and Abbeſſe, daughter to *Didan* Duke of *Oxford*, who being foilicited by one *Algarus* a noble yong man to yield vnto his luſt, eſcaped miraculouſly his violence, he being on the ſuddaine ſtroken blynd by Gods Iuſtice for offering the ſame. She was afterward made Abbeſſe of a Monaſtery erected by her Father in the ſame Citty: which Monaſtery in the tyme of King *Henry* the firſt was conuerted to a Priory of Chanons Regular, and ſo continued vntill King *Henry* the 8. when as *Cardinall VVolſey* obtayned the ſame of the Pope, towards the founding of Chriſts-Colledge, which is now built in the ſame place. She died in all ſanctimony and holines of life, about the yeare of Chriſt, ſeauen hundred thirty and nyne.

There

There is an ancient Chappell yet to be feene dedicated in her honour, in a Village of *Artoys* called *Bomy*, fome foure leagues diſtant from the Citty of S. *Omers*, where her feſtiuity is kept with due veneration of the Inhabitants.

THE fame day at *Maeſtricht* in *Brabant* the Tranſlation of S. *VVillebrord*, the firſt Biſhop of that Sea and Confeſſour, who being borne in *Yorkeshire*, went ouer into the low Countreyes with a dozen other Companions, all holy men, and conuerted the greateſt part of thofe Prouinces to the Chriſtian raith, and fo became their chiefe Apoſtle. He died in all fanctity and holines of life, about the yeare of Chriſt 736. and was afterward on this day tranſlated to *Maeſtricht*, and there is kept with great honour and veneration, as principall Patron of that Dioceſſe, where alſo his ſeaſt is celebrated with an Office of nyne leſſons.

Wion in Mart. Benedict. hæc die. Molan. in Indic. SS. Belgi

ALfo the fame day in *Ireland* the Depoſition of S. *Ethbyn* Abbot and Confeſſour, whofe godly liſe and miracles haue in tymes paſt byn ſamous through the Countreys round about. He died about the yeare of Chriſt, fix hundred and ten.

Mart. Rom. Molan. Petr. in Catal.

F

F   The twentith Day.

†aliter
Germany.

Peter
Cratep.
de Epif.
German.
Exegef.
l.11.Trit.
de Vir.
Illufir.
l.3. c. 79.
Molan.
Vion,
& alij
omnes
hac die.

AT *Toleys* in † *France* the depofition of *S.* *VVendelyn* Abbot & Confeſſour, Sonne to the King of *Scotland*, who forſaking all temporall preferments, and his owne inheritance to that Crowne and Kingdome, went ouer into *France*, and there became a Religious man and afterward Abbot of the Monaſtery of *Toleys*, where famous for ſanctity of life and Miracles, he repofed in our Lord, about the yeare of Chriſt, feauen hundred & twenty, and there lieth folemnly intombed. Ouer whofe body is alfo built a goodly Chappell, which for the côcourfe of people, that come thither on deuotion to viſit the fame, and the miracles that are dayly wrought therat, the Towne is now cômonly called by the name of S. *VVendelyns*.

G   The one and twentith Day.

AT *Cullen* in the higher *Germany* the Paſſion of *S. Vrfula* Virgin and Martyr, daughter to *Dionocus* King of *Cornwall*, who togeather with an eleuen thoufand other Britiſh Virgins (as ancient Authors do recount) being ſhipped at *London*, to paſſe ouer

into

into *France*, to be maried there to two Legions of British souldiers, vnto whome *Maximus*, that was by them chosen Emperour, had giuen the Countrey of *Armorica*, were by a contrary wynd driuen downe to the mouth of the Riuer of *Rhene*, and there, neere vnto *Cullen*, were all slayne by the barbarous *Hunnes* and *Pictes*, in defence of their Virginity, about the yeare of Christ, three hundred fourscore and three. Most of their bodyes were brought to *Cullen*, and there interred with great honour and veneration, and their memoryes celebrated vpon this day, throughout the Christian world. There was afterward a goodly Church built in *Cullen* in their honour, called the Church *Of the holy Virgins*, which alwayes hath byn had in such reuerence among the Inhabitants, that they neuer buried any other body there. Neyther will the ground or earth of that Church receyue any other body, no, not the corpes of yong Infants newly baptized, but, as it were, vomiting them vp againe in the night, they will be cast aboue ground, as hath oftentymes byn tried.

Gauf. Monum. l.5.c. 15. hist. Vet. Britan. Baron.in Annal. an.338. Rich. Vitus I. V.Doct. in hist. Britan. Mart. Rom. & omnes hac die.

A   The two and twentith Day.

Pet. de
Natal.
de vit.SS.
Vinc. in
spec.l. 11.
cap.74.
Mart.
Rom.
Molan.
& alij.

AT Roane in France, the Deposition of S. Mellon B.shop and Con ellour, who being a noble Britan by byrth, and sent to Rome in the tyme of Valerian the Emperour to pay Tribute for the Kingdome of Britany, was by Pope Stephen, instructed in the Christian faith and baptized, and after created the first Bishop of Roane, and sent into France to his Bishopricke: where in all kind of sanctity of life & miracles, he ended his blessed dayes, about the yeare of Christ, two hundred and fourscore. His body is kept vntill this day at Roane in the Cathedrall Church of that Citty, neere to the body of S. Nicasius with great honour & veneration of the inhabitants.

Mart.
Rom.
Molan.
in addit.
ad vsuar.
Rudolph.
in vita
Albert.
Magni p.
2.cap. 9.

THe same day at Cullen the passion of S. Cordula Virgin and Martyr, one of the eleuen thousand that suffered with S. Vrsula, who being terrified the first day with the slaughter of her companions hid herselfe: but on the morrow repenting her therof, & discouering herselfe to the Hunnes, was finally also crowned with Martyrdome, about the yeare of Christ 383. Albertus Magnus caused her body to be brought to Cullen, where the same is kept with great honour.

Also

ALſo the ſame day at *Feſuli* in *Tuſcane*, the Depoſition of S. *Donatus* Biſhop and Confeſſour, who borne in *Scotland* and deſcended of an honourable family, was created Biſhop of *Feſuli*; where famous for ſanctity of life and miracles in a good old age, he happily repoſed in our Lord. His feaſt is kept at *Feſuli* aforſaid on this day, with great ſolemnity and deuotion of the Inhabitants.

Franc.
Cattani⁹
Ep.Feſu-
lan. in
eius vit.
Mart.
Rom.
hac die.

B   *The three and twentith Day.*

AT the Monaſtery of *Brige* neere *Paris* in *France* the Commemoration of *S. Syra* Virgin, daughter to K. *Eugenius* the fourth of *Scotland*, who reiecting all worldly pōpe & preferments, in her tender yeares, went ouer into *France*, with her brother S. *Fiaker*, where ſhe receyuing the holy veyle of Chaſtity, became a Religious woman in the forſaid Monaſtery of *Brige*, vnder S. *Phara* Abbeſſe thereof: where excelling in a 1 kind of ſanctimony of life, and godly conuerſation, eſpecially in the vertue of humility, ſhe gaue vp her pure ſoule to her heauenly ſpouſe, about the yeare of Chriſt, ſix hundred and thirty, and was buryed in the ſame place.

*

Io. Leſl
Epiſco.
Roſſil 4.
de geſt.
Scot.
Wion
lib. 4.
lig.Vitæ.

C The foure & twentith Day.

Sur.to.5.
hac die.
Tritem.
de vir.
Illuftr. l.
3.c.50.&
L.4.c.47.
Mart.
Rom.
& Moli.

AT Paris in France the feftiuity of S. Maglore Bifhop and Confeffour, who being a noble Britan by birth, and kinfman to S. Sampfon, fucceeded him afterward in his Bifhopricke of Dole in little Britany, and laft of all became an Ermite in France, where leading a ftrict and auftere kind of life, famous for miracles, he finally repofed in our Lord, about the yeare of Chrift, 586. His body is kept with great veneration at Paris in a Monaftery there of his owne Name, commonly called S. Maglors, wherat it hath pleafed God in figne of his fanctity to worke many miracles.

THE fame day in France alfo, the Commemoration of S. Maxentia Virgin and Martyr, who being daughter to one Marcolane a noble man of Scotland, and promifed in matrimony to one of like dignity that was a Pagan, fhe contening the fame, fled fecretly into France with two of her truftieft feruants, and there lay difguifed for a tyme in a Village cal'ed Beauuaife, liuing in continuall prayer and contemplation, vntill being purfued b her pretended husband, was at laft found out and defcried. And when by no meanes fhe could be induced to yield vnto

Rob.
Buckl.
in eius
vita. lib.
M. S. de
vir.SS.
Mulier.
Angl.
fol.237.

his

his mariage, he turning loue into fury, prefently ftroke of her head with his owne hands, as alfo the heads of her two feruants *Barbantius* and *Rofebea.* The Innocency of whofe caufe was prefently mani:efted by a miracle, which was, that fhe taking vp her owne head from the ground, carried it to the place where it now remayneth, where afterward was a goodly Church crected in her honour, and God glorified therin by many miracles. Wnofe facred body *Charles* then King of *France* is faid to haue greatly reuerenced, & adorned with fundry Royall giftes.

D *The fiue & twentith Day*

AT the Towne of *Ceprano* in the Kingdome of *Naples*, the Commemoration of S. *Arduyne* Prieft and Confeffour, who borne in *England* of very worfhipfull parentes, and going to *Hierufalem* to vifit the holy Sepulcher of our Sauiour, in his returne backe from thence, came into *Italy*, where at that tyme the Plague forely infecting the Kingdome of *Naples*, in great fanctity of life, he there gaue vp his bleffed foule to reft. His body was with all folénity interred in the forfaid Towne of *Ceprano*, where vntill this day it is kept with great

Regiftr.
Ecclef.
Cepranéf.
*& in-
fcript.
eius Se-
pulturæ
ibidem
fculpt.*

honour and veneration of the Inhabitants,
for the dayly miracles it pleafeth God to
worke therat, in teſtimony of his holineſſe,
and increaſe of the peoples deuotion to that
place.

E   The ſix and twentith Day.

AT Lindisferne in the Kingdome of the
Northumbers, the Depoſition of S. Eatta
Confeſſour and Biſhop of that Sea, who
being firſt a Monke and then Abbot of the
Monaſtery of Mailros in the ſame Prouince,
was afterward ordayned Biſhop of Lindisferne (now tranſlated to Durham) and predeceſſour to S. Cuthbert, which when he had
gouerned in all kind of vertue and ſanctity
of life for fiue yeares or therabout, he was
remoued to the Church of Hagustald, reſig-
ning the Sea of Lindisferne to S. Cuthbert, and
within a while after in great holines, famous for Miracles, he departed to our Lord,
about the yeare of Chriſt, ſix hundred fourſcore and ſix.

THE ſame day in Lorayne, the Depoſition
of S. Albuine Biſhop and Confeſſour,
who being an Iriſhman by birth, and Moke
of a Monaſtery in the Iland of Hoy, neere
Scotland went ouer into Germany to preach
the Chriſtian faith, where he conuerted

the

the whole Dukedome of *Lorayne*, and became the Apoſtle of that *Prouince*. He was
afterward made Biſhop there of a place called *Friſlarium* in the Towne of *Burbach*; where
teaching and preaching continually to his
flocke, in great ſanctity of life & miracles, he
finally ended his bleſſed dayes, about the
yeare of Chriſt, ſeauen hundred and fifty.

in Catal.
Epiſſo.
Friſlar et
in Mart.
Benedict.

F   The ſeauen & twentith Day.

AT *Mechlyn* in *Brabant* the Tranſlation of
S. *Romuald* Biſhop and Martyr, Sonne
to the King of *Ireland*, who being ordayned Archbiſhop of *Dublyn* in the ſame Kingdome went to *Rome* for deuotion, and
thence backe into the lower Germany,
where in the Territory of *Mechlyn*, vnder
Count *Ado* of *Flanders*, he firſt planted the
Chriſtian faith, and became the Apoſtle of
that Prouince. He was afterward ſlayne in
hatred of Chriſt, by two ſoldiours, in the
ſame Territory, in the yeare, ſeauen hundred
threeſcore and fifteene. Whoſe venerable
body was afterward on this day tranſlated
to *Mechlyn* with great ſolemnity and vene-
tion, & put into a goodly Shrine of ſiluer
very richly ſet with precious ſtones, and
other ornaments, wherat it hath pleaſed
God to worke many miracles. He was ca-

† aliter
Scotland.

Io. Molā.
i addit.
ad Vſua.
et in Ind.
SS.Bel.ij

nonized for a Saint by Pope *Alexander* the fourth.

G *The eight & twentith Day.*

IN *Perſia* the Paſſiō of the glorious Apoſtle S. *Symon,* ſurnamed *Zelotes,* who according to diuers ancient wryters, among other his peregrinations, came into our Iland of Britany, about the yeare of Chriſt, fourty and ſix, and there preached the Chriſtian faith, baptized, ordayned Prieſts and Deacons, erected Churches and the like, wherby we may worthily call him our Apoſtle, and with greater ſolemnity celebrate his feaſt, by whome we receyued ſo ſingular graces and benefitts. He afterward went into *Perſia* with S. *Iude* to preach the Chriſtian faith to the Infidels of that Countrey, where at laſt he receyued the reward of his labours by Martyrdome, being nayled to a Croſſe: though *Dorotheus* wryteth, that he ſuffered, and was buryed in Britany.

THE ſame day at *VVincheſter* in Hápſhire the Depoſition of Bleſſed *Alfred* King of the *VVeſtſaxons* and Confeſſour, who after many glorious and victorious battayles achieued againſt the Pagá *Danes* that infeſted his realme; in great ſanctity and holines of life, he ended his bleſſed dayes, in the yeare

Niceph.
l.2.c.4.
Pol.Vir.
lib.7.
hiſt.
Weſt.
av.636.
& 652.
Doroth.
in Synop.

Abbo
Floriac.
in Chron.
Mar.
Scot. in
hiſt.

of

of Chrift, eight hundred fourfcore and
nynteene, and lieth buried at *VVinchefter*.
He founded diuers goodly Monafteryes, as
tha*t* of *Shaftesbury*, of *VVinchefter*, of *Ethelingfey*,
befides the famous Vniuerfity of *Oxford*.

Regift. de
Hide
Wion
& alij.

A *The nine & twentith* Day.

AT *Canterbury* the depofition of *S.Eadfine*
Bifhop and Conteffour, who being
Chaplyn to King *Harold*, was firft preferred
to the Bifhopricke of *VVinchefter*, and thence
to *Canterbury*, whofe innocency of life and
other vertues haue byn famous in our Iland
vntill thefe our dayes. He fpent the greateft part of his time in continuall prayer &
meditation of heauenly things. And when
he had gouerned the flocke committed vnto his charge for twelue yeares, in a venerable old age he gaue vp his foule to reft, in
the yeare of Chrift, one thoufand and fifty:
and was honourably interred in his owne
Cathedrall Church of *Canterbury*, where his
body was wont to be kept with great veneration, for the miracles that haue byn
wrought therat.

Henr.
Hūting-
ton. in
fua hift.
an. 1050.
Regift.
Ecclef.
Cant.
& Catal.
Epifco.
Cantuar.

THe fame day in *Scotland* the Commemoration of *S . Motifer* Monke and
Confeffour, who borne in *Ireland* and di-

*

fciple

Hect.
Boet. de
gest. Sco.
Io. Lesl.l.
4. hist.
Sc:t.

sciple to S. *Columbe* the Great, came with
him ouer into Scotland, & was his coadiutor
there in preaching the Christian faith to
the *Picts,* who in those dayes inhabited that
Kingdome, where famous for sanctity of
life, he made a holy end, about the yeare of
Christ, fiue hundred and icurscore.

B　　The thirtith Day.

Matth.
West.
an. 1038.
Tritem.
de Vir.
Illustr.
Pol.Vir.
l.7. in
fine. Nion
in Mart.
Benedict.

AT Canterbury the depositiō of S. *Egelnoth,*
surnamed the *Good,* Confessour and
Archbishop of the same Sea, sonne to Earle
Agelmare, and sometimes Deane of Chrits
Church in *Canterbury,* whose great holines
of life togeather with his learning and vertues haue byn famous throughout Christē-
dome, but especially in our iland of *Great
Britany.* He died on this day, about the yeare
of Christ, one thousand and fourty, hauing
byn Bishop seauenteene yeares, & was solemnly interred in his owne Church at
Canterbury, in the raigne of King *Harold* of
England. It is recorded that he going to
Rome to fetch his Archiepiscopall *Pall,*
brought thence with him an Arme of S.
Augustine the Doctor, and bestowed it vpon
the Abbey of *Couëtry* in *Warwickshire,* where
the same was kept with great reuerence,
vntill the tyme of King *Henry* the eight, and

decay

decay of that Monaſtery.

C   The one & thirtith Day.

IN *Hennalt* the Paſſion of *S. Foillan* Biſhop
and Martyr, Sonne to *Philtan* King of
Ireland, who being firſt a Monke, and then
Abbot of a Monaſtery called *Knobhersbunge* in
the Kingdome of the *Eaſtangles,* went to
Rome, and being there ordayned Biſhop by
Pope *Martyn* the firſt, was ſent backe into
Fráce & *Flanders* to preach the Chriſtiá faith,
whereat laſt as he was exerciſing of his Paſtorall function, he was ſlayne, togeather
with three other Companions, in the Territory of *Hennalt,* in the Dioceſſe of *Namures:*
whoſe death being reueyled to his brother
S. Vltan and *S. Gertrude* Abbeſſe of *Niuelle,* his
body was preſently ſought out, and being
found, was with all ſolemnity brought to
the Monaſtery of *Foſſis,* and there is yet conſerued with great veneration of the Inhabitants. He ſuffered about the yeare of Chriſt,
ſix hundred and fourty.

Vĕ. Bed.
l.3.hiſt.
Angl.
Petr. in
Catal.
Tritem.
de vir.
Illuſtr.
Vincent.
in ſpec.
lib. 22.
Io. Molā.
in addit
ad Vſua.
et in Ind.
SS. Belgij

THE
MONETH
OF NOVEMBER.

Â   *The first Day.*

V̄ē. Bed.
in Epit.
Sigeb.
in Chron.
Mar .
Scot. l.2.
hist . an .
717.
Wion
hac die in
Mart.
Benedict.

T *Fulda* in the higher *Germany* the Tranflation of S . *Boniface* Archbifhop of *Mentz* and Martyr, who borne in the Citty of *London* , and going into *Germany* to preach the Chriftian faith, went thence to *Rome* , and was there by Pope *Gregory* the fecond ordayned the firft Bifhop of *Mentz* , and fent backe to his Bifhopricke; where teaching and preaching the faith of Chrift to the *Germans* , he conuerted the greateft part of that Countrey, & became their Apoftle . He was finally martyred in *Frizeland* , at a towne called

Dockum

Dockum, with fifty other companions, about the yeare of Chrift, feauen hundred fifty & foure. His body was afterward of this day tranflated to the Monaftery of *Fulda*, which himfelfe had founded, where the fame is kept with great honour and veneration, for the miracles that haue byn wrought therat.

THE fame day in the Monaftery of *Hampole* neere *Doncafter* in *Yorkeshire*, the Cõmemoration of Bleffed *Richard* Confeffour & Ermite, whofe fingular fpirit of piety & deuotion, is left written, and manifeft to the world by his owne workes yet extant. He was firft a Doctor, and then leauing the world became an Eremite, and led a folitary life neere to the forfaid Monaftery of *Hampole*: to which place he was wont often to repayre, to fing pfalmes and hymnes in honour of God, as himfelfe teftifieth in his workes. And after many fpirituall bookes and treatifes by him wrytten, full of great fanctity of life and venerable old age, he finally refted in our Lord, about the yeare of Chrift, one thoufand three hundred fourty and nyne: and was buryed at *Hampole*.

*

Sixtus Senenf. in Biblioth. Script. Illuftr. lit. R. Codex M.S. in Coll. Angl. Duacenf.

E

E　*The second Day.*

Chron.
Camerac.
Lamb.de
Loos
Monach.
S. Aut-
bert . &
Molan.
in Indic,
SS.Belgij

AT *Lens* in the Prouince of *Artoys*, the eftiuity of *S. Vulganius* Bifhop and Confeffour, who borne in *Ireland*, and going thence with the Saintes *Foillan, Obodius*, and others of that Nation, into the lower *Germany*, began there to preach the Chriftian faith, and was at laft confecrated Bifhop. Where after infinite labours and trauayles taken for the loue of Chrift, in propagating his name and faith among the Infidells of thofe partes in all fanctity and holines of life, he ended his bleffed dayes about the yeare of Chrift, feauen hundred and foure. His body is yet kept with great honour and veneration at the forfaid towne of *Lens*, in the Monaftery there of the Chanons-regular, where his feaft is yearly celebrated on this day with great folemnity and deuotion of the Inhabitantes of that place.

F　*The third Day.*

IN *North-wales* the Depofition of *S. VVenefride* Virgin and Martyr, daughter to a noble Britan of thofe partes, called *Trebuith*, whofe head being cut of by *Cradocus* Sonne

to *Alane* King of *North-wales*, for not con-
fenting to his vnlawfull luft, was by her
Maifter *S. Beno* fet on againe, fhe liuing
fifteene yeares a ter, to the admiration of
the whole world for fo famous a miracle. In
the place where fhe was beheaded, prefently
fprang vp a miraculous fountayne, very
foueraigne for the curing of many difeafes:
which vntill this day is a great pilgrimage
and place of deuotion for all Catholickes
of *England*, commonly called S. *VVenefrides*
well. Her body was afterward tranflated to
Shrewsbury, about the yeare of Chrift, one
thoufand one hundred thirty and eight.
This feftiuity of hers was wont to be celebrated in our Catholicke Church of England with an Office of nyne leffons, according to the vfe of S*arum*, and in many places
kent holiday.

THE fame day at *VVilton* in *Wilshire* the
Tranflation of *S. Edith* Virgin, daughter to holy Edgar King and Monarch of
England, who a ter the death of her Mother
VVilfred, was ordayned Abbeffe of the Monaftery of *VVilton* aforfaid: where in all fanti-
mony and holines of life, fhe gaue vp her
foule to reft, and was buryed there in the
Church of *S. Dionyfe*, which herfelfe had
fomtyme built, about the yeare o Chrift
984. whofe body was afterward on this day
taken vp, and tranflated to a more eminent

place

Sur.to 6
de vit.SS.
Robert.
Salop.
in eius
vita.
Breuia
Sarum.
Mart.
Rom.
& alij.
omnes
hac die.

Sur.to.5.
17.Septe.
wion in
Mart.
Bened.
hac die.

place of the fame Church , wherat it is recorded many miracles to haue byn wrought This woman is commonly called by the name of S. *Edith* the yonger.

G   *The fourth Day.*

IN *France* the Paffion of *S. Clare* Prieft and Martyr, who defcended of a worthy Britifh ftocke, and borne in the Citty of *Rochefter* in *Kent*, his worldly friends would haue had him to marry a wife againft his will, for which he forfaking both Coûtrey & friéds, went ouer into *Normandy*, where he taking holy Orders , was made Prieft : and afterward going thence into France , for that he refufed to yield to the luft of a noble womã of that Coûtrey , was flayne by her procurement in defence of his chatity , about the yeare of Chrift, fix hundred threefcore and fix. His body was buryed there in a Village called *Volcaßine* , wherat it pleafed God in figne of his innocency to worke many miracles.

Io.Capg. in Catal. SS. Brit. Mart. Rom. & Vfua. hac die.

A   *The fifth Day.*

AT *Clareuallis* in the Territory of *Lãgres* in *France*, the feftiuity of *S. Malachy* Bifhop ſhop & Cōſeſſour, who being firſt a Monke of *Benchor* in *Ireland*, & then Abbot,was after ordayned Biſhop of *Connerthen* in the ſame Ilád, & laſt of all Archbiſhop & Primate of *Ireland*. He liued and died in the tyme of *S. Bernard*,about the yeare of Chriſt,one thouſand one hūdred fourty & eight,who wrote vnto him diuers learned Epiſtles , as alſo his whole life, yet extant among *S. Bernards* workes. He deſceaſed rhe ſecond day of this moneth in the forſaid Monaſtery of *Clareuallis*,though his feſtiuity be cōmonly celebrated on this day, becauſe on the other is kept the Commemoration of *All-Soules*, eſpecially among the Monkes of the Venerable Order of *Ciſterce*.

Sur.to.6. hac die. vna cum Molan. in additᵒ ad Vſuar. Baron. in not ad Mart. Rom. 3.nonas Noūēb. Bernard. in eius vita et in Epiſt . Mombr. tom. 1. vit. SS-

B   *The ſixt Day.*

IN the Monaſtery of *VVoromholt* by *Berghen* in *Flanders* the depoſitiō of S.*VVinocke* Abbot and Confeſſour , who deſcended of a moſt noble & Royall bloud in *Britany*,went ouer into the lower *Germany* to *S.Bertin*,who then liued there in great fame for his holynes, and was by him ordayned Abbot of a Monaſtery erected in *Flanders*, called Woromholt: where full of wonderfull holines & ſanctity of life, togeather with working of many miracles, he repoſed in our Lord,

Sur.to.6. Marcell. in vita.S. Switber. Molan. in addit. ad Vſua. et in Ind. SS.Belgij

V   about

Iacob.
Meyrus
in Anv.
Flandr.
lib.1.

about the yeare of Chrift, feauen hundred and fixteene. His body was afterward tranflated to *Berghen* aforfaid, where the fame is preferued,euen vntill thefe our dayes with great veneration of the Countrey round about : In whofe honour the faid Towne is now alfo commonly called of him by the Name of *VVinockes-Berghen*.

C *The feauenth* Day.

Sur.to.6.
Marcell.
in vita S.
Simib.
Molan.
in addit.
& Vfua.
et in Ind.
SS.Belgij

AT *Epternake* in the higher Germany the depofitiō of S. *VVillebrord* Bifhop & Cō-feffour,who being a Mōke of *Rippon* in *Torke-shire*, was fent out of *England* by the holy Ab-bot *Egbert*, with a dozen other Companions to preach the Chriftian faith in the Low-Countreys and Germany ; and going thence to *Rome*, was by Pope *Sergius* confecrated Archbifhop of *Maeftricht* in *Brabant*, and fent backe to that Sea. Where after the conuer-fion of many thoufand foules to the true worfhip of one God, he there ended his bleffed dayes,in a Monaftery at the forfaid place of *Epternake*, in the Dioceffe of *Treuers*, which himfelfe had built, in the yeare of Chrift, feauen hundred thirty and fix.

THE fame day at *Strasburge* in the higher Germany alfo, the depofition of S. *Florentius* Bifhop and Confeffour,who being

borne

borne in *Scotland* of an honourable parentage, went ouer into Germany, in the tyme
of King *Dagobert* of *France*, whose daughter
being dumbe and blind from her natiuity,
he by his prayers reſtored both to ſpeach
and ſight. And after going into the Prouince of *Alſatia*, was ordayned Biſhop of
Strasburge : where in all holines of life, attending diligētly to his charge, he gaue vp his
ſoul to reſt, about the yeare of Chriſt, ſix hūdred threeſcore an̄ fifteene, and was buried
there in a Monaſtery neere to the Riuer of
Bruſch, which himſelfe had founded a little
berore, for the Scottiſh nation.

Mart.
Rom.
hac die.
Leſl.l. 4.
de geſt.
Scot.
Democ.
tom.2. de
ſacrif.
Miſſæ
cap.35.

D   *The eight Day.*

AT *Bremen* in *Eaſt-frizland* the depoſition
of *S.VVillehade* Confeſſour & firſt Biſhop of the ſame Sea, who going out of
England, where he was borne, for the Cō-
uerſion of his Neighbour-countreys, after
he had preached to the *Saxons* & *Frizians* for
more then fifty yeares togeather, & cōuerted
many thouſands to the Chriſtian faith, was
at the requeſt of Charles the great, ordayned Biſhop of *Bremen* in Frizland. Where
after he had paſſed a venerable old age, ioyned with ſanctity of life, he finally reſted in
our Lord, abour the yeare of Chriſt, ſeauen

Albert.
Cranz.
lib. 2. c.
14.& 15.
Io. Mola.
in addit.
ad Vſua.
et in Ind.
&S. Belgij
Mart.
Rom.
Sur.to.6.
Tritem.
de vir.
Illuſtr.

hundred fourfcore and eleuen. His body
was buryed in the Cathedrall Church of
that Citty dedicated to S. *Peter*; which himfelfe had built, and was there wont to be
kept with great honour and veneration of
the Inhabitants, as chiefe Patrone and Apoftle of that Prouince, euen vntill thefe our
later dayes of fchifmes and herefyes in thofe
partes.

E   *The ninth Day.*

*

Pol.Vir.
*l.*4. *hiſt.*
Angl.
Wi̅ *l.*4
lig.vita.

AT *VVhitby* in *Yorkeshire* the Commemoration of *S. Congilla* Virgin and Abbeſſe
whofe godly and vertuous life, togeather
with the obferuation of Monafticall difcipline, hath deferued to be famous, in Catholicke tyme, throughout England. She
was co̅ftituted Abbeſſe of an ancientMona-
ftery now called *VVhitby*, which *Ofwy* King
of the *Northu̅bers* had newly fou̅ded; wherin
he caufed his owne daughter *Ethelɟred* to be
brought vp, vnder the care and gouerment
of the forfaid *Congilla*; who famous for fanctimony of life and miracles, gaue vp her
foule to her heauenly fpoufe, about the
yeare of Chrift, fix hundred threefcore and
eleuen.

F   *The tenth Day.*

AT *Canterbury* the Depoſition of S. *Iuſtus* Archbiſhop of the ſame Sea and Conſeſſour, who comming into England with S. *Auguſtine* and his fellowes, was firſt ordayned Biſhop of *Rocheſter*, and after of *Canterbury*, where in all holines of life, he deſceaſed, about the yeare of Chriſt, ſix hundred thirty and two, and was buryed at *Canterbury*.

THE ſame day at *Michelmburgh* in *VVandalia* the paſſion of S. *Iohn* Biſhop and Martyr, who being an *Iriſhman* by byrth, & a Monke, went ouer into the lower *Germany*, and thence into *VVandalia* to preach the Chriſtian faith; where being conſecrated Biſhop of *Michelmburgh*, was at length taken by the Infidels of that Countrey, and ſorely beaten with cudgells. And when they could not auert him from calling vpon the name of I E S V S, they firſt cut of his hands, and then his feet, and laſt of all his head, about the yeare of Chriſt, one thouſand threeſcore and ſix.

Bed.l.1.c.
29.et l. 2.
c. 3. 5. 8.
Mart.
Rom.
Molan.

Albert.
Stadenſ.
in Chron.
hac die.
Helmod.
in Chron.
Sclau.
l. 1. c. 23.
Cranʒ.
Metrop.
l. 4. c. 43.
Truem.
de vir.
Illuſtr.

G   The eleuenth Day.

IN the Monaſtery of *Malòn* in the Territory of *Namures*, the Depoſition of S.
Bertuine Biſhop and Conteſſour, who borne
in *Ireland* of a noble parentage, and going
ouer into the Lower *Germany*, to preach the
Chriſtian faith, built himſelfe a little Oratory in honour of our Bleſſed Lady, in a
Village called *Malòn* in the forſaid ſerrito-
ry of *Namures*, where in very great auſterity
& holineſſe of life, he gaue himſelce wholy
to contēplation and meditation of heauenly things, vntill his dying-day, which happened full of miracles, about the yeare of
Chriſt, ſix hundred fifty and one. In the
ſame place where he had built his ſaid Oratory, was afterward erected a goodly Monaſtery of the Inſtitute of *S. Auguſtine*, where
his body is yet kept with great veneration
of the Inhabitants therabout.

Io. Molā.
in addit
ad Vſua.
et in Ind.
SS. Belgij

A   The tweluth Day.

AT *Aſche* in *Flanders* the Paſſion of S.
Liuinus Biſhop & Martyr, who being
borne in Scotland, & ſcholler to S. *Auguſtine*
our Engliſh Apoſtle, went ouer into *Flanders*

with)

with three other Companions to preach the faith of Chriſt, where he was ſlayne in hatred therof by the Pagans of that Countrey, about the yeare of Chriſt, ſeauen hundred and three. They firſt cut out his tongue, which being miraculouſly reſtored vnto him againe, he was finally beheaded. His body was firſt buryed at *Hauten*, but afterward tranſlated to *Gaunt* in the yeare 1007. THE ſame day in *Oueryſle* of *Gelderland* the feſtiuity of *S. Lebuine* Prieſt and Confeſſour, who being a Monke of *Rippon* in *Yorkeſhire*, and diſciple to *S. VVillebrord*, went ouer to *S. Gregory* Biſhop of *Maeſtricht* in *Brabant*, of whome he was ſent to preach to the *Saxons* beyond the Riuer of *Yſle*; where after he had conuerted many thouſands to the faith of Chriſt, full of ſanctity and miracles he ended his bleſſed dayes, about the yeare of Chriſt, ſeauen hundred and threeſcore. His body was afterward tranſlated to *Dauentry*, and there is kept in the Cathedrall Church of that Citty with great veneration, as one of the chiefe Patrons of the Dioceſſe.

Io.Molā. in addit. ad Vſuar. et in Ind. SS.Belgij Marcell. in vita.S. Bonifac. Suitbert. & eius.

Sur.to.6. Tritem. lib. 3. de vir. Illuſtr. cap. 146. Molan. in addit. ad Vſuar. et in Ind. SS.Belgij

B   The thirteenth Day.

IN the Territory of *Arras* in *Artoys* the Depoſition of S. *Kilian* Biſhop & Confeſſour,

V 4   who

who defcended of the bloud-roall of *Scotland*
and Kinfman to King *Eugenius* the fourth of
that Name, defpifed, for the loue of God,
all worldly prefcrments , and went ouer

into the lower *Germany*, to preach the Chriſtian faith ; where when he had reduced
many thoufands to Chriſtes flocke , repleni-
ſhed with fanctity of life , he ended his bleffed dayes, in a venerable old age , about the
yeare of Chriſt, fix hundred and fourty.His
body is kept vntill this day in a Village called *Albiniacke*, in the Dioceſſe of *Arras*,where
there is a goodly Priory of *Chanons-Regular*
erectd in his name , commonly called the
Priory of S. *Kilian*. This man is different
from the other S. *Kilian* of the fame Name
mentioned vpon the eight of Iuly , who
was of the Iriſh Nation, and a Martyr.

C   *The fourteenth* Day.

AT *London* the Tranflation of S. *Erconwald* Confeſſour and Biſhop of the
fame Sea, Sonne to Offa King of the *Eaſt-
faxons*, whofe fame of fanctity and holines
of life,togeather with working of miracles,
hath byn notorious throughout Chriſtendome, but efpecially in England. He died
in the yeare of Chriſt, fix hundred threefcore
and fifteene, and was buryed at *London* in S.

Paules Church, but afterward taken vp on this day, and tranflated to a more eminent place of the fame Church in the yeare of Chrift 1148. At whofe body it is recorded many miracles to haue byn wrought.

THE fame day at *Ewe* in *Normandy* the depofition of S. *Laurence* Bifhop and Confeffour, who being firft a Monke and then Abbot of *Glindalacke* in *Ireland*, was laftly ordayned Bifhop of *Dublyn* in the fame Kingdome : And thence going ouer into *Normandy* in great holines of life and miracles, ended his bleffed dayes. He was afterward canonized for a Saint by *Pope Honorius* the third, in the yeare of Chrift, one thoufand three hundred and fix. His body ftill remayneth at *Ewe* aforfaid, where it is kept with due veneration of the Inhabitants of that place. *(margin: Mart. Rom. cū Barō. Molan. in addit. ad yfuar. Sur.10.6. Wion in Catal. Epifco. Dublinē.)*

ALfo the fame day in *Bardfey-Iland* in *North-wales* the depofition of S. *Dubritius* Confeffour, Archbifhop of *Carleon* vpon *Vske*, & Primate of the old Britans of VVales, who refigning his Sea to S. *Dauid*, King *Arthurs* vncle, became an Ermite in the wild Mountaynes of *North-wales*; where in very great aufterity of life, full of miracles, in a venerable old age, he finally repofed in our Lord, about the yeare of Chrift, fiue hundred twenty and two; and was buryed in the aforfaid Iland of *Bardfey*. *(margin: Matth. Weft. an. 507. Gaufr monum. l. 9. c. 4. & 13. hift. Britan.)*

D

D The fifteenth Day.

AT Sainctes in France the Deposition of S. Macloue Bishop and Confessour, who being descended of a noble British bloud, & Mōke of the Monastery of Bangor in Caerneruanshire of VVales, was thence promoted to the Bishopricke of Althene in little Britany (now called of his name in that vulgar language San-Macloue) and consecrated therto by Leontius Bishop of Sainctes : which Sea when he had gouerned most worthily for many yeares, in all sanctity of life and laudable vertues, comming to Sainctes aforsaid, in a good old age gaue vp his soule to rest, about the yeare of Christ, fiue hūdred threescore and foure. His Reliques were afterward translated to the Monastery of Gemblacum, where the same are yet preserued with great honour and Veneration, for the manifold miracles, that in tymes past haue byn wrought therat.

E The sixteenth Day.

AT Pontoyse in France the Deposition of S. Edmund Bishop and Confessour, who being somtyme Treasurer of the Church of

Salis-

Salisbury, was ordayned Archbifhop of *Canterbury*: which Sea when he had gouerned for fix yeares in all godly manner, being many wayes iniured by King *Henry* the third and *Cardinall Otho*, he refigned the fame, went ouer into *France*, and liued in voluntary banifhment, fpending the reft of his dayes in continuall prayer and meditation, in a Monaftery of Chanons-Regular at *Soyfon*: where in very great fanctity of life he departed this world, in the yeare of Chrift, one thoufand two hundred and fourty. His body was brought with all folemnity to *Pontoyfe*, where the fame is kept with great honour and Veneration vntill this day. He was canonized for a Saint by Pope *Innocentius* the fourth, fix yeares after his death. This day was afterward commaunded to be kept holy in his memory throughout England. King *Lewes* of France caufed his body to be tranflated to a more honourable place of the Church in *Pontoyfe*, and beftowed theron a fumptuous fhryne of filuer, guilt & richly adorned with many precious ftones.

Pol. Vir. lib. 16. Sur. to. 6. de vit. SS Matth. Weft. an. 1246. Mart. Rom. Molan. & alij,

THE fame day in *Scotland* the depofition of S. *Margaret* Queene, wife to holy King *Malcolme* the third of that Name, and daughter to Prince *Edward* of England, furnamed the *Out-law*, whofe wonderfull life and vertues, efpecially in deuotion and li-

Sur. to. 3. & Mart. Rom. 10. Iunij. Io. Mola. in addit. ad V fua. hac die.

berall

berall almes to the poore, are famous to pofterity. Her principall feftiuity is celebrated vpon the tenth of *Iune*, though fhe died
on this day, in the yeare of Chrift, one
thoufand fourfcore and twelue, and in the
raigne of K. *VVilliam Rafus* of England.

F   *The feauenteenth Day.*

Pol.Vir.
*l.*13.14.
& 15.
Petr.
Sutor de
Yita Car-
thufiana
*l.*2.*c.*5.
Silu.
Girald.in
eius Yita
Weft.
*an.*1297.
Mart.
Rom.
Molan.
& alij
omnes
hac die.

AT *Lincolne* the depofition of S. *Hugh*
Confeffour and Bifhop of the fame
Sea, who borne in *Burgundy*, was fent for
into England by King *Henry* the fecond, and
firft made Prior of the Charterhoufe-Monks
at *VVittam* in *Somerfetfhire*, and thence elected
and ordayned Bifhop of *Lincolne*. In which
function he fo excelled in all kind of vertue
and holines of life, that his merits deferued
to haue the fame manifefted to the world,
by the wonderfull miracles wrought at his
body. He newly built the Cathedrall
Church of *Lincolne* from the foundations.
And when he had moft laudably gouerned
his flocke for fourteene yeares, full of venerable old age, he gaue vp his foule to reft at
London, in the yeare of Chrift, one thoufand
and two hundred. His body was prefently
brought to *Lincolne*, at what tyme there happened to be prefent King *Iohn* of England,
and *VVilliam* King of *Scots*, with very many

of

of the Nobility of both Realmes. The two Kinges for the great reuerence they had vnto his holines, bare-headed carried his body from the gates of the Citty vnto the Church, where the same being most solemnly receyued by the Prelates & Clergy, was buryed behind the high Altar, neere vnto the Chappell of S. *Iohn Baptist*. He was afterward canonized for a Saint by Pope *Honorius* the third, in the yeare of Christ 1220.

THE same day at *Strenshalt* in the Kingdome of the *Northumbers* the Deposition of S. *Hilda* Virgin and Abbesse, descended of the bloud royall of the Kinges of that Prouince, who forsaking the vanityes of the world became a Religious woman first in a little Nunry neere to the riuer of *VVire*, and then Abbesse of the Monastery of *Hartsey* (now called *VVhitby* in *Yorkeshire*) & afterward of *Strenshalt*, where in very great sanctity of life, she ended her blessed dayes, about the yeare of Christ, six hudred & fourscore. Her feast is in many places obserued vpon the fifteenth of December, where also we haue againe made mention of her.

Vē. Bed. *l. 3. c. 24.* *& lib. 4.* *cap. 23.* *Lippomannus tom. 2.* *West.* *an. 680.* *Tri: em. de Vir. Illustr.*

G   The eighteenth Day.

AT *Santo-Padre* a Village in the Kingdome of *Naples*, the Commemoration
of S.*Fulke* Côteſiour,who being an Engliſhman by byrth, and deſcended of a noble
family in our Iland, tooke vpon him for
the loue of Chriſt, a long peregrination, to
viſit the holy Sepulcher at *Hierufalem*. And as
he returned homeward by *Italy*, the plague
at that tyme ſorely raging in thoſe partes, in
very great ſanctity and holines of life, he
receyued the reward of his labour, and ended his bleſſed dayes in reſt. His body is
vntill this day kept with great honour and
veneration in the forſaid Village, called by
the Italiás *Santo-Padre*, for the manifold miracles that are dayly wrought therat:wher-
by the ſame place is now become a pilgrimage of deuotion to viſit his body, eſpecially among the *Neapolitans*, and people of
Calabria.

A   The ninteenth Day.

IN *Kent* the feſtiuity of S. *Ermenburge*
Queene and Abbeſſe, daughter to *Ercombert* King of *Kent*, and wife to *Merual-*

dus

dus King of the Mercians (or midle Englifhmen) and mother to the three famous
Virgin-Saintes *Milburge*, *Mildred*, and *Milwyde*:
who hauing built a goodly Church and
Monaftery in *Kent*, in honour of her two
kinfmen *Ethelbrit* and *Ethelred* Martyrs, gathered togeather feauenty other Virgins
and holy women, and with confent of her
husband, entred into the fame, as Abbeffe
and Gouerneffe of the reft: where in all fan-
&imony of life and vertuous conuerfation,
fhe ended her bleffed dayes, about the yeare
of Chrift, fix hundred fifty and foure, and
was buryed in the fame place.

Matth.
Weft.
an. 654.
& 676.
Pol. Vir.
l. 4. hift.
Angl.
& alij.

B   The twentith Day.

A T *Hexam* in *Northumberland* the Paffion
of *S. Edmund* King and Martyr, who
being a Saxon by bloud, borne in the Citty
of *Noremberge* in that Prouince, and nephew
to *Offa* King of the *Eaftangles*, was by him
adopted fucceffour and heyre of that Kingdome. And when had moft Chriftianlike
gouerned the fame for fifteene yeares, was in
the firft *Danish* perfecution, vnder the Cap-
taines *Hinguar* and *Hubba*, for the Confeffion
of Chrift, firft whipped forely, and then
tied to a tree, and his body fhot full of ar-
rowes, was finally beheaded. Whofe head

Abbo
Floriac.
in eius
vita.
Petr.
in Catal.
Ofbert. de
Stokes in
eius vita
Mart.
Rom.
& omnes
hac die.

the

the *Danes* carrying into a wood neere by, caſt among briars and buſhes. And when the Tyrants forſooke thoſe partes, and the Chriſtians ſeeking for the ſame, loſt themſelues in the forſaid wood, and one calling vpon another, asking with a loude voyce, *VVhere art? where art? where art?* the bleſſed Martyrs head anſwered, *Heere, Heere, Heere.* By which miraculous voyce they found out the ſame. He ſuffered in the yeare of Chriſt, eight hundred and ſeauenty.

THE ſame day, and ſame place alſo, the paſſion of *S. Humbert* Biſhop and Martyr, who being Counſellour and companion to the forſaid *King Edmund* in the adminiſtration of his Kingdome, deſerued to be made partaker with him of his martyrdome, & ſo obtayned a crowne of glory, in the yeare of our Lord aboue mentioned.

Weſt.
an. 870.
& 855.

C   *The one and twentith Day.*

AT *Bobia* in *Lombardy* the depoſition of *S. Columbane* Abbot & Confeſſour, who being an Iriſhman by byrth, and firſt a monke, then Abbot of the Monaſtery of *Benchor* in the ſame Kingdome, went ouer into France, & there founded a Monaſtery at *Luxouium,* and thence paſſing into *Italy,* he there alſo founded another at *Bobia,* by the

Vĕ· Bed.
in eius
vita.
Mart.
Rom.
& Molã.
hac die.

help

helpe of *Agilulph* King of the *Lombards*, of which himleite became Abbot. And after all tnele, and diuers other labours and toyles taken for the aduancement ot Chriltian Religion in Gods Church, full of wonderfull fanctity of life and miracles, he ended his venerable dayes, about the yeare ot Chrift, fix hundred and fourteene, and was buried in the forfaid Monaltery of *Bobia*.

Io. Lefl.
de gelt.
Scot.
Hect.
Boet.
ibid. in
Eugenio
4.*Carol.*
Sigon.
de regno
*Italiæ.l.*2

D   *The two and twentith Day.*

IN *France* the Cõmemoration of S. *Ofmane* Virgin, delcended of the Bloud - Royall of *Ireland*, whole parentes being Pagans, fhe notwithftãding in her tender years was priuately inftructed in the Chriftian faith. But afterward being to be elpouled to a Noble mã of the fame Kingdome but an Ethnicke, forfooke both Countrey and friends and fled fecretly ouer into *France*, accompanied only with a mayd-feruant, that wayted on her called *Aclitenis*, where in a wood neere to the Riuer of *Loyre*, fhe liued a very auftere life, being clad with a coate made of bulruthes, and feeding her hungry body only with hearbes. It chanced one day, that a wild boare being chafed in that wood by the hunters, came running to her, as it were, for fuccour. The huntefmen eagerly

Vide
fufius
eius vitã
l. Manu-
fcript.
Rob.
Buckl. de
vita SS.
Mulier.
Angl.
pag. 239.
ex antiq.
monum.
Hiberniæ
et Fraciæ

purſuyng the beaſt, ſtroke him with their ſpeares with all their force, but could not once pearce his skynne. Heerupon the Virgin being diſcouered, was ſuſpected to be a witch; & being brought to the Biſhop, and found to beliecue in Chriſt, was by him baptized, & had a little territory aſſigned her, & a Gardener appointed to cultiuate the ſame, for her bodily reliefe and ſuſtenance: who being on a tyme deluded by the diuell to attempt ſome thing againſt her, was by diuine iuſtice ſuddainly ſtroken blynd: wherof he repenting himſelfe, was by her prayers againe reſtored to his ſight. And ſo ſhe perſeuering a longe tyme in that holy conuerſation, full of ſanctimony of life, was finally called thence vnto Chriſt her ſpouſe, whome ſhe had ſo entyrely loued and ſerued.

E   *The three and twentith Day.*

AT *Chepſtow* in *Monmouthſhire* of *Wales*, the Comemoratiō of *S. Tathar* Confeſſour and Eremite, who being deſcended of a noble Britiſh lynage, cōtemned the world, & became an Ermite in the Mountaynes of *Monmouthſhire*, in the raigne of *Cradocke* King of *South-wales*; about which tyme alſo in great ſanctity of life and miracles, he ended

his

his bleſſed dayes: He built of his owne inheritance a goodly Church in the forſaid
Towne of *Chepſtow*, togeather with a fayre
Schoole for the education of youth in learning and vertue : for which his memory is
yet famous in jour Iland, eſpecially among
the ancient Britans of *South-wales*.

F *The foure & twentith* Day.

AT *Strenſhalt* in the Kingdome of the
Northumbers the Commemoration of
Bleſſed *Eanſlede* Queene, daughter to *Edwyn*,
and wife to *Oſwy* Kinges of *Northumberland*;
who after the death of her Lord, and
husband, ſetting aſide all worldly pompe
and pleaſure, tooke a Religious habit. and
became a Nunne in the Monaſtery of S.
Peter at the forſaid place of *Strenſhalt*, vnder
the care and Gouernement of her owne
daughter *Ethelfred* that then was Abbeſſe of
the ſame. Where in all kind of profound
humility, ſanctimony of life, and other vertues, ſhe ended her bleſſed dayes, about the
yeare of Chriſt, ſix hundred and ſourſcore.

✳
Bed. l. 4.
hiſtor.
Angl.
cap. 26.
Arnol.
W*ion*
lib. 4.
lig. vitæ.

G   *The fiue & twentith* Day

*
Regist.
Ecclef.
Landaf.
& Catal.
Epifco.
eiufdem
Eccl . ex
antiq.
monum.
Cambriæ

AT *Landaffa* in *Clamorganshire* of *VVales* the Commemoration of *S. Telean* Martyr, and fecond Bifhop of the fame Sea, whofe rare life, learning, & other eminent vertues haue in tymes paft byn famous throughout *England*, efpecially among the ancient Britans of our Nation, where his memory is frefh euen vntill this day. He was very nobly borne, and brought vp vnder S. *Dubritius* Archbifhop and Metropolitan of *VVales*, togeather with S. *Dauid*. And a little after his comming to his Bifhopricke, he was conftrayned, through a vehement plague infecting thofe partes, to go ouer into *France*. The which being ceafed and he returned, was foone after flayne by a certaine noble Man of that Countrey, called in the Britifh tongue *Gueddan*, about the yeare of Chrift, fix hundred twenty and fix. His body was buryed in his owne Cathedrall Church of *Landaffa* (to whome the faid Church is now dedicated) where the fame was preferued with all honour and veneration, euen vntill the dayes of King *Henry* the eight of *England*.

A

A   The six and twentith Day.

AT *Fulda* in the higher *Germany*, the Commemoration of S. *Egbert* Abbot and Confessour, who being a Scottishman by birth, and descended of a noble family in that Kingdome, forsooke his Countrey, and went ouer into *Germany* in that Primitiue Church, and there became first a Monke, and after Abbot of a Monastery which S. *Boniface*, Archbishop of *Mentz* and Apostle of the *Germans* had newly erected at *Fulda* aforsaid. Where in very great sanctity of life and doctrine, especially in the obseruáce of Monasticall discipline he finally reposed in our Lord. Where also his body is yet kept with great honour & veneration of the Inhabitants of that place. This man is different from the other S. *Egbert* of the same Name, that was Abbot of S. *Columbs* in *Scotland*, whose feast is obserued vpon the foure and twentith day of Aprill.

Io. Lesl.
Episco.
Rossens.
l.5. de
gest.
Scot.
Wion *in*
append.
ad lib.3.
lig. vitæ,

B   The seauen & twentith Day.

AT *Rhode* in *Brabant* the deposition of S. *Oda* Virgin, who borne in *Scotland*

or the Roall bloud of that Kingdome , and
being ſtrokē blind, wēt ouer into the lower
Germany to the body of *S. Lambert* at *Liege*,
where by his merits and her owne prayers

Io. Moli.
in addit.
ad vſuar.
et in Ind.
SS. Belgij
hac die.

ſhe receyued againe her ſight, vowing perpetuall Chaſtity to God, that had ſo miraculouſly deliuered her of that infirmity.
Her Father, notwithſtanding, would haue
had her to marry;but ſhe deteſting the ſame,
neuer returned backe into her Countrey,
but lead a ſolitary and moſt holy life in the
Territory of *Liege*: where in all ſanctimony
ſpending the reſt of her dayes in continuall
prayer and contemplation of heauenly
things, ſhe gaue vp her ſoule to her heauenly ſpouſe, about the yeare of Chriſt ſeauen
hundred & thirteene. Her body remayneth
in the forſaid Village of *Rhode*, and there, as
Patroneſſe of that Towne, is kept with
great veneration, for the often miracles that
haue byn wrought therat.

C *The eight & twentith Day.*

Gul.
Malmeſ.
l. de Pot.
Angl.
hac die.
Herebert.
in faſt. SS.

AT *Dorcheſter* in *Oxfordſhire* the depoſition of *S. Edwold* Confeſſour and Ermite, brother to King *Edmund* the Martyr,
who refuſing the Kingdome of the *Eaſtagles*,
after his Brothers paſſion, gaue himſelfe
wholy, for the loue of Chriſt . to a kind of

ſo-

solitary life and heauenly contemplation. In which after he had liued many yeares with great fignes of fanctity & holines, ended his bleffed dayes in an old Monaftery, at *Dorchefter* aforfaid, fomtime called *Corn-houfe*, and was there with great veneration interred, about the yeare of Chrift, eight hundred threefcore and eleuen.

D The nine & twentith Day.

IN *Clamorganfhire* of *VVales* the Comemoration of *S. Barucke* Confeffour and Ermite, who being defceded of a noble Britifh race in our Iland, did for the loue of God contene the world, and become an Ermite, leading a moft ftrict and feuere kind of life in a little Iland of the fea, in *Clamorganfhire*, called afterward of his Name, *Barucks-eye* (but now more corruptly *Bardfey:*) where in very great holines &, fanctity of life, he gaue vp his bleffed foule to reft in our Lord. His memory is yet very famous in the forfaid Prouince of *Clamorgan*, as alfo among the ancient Britans of our Iland.

Ex antiq. Monum. Cambr. de Prou. Clamorg.

E *The thirtith Day.*

*

*Eius Vit.
extat M.
S. à Rob,
Buckl
inter Vit.
SS. Mul.
Angl.*

AT *Derham* in *Norfolke* the Comemoration of *S. VVithburge* Virgin ,daughter to *Annas* King of the *Eaftangles,* and fifter to *S. Audry* and *S. Sexburge* Queenes who building with her owne patrimony a Nunry at *Derham,* entred therin & receiued a Monafticall habit. Where after fhe had fpent her dayes in great holineffe and fanctimony of life, finally refted in our Lord , about the yeare of Chrift , fix hundred and threefcore. S. *Ethelwold* Bifhop of *VVinchefter* in the yeare of Chrift 974. hauing repayred the Abbey of *Ely* defaced by the Danes, and adioyning vnto it this forfaid Nunry of *Derham,* caufed her body to be taken vp (which was found whole and vncorrupt, after aboue 300. yeares from her death) and tranflated to the Abbey of *Ely,* by Abbot *Brithnote,* and there placed neere to the holy body of S. *Audry* her fifter. The faid Monaftery which fhe built, being afterward conuerted into a parifh Church, remayneth vntill this day in *Norfolke,* ftill retayning the forfaid name of *Derham.*

THE
MONETH
OF DECEMBER.

F   *The first Day.*

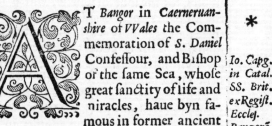

AT *Bangor* in *Caerneruan-shire* of *VVales* the Commemoration of *S. Daniel* Confessour, and Bishop of the same Sea, whose great sanctity of life and miracles, haue byn famous in former ancient tymes throughout our whole Iland, both aliue and dead, especially among the anciet Britans of *VVales*. His body was buryed at *Bangor* aforsaid, where the Cathedrall Church of that Bishopricke, that now is, was erected and dedicated in his honour. He was the first Bishop of that Sea, and liued about the yeare of Christ, fiue hundred

*

Io. Capg. in Catal. SS. Brit. ex Regist. Ecclej. Bangorē.

and

and fixteene, and in the Raigne of King
Arthur of *Britany.*

G   *The ſecond Day.*

*

⁹ *alias*
Eue

AT *Dormundcaſter* two miles from *Peter-*
burrow in *Northamptonſhire* the Commemoration of † S. *VVeede* Virgin and Abbeſſe, daughter to *Penda* a Pagan King of
the *Mercians*, and ſiſter to the holy Virgins
Kinneburge, Kiniſdred, Kiniſwide and *Edburge*,
who conténing all worldly pompe and delightes, for the loue of Chriſt, entred into

Wiol. 4
lig. vitæ
Chron.
Britan.
fol. 276.
Regiſt.
Ecclеſ.
Petribur.

the Monaſtery of *Dormundcaſter* aforſaid, and
there tooke the holy veyle of chaſtity and
monaſticall habit, vnder the gouerment of
her owne ſiſter *Kinneburge* that then was Abbeſſe of the ſame; where after the death of
her ſiſter *Edburge,* that ſucceeded *Kinneburge,*
ſhe was eleꞔted alſo to that Office. Which
three ſiſters one ſucceding another in the
ſame dignity of Abbeſſe, did, as it were, by
an hereditary right, leaue one the other their
ſanꞔtimony and holines of life, which each
one conſerued and augmented vntill her
dying day. This was the yongeſt of fiue
ſiſters, all Saintes, and died about the yeare
of Chriſt, ſix hundred fourſcore & twelue.
Her body was tranſlated to *Peterburrow,* and

                                there

there intombed very richly with the reſt of her ſiſters

A   The third Day.

AT *Chure* in *Heluetia* the Paſſion of S. *Lucius* the firſt Chriſtian King of *Britany* and Martyr, who being conuerted to the faith of Chriſt by the Saintes *Fugatius* & *Damianus*, ſent from *Rome* by Pope *Eleutherius*, afterward became himſelfe a preacher of the ſame Doctrine, and went ouer into *France* and thence into *Germany*, where after many perſecutions ſuſtayned for the confeſſion of Chriſt, being at laſt (according to ancient traditions) ordayned the firſt Biſhop of *Chure*, was there finally put to death by the incredulous people of that Nation, about the yeare of Chriſt, one hūdred fourſcore & twelue. His feaſt is very ſolénely celebrated with *Octaues* at *Chure* aforſaid, as is to be ſeeñe in the Breuiary of that Dioceſſe, wherin the whole ſtory of his life is recounted at large.

THE ſame day at *Dorceſter* in *Dorcetſhire* the depoſition of *S. Birine* Confeſſour, and firſt Biſhop of that Prouince, who conuerted the *Weſtſaxons* to the faith of Chriſt, togeather with their King *Kinegilſus*, and ſo became their Apoſtle. He died in the yeare of Chriſt, ſix hundred and fifty, and

was

Eyſengr. cent. 2. p. 5. diſt. 2. p. 2. d. 7. p. 3. d. 2. p. 4. d. 2. Io. Nauc. vol. 8. gē. 6. Petr. de Natal. l. 1. c. 24. Annal. Curienſ. Ratisbō. Bauar. et Monaſt. S. Lucij ibidem. Bernard. Guido in Catal. Pōt. ſub Eleuth.

Vē. Bed. l. 3. c. 7. Weſt. an. 637. & 644. Mart. Rom.

Gul.
Ramefius
in eius
vita.
Wiõ l.2.
lig. vitæ.
in Catal.
Epifco.
Dorce-
ſirenſ.

was buryed at the forſaid towne of *Dorceſter*, but afterward tranſlated to *VVincheſter* by S. *Hedde* Biſhop of that Citty, and there with great ſolemnity and veneration being placed in the Cathedrall Church of *S. Peter* and *S. Paul*, deſerued to be honoured with this Epigram of an ancient Poet, that wrote his life in verſe.

> *Dignior attolli quàm ſit Tyrinthius heros,*
> *Quam ſit Alexander Macedo. Tyrinthius hoſtes*
> *Vicit, Alexander mundum, Birinus vtrum q̃.*
> *Nec tantùm vicit mundum Birinus & hoſtem ;*
> *Sed feſe bello vincens, & victus eodem.*

I N like manner the ſame day in the Territory of *Liege* in the *Lower Germany* the depoſition of *S. Eloquius* Prieſt & Confeſſour, who borne in *Ireland*, went ouer the ſea, with diuers other Companions to preach the Chriſtiã faith to the *Netherlanders*; where after much fruite reapt in that kind, in great ſanctity of life he ended his bleſſed dayes, about the yeare of Chriſt, ſix hundred fifty & one : whoſe body was afterward tranſlated to the Towne of *VValciodore*, and there is kept with great veneration, as Patrone of that place.

Io. Molã.
in addit.
ad Vſuar.
et in Ind.
SS. Belgij

B   *The fourth Day.*

AT *Salisbury* in *VViltshire* the depofition of S. *Ofmund* Confeffour and Bifhop of the fame Sea, who being a *Norman* of noble birth, came into England with King *VVilliam* the *Cöquerour*, by whome he was firft made Chancellour of the Realme, and Earle of *Dorfet*, and afterward, for that he was a moft vertuous and learned man, he was elected Bifhop of *Salisbury* : which Church being begon by his Predeceffour he finifhed, adding therto a goodly Library, which he furnifhed alfo with many excellent bookes. And when he had moft laudably gouerned his flocke for fixteene yeares, in great fanctity and holines of life, he happily repofed in our Lord, in the yeare of Chrift, one thoufand fourfcore and nynteene, and was buryed in his owne Cathedrall Church of *Salisbury*, at whofe body it pleafed God to worke miracles. He was canonized for a Saint by Pope *Calixtus* the third, two hundred and fifty yeares after his death.

Ranulp.
Ceftrenf.
in eius
vita.
l.7.c.3.
Mart.
Rom.
& alij
omnes
hac die.

THE fame day at *Trinis* in the Territory of *Chure* in the Prouince of *Heluetia* in *Germany*, the feftiuity of S. *Emerita* Virgin & Martyr, fifter to King *Lucius* of *Britany*, who

going

Eyfengr.
p.3.Cent.
2.d.1.
Breuiar.
Curienf.
in Offic.9.
lection.
hac die.

going into *Germany* with her faid brother, was by the pagã people of that Coũtrey, for the confeſſion of Chriſtian faith, put to death, ending her glorious martyrdome by fire, about the yeare of Chriſt, one hundred fourſcore and thirteene. The whole ſtory of her life is ſet forth at large in the *Breuiary* of the Dioceſſe of *Chure* aforſaid, in her Office on this day.

C   *The fifth Day.*

✱

Matth.
Weſt.
an.1067
Parif.
eodem
an. &
1209.
Pol.Vir.
lit.s.hiſt.
Angl.

AT *VVincheſter* in *Hampshire* the Commemoration of *S. Chriſtine* Virgin and Abbeſſe, daughter to Prince *Edward* ſurnamed the *Out-law*, and ſiſter to the famous S. *Margaret* of *Scotland*, who togeather with her mother *Agatha*, entred into the Monaſtery of *VVincheſter*, and there became a Religious woman firſt, and afterward Abbeſſe of the whole houſe. In which dignity ſhe perſeuering in all kind of exemplar ſanctimony of life, and Monaſticall diſcipline, gaue vp her ſoule at laſt to her heauenly ſpouſe, about the yeare of Chriſt, one thouſand and fourſcore, and in the raigne of King *VVilliam* the *Conquerour.*

D   *The fixt Day.*

IN *Ireland* the Commemoration of S. *Congellus* Abbot and Confeſſour, who being a moſt venerable Monke of the Order of S. *Benedict,* and liuing with S. *Malachias,* at that tyme Biſhop of *Connerthen* in *Ireland,* was by him ordayned Abbot of an ancient Monaſtery neere to the forſaid Biſhops Sea in the ſame Kingdome; where in very great ſanctity or life & miracles he ended his bleſſed dayes, about the yeare of Chriſt, one thouſand, one hundred and fourty.

THE ſame day at *Cullen* in *Germany* the Commemoration of S. *Florentina* Virgin and Martyr, who being one of the number of the eleuen thouſand holy Britiſh Virgins martyred with S. *Vrſula,* was for defence of her Chaſtity there put to death with the reſt of her fellowes, about the yeare of Chriſt, three hundred fourſcore and three, herſelfe afterward miraculouſly reueyling her name.

*Bernard.
in vita
S. Malac.
Epiſcop.
Wion in
append.
ad lib. 3.
lig. vitæ.*

*Tabulæ
Coleniéſ.*

E   *The ſeauenth Day.*

AT *Durham* in the *Bishopricke,* the Cōmemoration of S. *Odwald* Abbot and Cōfeſſour, feffour, who of a Monke of wonderfull Innocency, and godly conuerfation, was elected Abbot of the monaftery of *Lindisferne* in the Kingdome of the *Northumbers,* where in all kind of holines of life and Monafticall difcipline, full of miracles, he repofed in our Lord, about the yeare of Chrift, eight hundred and fix, and was afterward buryed at *Durham* aforfaid.

THE fame day in *Scotland* the Commemoration of *S . Gallanus* Monke and Confeffour, who borne in *Ireland*, and defceded of a noble bloud in that Kingdome, came ouer into *Scotland* with *S . Columbe* the *Great*, whofe fcholler and difciple he was, where teaching & preaching the Chriftian faith to the *Pictes* that in thofe dayes inhabited *Scotland,* famous for fanctity of life and miracles, he departed this world, about the yeare of Chrift, fiue hundred and fourfcore.

F   *The eight Day.*

THE CONCEPTION of the moft glorious and immaculate Virgin MARY mother of God, by the grace and power of her Sonne , that preferued her from all inquination of fynne : which feaft being firft of all begun to be celebrated in our Iland of

Great

Great Britany in the tyme of S. *Anselme* Archbishop of *Canterbury*, and King *VVilliam* the
Conquerour, about the yeare of Chrift, one
thoufand threefcore & ten, by the Monkes of
the Venerable Order of S. *Benedict*, to the
honour and glory of the bleffed Virgin; was
afterward confirmed by our Mother the holy Roman Church, and cõmaunded to be
kept holiday throughout Chriftendome, to
the increafe of deuotion towards fo mighty
a Patroneffe.

THE fame day at *VVinchefter* in *Hampshire*
the Commemoration of Bleffed *Agatha*
Queene, daughter to *Salomon* King of *Hungary*, and wife to Prince *Edward* of *England*
furnamed the *Outlaw*, and Mother to the
two famous Saintes *Margaret* and *Chriftine*,
who when, after the death of her husband,
fhe faw her Sonne *Edgar*, to whome the
fucceffion of the *Crowne* of *England* by right
belonged, to be iniuftly depreffed and mo-
lefted by the inuafions of King *Harold* firft,
and after of the *Conquerour*, and therby fru-
ftrated of the recouery of the Kingdome,
fhe with her two daughters, refolued to take
their iourney backe towards *Hungary* by fea;
but being driuen by tépeft into *Scotlãd*, they
were very honourably receyued by King
Malcolme, who tooke the forfaid *Margaret* to
wife. And after a while that they had ftayed
there, *Agatha* the Mother, and *Chriftine* the

*Petr. in
Catal.l.i.
c.41.Sixt
PP.4.
Extrau.
commun.
tit.de Re-
lig. &
Vener.
SS.Conc.
Trid.
Baron.in
Not. ad
Mart.
Rom.
hac die.*

✱

*Hiftor.
Scot.
excufa
Francof.
an. 1584.
lib. 7.
Matth.
Weft.
& Parif.
an. 1067.
Wiõl. 4
lig. vitæ*

Y   other

other daughter, returned into *England*, entred both into the Monaſtery of Religious
women at *VVincheſter*, where in very great
ſanctimony of life, they finally ended their
bleſſed dayes ; the Mother deſceaſing about
the yeare of Chriſt, one thouſand threeſcore
and twelue : whoſe body being interred in
the ſame Monaſtery, hath byn kept with
great veneration, euen vntill our dayes.

G   *The ninth Day.*

Matth.
Weſt.
an. 871.
& 888.
Gene.l.
Alfredi
Regis
an. 870.
Pol. Vir.
lib. 5.
& alij.

AT *Shaftesbury* in *Dorcetſhire* the Commemoration of *S. Ethelgine* Abbeſſe, daugh-
ther to *Alfred* King of the *VVeſtſaxons*, who
deſpiſing all temporall and worldly preferments, tooke a Religious habit, and became a Nunne in the Monaſtery of the forſaid Towne of *Shaftesbury*, which her Father had there newly erected : wherof at laſt
ſhe being ordayned Abbeſſe, gouerned the
ſame in all ſanctimony of life, and exact
Monaſticall diſcipline, vntill her dying
day, which happened about the yeare of
Chriſt, eight hundred fourſcore and ſixteene.

A

A   The tenth Day.

AT *Glower* in *Clamorganshire* of VVales the Commemoration of S. *Chined* Confeſſour and Eremite, who borne in Wales, and there deſcended of an ancient and noble Britiſh lynage, contemned the vanityes of the world, and for the loue of Chriſt, became an Eremite, leading a moſt ſtrict and ſeuere kind of life in the Mountaynes of the forſaid Prouince of *Clamorgan*, where in very great ſanctity and holines of life, he finally ended his happy dayes. His body was buryed at the forſaid Towne of *Glower*; whoſe memory hath in tymes paſt, byn very famous throughout England, but eſpecially among the ancient Britans of VVales.

Io. Capg.
in Catal.
SS. Brit.
ex antiq.
Monum.
Cambriæ

B   The eleuenth Day.

IN *Morauia* the Commemoration of S. *Geruadius* Biſhop and Confeſſour, who borne in *Scotland* and deſcended of a noble parentage in that Kingdome, tooke a Religions habit, and became a Monke there of the Venerable order of S. *Benedict*, and thence went ouer into *Germany*, and laſtly into *Morauia*, where being created Biſhop, he preached the Chriſtian faith inceſſantly to that

Io. Leſl.
Epiſcop.
Roſſ.
l. 5. hiſt.
Scot.
Wion in
append.
ad lib. 3.
lig. vitæ.

Nation, and became their Apoſtle. And after that he had brought many thouſands from their Idolatry to the true worſhip of one God, full of venerable old age, in great ſanctity and holines of life, he finally reſted in our Lord, about the yeare of Chriſt, eight hundred and foure.

C The tweluth Day.

IN the Ile of *Crowland* in *Lincolnſhire* the Commemoration of S. *Elfrede* Virgin, daughter to *Offa* the Pagan King of *Mercia,* who being conuerted to the Chriſtiā faith principally by the murder cōmitted by her Mother vpon King *Ethelbert* of the *Eaſtangles* that came to demaund her in Marriage for his wife, forſooke her ſaid parents, friends and all other worldly preferméts, and tooke a Religious habit, in the Monaſtery of S. *Guthlacke* in the forſaid Ile of *Crowland,* where in great ſanctimony of life, and obſeruance of Monaſticall diſcipline, ſhe gaue vp her ſoule to her heauenly ſpouſe, about the yeare of Chriſt, ſeauen hundred fourſcore and thirteene,

*

Pol. Vir.
l. 4. hiſt.
Angl.
Steph.
Luſingā.
cor. 4. c.
9. Wion
lib. 4.
lig. vitæ.

D

D The thirteenth Day.

AT *Pontoyfe* in *France* the Depofition of S. † *Iudocus* Confeffour and Ermite, who being defcended of a moft noble Britifh bloud, forfaking all worldly prefermentes, went ouer into *France*, and there for the loue of Chriſt, became an Ermite. In which kind of life he fo excelled in fanctity and holines, that it pleafed God to manifeft the fame by the incorruptibility of his body, which is kept whole vntill this day with great veneration at the forfaid Towne of *Pontoyfe*. He gaue almes foure tymes to Chriſt vifibly in the habit of a poore man, that demaunded the fame; and died in the yeare of Chriſt, fix hundred fifty and three. Whofe worthy praife this diſtich declareth.

Regia Progenies veterum ſtyrps clara Britannûm,
Ecce nitet rutila Iudocus *luce per Orbem.*

THe fame day in the Ile of *Thanet* in *Kent*, the depofition of *S. Edburge* Virgin and Abbeffe, daughter to bleffed *Ethelbert* the firſt Chriſtian King of that Prouince, who being baptized and inſtructed in the Chriſtian faith by *S. Auguſtine* our Apoſtle, forfooke the world, and entred into the Monaſtery of holy Virgins erected in the Ile of *Thanet* aforfaid, vnder the gouerment of her

Marginal notes:
† *Ioyce.*
Sur.to.6.
Petr.in Catal.l.1. cap. 25. Vincent. in ſpecul. Wiō l.4 lig. vitæ. Rodulp. Agricol. in diſtich.

Regiſtr. Eccleſ. Cantuar. & Rob. Buckl. in eius vita l.M. S. de SS. Mulier. Angl. pag. 115.

neece *S. Mildred*, after whofe death fhe became Abbeffe of the fame place : where in
all fanctimony of life, fhe ended her bleffed
dayes. *S. Lanfranke* Archbifhop of *Canterbury*
in the yeare of Chrift , one thoufand fourfcore and fiue , tranflated her body, as alfo S.
Mildreds, vnto *Canterbury*, and placed them
there in the Church of S. *Gregory*, which
he had newly repayred , and enriched ,
wherat miracles are recorded to haue byn
wrought.

E   *The fourteenth* Day.

Io.Lefl.
Epif.
Roff l.4.
Hiftor.
Scot.
Arnol.
Wiõ. in
append
ad lib.3.
lig.vitæ.
Regift.
Monaft.
S. Mart.
Colon .

AT *Cullen* in *Germany* the Cõmemoratiõ
of *S. Mimborine* Abbot and Confeffour,
who borne in *Scotland* , and defcended of a
noble bloud in that Kingdome , defpifed
the world, and became firft a Monke of the
Venerable Order of S. *Benedict*, and afterward went ouer into Germany, and there
was made Abbot of a Monaftery dedicated
to *S. Martin* in *Cullen* : which when he had
moft laudably gouerned for twelue yeares
or therabout, in great fanctity of life and miracles he ended his bleffed dayes, in the yeare
of Chrift, nyne hundred fourfcore and thirteene, and was buryed in the fame place.

F   *The fifteenth Day.*

AT *Strenshalt* in the Kingdome of the *Nor-thumbers*, the Tranſlation of S. *Hilda* Virgin and Abbeſſe, daughter to Prince *Herericke* nephew to *Edwyn* King of the ſame Prouince, who from her infancy giuing herſelfe wholy to deuotion and piety became a Religious woman firſt in a little Nunry by the Riuer of *Wyre*, and then was ordayned Abbeſſe of a Monaſtery erected in the forſaid Kingdome, neere to the ſea ſide called *Hartſey* (at this day commonly knowne by the name of *VVhitby* in *Yorkeſhire*) & afterward of another Monaſtery alſo in the ſame Prouince called *Streshalt*, which herſelfe had built; where in all kind of holines of life & excercife of Monaſticall diſcipline, glorious for miracles ſhe finally went vnto her ſpouſe, in the yeare of Chriſt, ſix hundred and fourſcore. Her body was after many yeares taken vp, and ſet in a more eminent place of the forſaid Church of *Strenshalt*, where before ſhe lay buryed, wherat it pleaſed God to worke many miracles.

Vë. Bed. l.3.c. 24. & l.4.c. 23. Weſt an. 665. & 680. Trit. de vir. Illa. l.3.c.123.

G   The *sixteenth* Day.

Mart.
Rom.
Io. Molā.
in addit.
ad vſuar.
ex vet.
manuſcr.

*

De hac
vid. l. ma-
nuſcript.
de vit. SS.
Mulier.
Angl.
pag. 177.
Regiſt.
Eccleſ.
Petribur.

AT *Aberdine* in *Scotland* the depoſitiō of S. *Bean* Confeſſour and Biſhop of the ſame Sea, whoſe wonderfull holines of life, togeather with the Miracles he wrought both aliue and dead, haue in tymes paſt byn famous throughout the Chriſtian world, but eſpecially in *Scotland* and *Ireland*, where alſo many goodly Churches & Altars haue byn erected and dedicated in his honour.

THE ſame day at *Dormundcaſter*-Monaſtery two miles from *Peterburrow* in *Northāptonshire*, the Commemoration of S. *Tibbe* Virgin and Anchoreſſe, who deſcended of a noble bloud in our Iland, and Kinſwomā to the Saints *Kiniſdred* and *Kiniſwide*, forſooke the pleaſures of the world, and became an Anchoreſſe for the loue of Chriſt, liuing a moſt ſtrict and ſeuere kind of recluſed life in great holines and ſanctimony vntill her dying day, which happened about the yeare of Chriſt, ſix hundred threeſcore and nyne, and was buryed with her forſaid Kinſwomen at *Dormundcaſter*.

A

A   *The seauenteenth Day.*

AT *VVimborne* in *Dorcetshire* the Commemoration of *S. Tetta* Abbesse, sister to
Cuthredus King of the *VVestsaxons*, who forsaking the vanityes of the world, and receyuing the holy veyle of Chastity in the Monastery of *VVimborne* aforsaid, was after the
death of S. *Cuthberge* foundresse therof, made
Abbesse of the same place, where in very
great sanctimony of life, & obseruance of
monastical discipline, she gaue vp her blessed
soule to rest, about the yeare of Christ, seauen hundred and six. There is a letter yet
extant wrytten by S. *Boniface* Archbishop of
Mentz to this S. *Tetta*, for the sending of the
Virgins *Tecla, Lioba, Agatha,* and others out of
her Monastery into *Germany*, in the beginning of that Primitiue Church, to be made
Abbesses and directresses of diuers new Monasteryes, which S. *Boniface* aforsaid had
erected in that Countrey.

Rodulph.
Monac.
in vita S.
Liobæ
apud
Sur. to. 5.
28. Sept.
Wion
lib. 4.
lig. vitæ.
Vita S.
Bonifac.
Episcop.
Mogunt.
et Germ.
Apost.

B   *The eighteenth Day.*

AT *Heydelmayne* in *Franconia* the Deposi-
tiõ of S. *VVinibald* Abbot & Cõfessour,
Sonne to S. *Richard* King of the English,

who

who going ouer into the low-Countreys
and Germany with S. *Boniface* his Vncle,
Archbifhop of *Mentz* and Apoftle of the
Germans, was by him ordayned Abbot of a
Monaftery which himfelfe had there founded in the fame Prouince,called *Heydelmayne*;
which when he had gouerned for ten
yeares in great fanctity of life, glorious for
miracles and other renowned vertues, he
ended his blefled dayes in reft, in the yeare
of Chrift, feauen hundred and threefcore,
and was buryed in the fame Monaftery,
with this Epitaph engrauen on his tombe.

Hic VVinibaldus Richardi filius almus,
Qui Regnū Anglorū mox linquens, hoc Monachorū
Clauftrum fundauit, Benedictiǫ, dicauit
Nomine, feptingento quinquagefimoǫue anno.

His body was afterward tranflated to *Eyft*
in Germany, and there interred with his
brother S.*VVillebald,* where it is kept with
great Veneration.

C The ninteenth Day.

AT *VVirtzburgh* in the higher *Germany* the
Commemoration of S. *Macharius* Abbot and Confeffour, who borne in *Scotland*
of a worthy family, and taking vpon him
a Monafticall habit in the fame Kingdome,
went ouer into *France,* and thence into *Ger-*

many, and was ordayned Abbot there of an ancient Monaftery in the forfaid Citty of *VVirtzburgh*, where in very great fanctity of life, renowned for miracles, he ended his bleſſed dayes in peace, about the yeare of Chriſt, one thoufand one hundred and fourty. Among other his Miracles one is recounted, that fitting at a banquet, he turned wyne into water, to the aftoniſhment of all the behoulders there prefent.

Wiõ in append. ad lib. 3. lig. vitæ.

D   The *twentith* Day.

IN *Ireland* the Commemoration of S. *Comogel* Abbot and Confeſſour, whoſe holy life and doctrine haue byn famous in tymes paſt in the Kingdome of *Ireland*, eſpecially for the reformation & obſeruance of Monaſticall diſcipline. He was Abbot of the great and ancient Monaſtery of *Benchor* in *Ireland*, & maiſter to the famous S. *Columbane* of that Nation, whome he inſtructed in all kind of good learning and other vertues, before his fending into *France* and *Italy*. And when he had gouerned the fame Monaſtery for many yeares, full of fanctity and venerable old age, he finally gaue vp his foule to reſt in our Lord, about the yeare of Chriſt, fix hundred and foure.

Vita S. Columb. apud Bedam tom.3. Wiõ l.3. lig. vitæ in not. ad Mart. Bened.

E

E   The one and twentith Day.

Chronog.
Britan.
fol. 276.
Arnol.
Wiṅ.l.4
lig. Vitæ.

AT Dormundcaster two myles from Peter-burrow in Northamptonshire, the Comme-moration of S. Edburge Virgin and Abbesse daughter to Penda the Pagan King of the Mercians, who contemning all worldly and temporall pleafures, became a Religious woman in the Monaftery of Dormundcafter aforfaid, vnder the care of S. Kinneburge her fifter ; after whofe death, fhe being chofen Abbeffe, gouerned the fame in all fanⅆti-mony of life and other vertues, vntill her dying day,which happened about the yeare of Chrift, fix hundred and fourfcore , and was buryed in the fame place neere to her faid fifter . This holy woman is different from the other three of the fame Name ,

In Vita S.
Edburgæ
Abbatiſſ.
Thanat.
infulæ
13.Deceb.

whofe feftiuall dayes are celebrated vpon the fifteenth of Iune, eighteenth of Iuly , and thirteenth of December. And befides thefe, there was another Edburge alfo, Virgin and Abbeffe, daughter to Ethelnulph King of the VVeftfaxons, who gouerned the Monafte-ry of holy Virgins at VVinchefter in Hampshire, full of renowned holynes and fame , about the yeare of Chrift, eight hundred and three-fcore.

F The two and twentith Day.

AT *Barking* in *Essex* the Commemoratiõ of S. *Hildelide* Virgin and Abbesse, who for her great vertue and sanctimony of life was made Abbesse of the Monastery of holy Virgins at the forsaid towne of *Barking*, and succeeded in that office S. *Edilburge*, sister to to S. *Erconwald* Bishop of *London*, by whome the said Monastery was erected : where in the exercise of all kind of vertue &obseruáce of Monasticall discipline, renowned for miracles, she ended her blessed dayes, about the yeare ofChrist, seauē hūdred. There is a story recorded, how that three blynd womē on a tyme came to this said Monastery of *Barking* to beseech the help and patronage of three holy Virgins there desceased, and all famous for holines , to wit , the forsaid *Edilburge* *VVulfhild* , and this our *Hildelide* , and there praying a long tyme, they were at last restored to their sight; but ech one by the intercessiõ of that particular Saint, to whome she prayed. This Monastery was afterward in the Danish persecution burned to the ground, defaced and spoyled, to the great lamentation of all England.

Vē. Bed.
l.4.c.20.
Io. Trit.
l.3.c. 121.
Wion *in*
append.
ad lib. 3.
lig.vitæ.
Rob.
Bu.kl. in
eius vita
l.M.S.
pag. 183.

G

C *The three and twentith Day.*

IN *VVales* the Commemoration of S. *Inthware* Virgin and martyr, who being defcended of the ancient Britifh bloud in our Iland, liued a moft godly and vertuous life in her Fathers houfe, being wholy occupied in intertayning & feruing of pilgrims and ftrangers that reforted thither. After her Fathers death, fhe being enuied for her holines of life by her ftepmother, was by a malitious deuife of hers, accufed to her own brother, called *Bana*, to be an harlot: wherevpon in this rage, he flew her with his owne hands, as fhe came one day from the Church. Whofe innocency was prefently teftified by this wonderfull miracle; that hauing her head cut of, fhe inftantly with her owne handes tooke it vp from the ground, and carried it to the Church from whence fhe came: as alfo in the fame place where fhe was beheaded, there fprang vp a fountaine of cleere water, very foueraigne for many difeafes. She fuffered about the yeare of Chrift, feauen hundred. About which tyme alfo there liued three fifters of hers, all very holy women, called *Edware*, *VVilgith*, and *Sidewell*; who as they were conioyned to her by neernes of bloud and

byrth;

byrth; fo where they alfo vnited in fingular fanctimony of life.

F   *The foure & twentith Day.*

IN *Scotland* the Commemoration of S.
Ruthius Monke and Confeffour, who
being an Irifhman by byrth, defcended of a
noble bloud in the fame Kingdome, became
a difciple firft to S. *Columbe* the *Great* of that
Nation,and afterward comming ouer with
him into *Scotland*, was his coadiutor in the
Cóuerfion of the *Pictes* to theChriftiã faith,
that in thofe dayes inhabited that Kingdome :where after the reducing of many
foules from their errours, to the knowledg
& worfhip of Chrift,famous for fanctity of
life & grace of Miracles he finally repofed
in our Lord, about the yeare of Chrift 588.

*

*Hect.
Boet .de
gest. Sco.
Io.Lest.
Episco.
Rofs.l.4.
hist. Sco.
pag. 150.*

B   *The fiue & twentith Day*

IN the Monaftery of S. *Meginhard* in the
higher Germany the Commemoration
of S. *Gregory* Prieft and Confeffour, Sonne
to King *Edward* of the VVeftfaxons, furnamed
the *Elder*, and brother to the holy Virgin S.
Edvurge of *Wilton*,who being admonifhed by
an Angell, forfooke both Countrey and

*

*Io. Trit.
de vir.
Illu. ord.
D.Bened.
l.3.c. 225.*

friends

Arnol.
Wiõ.l.4
lig. vitæ.
pag. 510.

friends, in the troublefome tyme of his
Fathers raigne and incurfions of the *Danes*,
and went ouer into *Germany* to S. *Eberhard*
a monke then famous in thofe partes both
for fanctity of life and gift of prophefy;vnto
whome he affociating himfelte in the forfaid Monaftery of S. *Meginhard*, became a
Monke in the fame place: where in very
great holines of life, he ended his bleffed
dayes, about the yeare of Chrift, nyne hundred fourty and fiue.

C   The *fix and twentith* Day.

Pol.Vir.
l.4.hift,
Angl.
Wiõ l.4
lig.vitæ.

AT *VVhitby* in *Yorkeshire* the Commemoration of Bleffed *Ethelfrede* Virgin,
daughter to *Ofwy* King of the *Northumbers*,
who contemning all worldly pompe and
trafitory glory, tooke a Religious habit, togeather with the holy veyle of Chaftity,in
a Monaftery of the fame Prouince, called
afterward *VVhitby*, which her faid Father
had there newly founded ; where vnder the
Gouernment of S. *Congilla*, that was then
ordayned Abbeffe therof, in all humility &
fanctimony of life, fhe made a holy end, and
gaue vp her foule to her heauenly fpoufe,
about the yeare of Chrift, fix hundred and
feauenty.

D

D   The seauen & twentith Day.

AT *Gallinaro* a Village in the Kingdome of *Naples*, the Commemoration
of *S. Gerard* Conteffour, who being an Englifhman by byrth, and defcended of a
a worthly parentage in our Iland, tooke
vpon him for the loue of God a long peregrination to vifit the holy Sepulcher of
Chrift in *Hierufalem*, which when he had
performed and returning backe by *Italy*,
where at that tyme the plague forely raged,
in very great fanctity of life, gaue vp his
foule to reft in our Lord. His body is vntill
this day kept with great honour and veneration, in the forfaid Village of *Gallinaro*,
wherat in teftimony of his holy life, miracles are yet daily wrought. So as the place
is therby become a great pilgrimage, efpecially for the *Neapolitans* & people of *Calauria*.

Registr.
Eccl.
Gallinar.
& In-
script.
ipsius
sepulchri
ibidem
sculpt.

E   The eight & twentith Day.

AT *Canterbury* the Tranflation of *S.
Elphege* Bifhop and Martyr, who being
firft Abbot of a Monaftery neere vnto *Bath*
in *Somerfetshire*, was thence promoted to the
bifhoprick of *VVinchefter* & laftiy to *Canterbury*.

Sur.to.5.
19. Agr.
Pol.Vir.
l.7. hift.

Z   He

Io.Capg.
& Breu.
fec.)su
Sa: um
Pet.in
Cat.Osb.
in cius
)ita.
Mart.
Rom.19.
Apr.
Mavrol
& Wio
bac die.

He was flayne at *Greenwich* in *Kent* in the second *Danish* persecution by those barbarous people in defence of his Church of *Canterbury*, and for not deliuering them three thousand Markes of money belonging to the said Church, in the yeare of Christ, one thousand and twelue. His body was first brought to *London*, and afterward on this day solemnely tranflated to *Canterbury*, and there placed in his owne Cathedrall Church of that Citty, where it was wont in Catholicke tyme to be kept with great honour and Veneration.

F   *The nine & twentith Day.*

Sur.to 5.
bac die
B euior.
fec.)sum
Sarum
Mart.
Rom.
Eius)it.
babetur
in bift.
quadrip.
impreff.
Parifijs
an.Dom.
1495.

AT *Canterbury* the Paffion of S. *Thomas* Archbifhop of the fame Sea, Legate Apoftolicall and Primate of *England*, who for defence of the liberties of the Church, being many wayes iniured by King *Henry* the fecond, was forced to appeale to Pope *Alexãder* the third; of whome being acquited of all the calumniations and flaunders laid to his charge, was againe reftored to his Bifhopricke, but within a while after being violently oppreffed by fome of the forfaid Kinges feruants, to wit, *Syr William Tracy, Syr Reynold Fitzvrfon, Syr Hugh Moruill, Richard Breton,* and others, was flayne in his owne

Church

Church of *Canterbury*, in the tyme of Euenſonge, before the high Altar, in the yeare
of Chriſt, one thouſand one hundred threeſcore and eleuen. Whoſe martyrdome is
heere deſcribed in theſe old verſes:

Staplet.
de trib.
Thomis
& omnes
alij hac
die.

Richardus Breton , *nec non* Moruilſius *Hugo,*
Guillelmus Tracy , *Reginaldus* Filius-vrſi,
Thomam *Martyrium fecére ſubire beatum.*
Fortis & inuictus his quattuor enſibus ictus
Primas Anglorum Thomas *petit alta polorum.*

His body was ſhortly afterward put into a
goodly ſhrine, beſet with coſtly iewells &
pretious ſtones, and placed in his owne
Cathedrall Church of *Canterbury*, wherat
infinite miracles were wrought ; and ſo
continued vntill the tyme of King *Henry*
the eight, by whoſe commandement the
ſaid monument was vtterly deſtroyed, and
his ſacred Reliques burned to aſhes, in the
yeare of Chriſt 1538.

Nicol.
Sand. l. 1.
de ſchiſ.
Angl.

G   *The thirtith Day.*

IN the Abbey of *Flay* the Commemoration of S. *Euſtach* Abbot and Confeſſour,
who for his ſingular vertue and innocency
of life, being firſt a Monke, was ordayned
Abbot of the forſaid Monaſtery of *Flay*. In
which dignity he ſo excelled, in all kind of
profund humility, charity to poore Or-

*
Matth.
Weſt.
in Hiſt.
maiori
ad an.
1200.

Wiō in
append.
ad lir.3.
lig. vitæ.

phans, and other eminent vertues, especially in the exercise and observance of Monasticall discipline, that his name deserued to be famous throughout our whole Iland, in former Catholicke tymes. He died about the yeare of Christ, one thousand and two hundred. At whose body it pleased God afterward, in testimony of his holy life, to worke miracles.

A   The one & thirtith Day

Io.I est.
lib.4.de
gest.Sco.
Wion in
append
ad lib. 3.
lig. vitæ.

IN Scotland the Commemoration of S. ternane Monke and Confessour, Nephew to S. Columbe the Great of Ireland, who contemning all worldly honours and prefermentes, tooke a Religious habit, and became a Monke of the Order of S. Benedict in a Monastery in the Iland of Hoy by Scotland, vnder the gouerment of his forsaid vncle S. Columbe; where in all kind of sanctity of life, he ended his blessed dayes, about the yeare of Christ, fiue hundred fourscore and eighteene. Whose memory hath continued famous both in Scotland where he liued, and in Ireland where he was borne, euen vntill this last age.

Laus Deo & Beatiss. Virg. Mariæ.

AN
ALPHABETICAL
TABLE OF THE
SAINTES NAMES
CONTEYNED
in the former Martyrologe.

A

 *Aron Martyr 1. Iuly.*
Acca B. 19. Feb.
Adaman Ab. 2. Sept.

Adaman Confeſſ. 31. Ianuar.
Adelme B. 31. Mar. 15. May.
Adalbert conf. 25. Iune.
Adelhere Mart. 5. Iune.
Adlar Mart. 20. Apr. 5. Iune.
Adrian Abbot. 9. Ianuar.
Adrian Prieſt 1. April.
Adolph Mart. 5. Iune.

Agatha Virgin 12. Iune.
Agatha Queene 8. Decem.
Agnes Virg. Mart. 28. Auguſt.
Aidan Bishop 31. Auguſt.
Alban Protomart. 16. Apr. 16. May & 22. Iune.
Albuine Bishop 26. Octob.
Aleuine Abbot 19. May.
Alkmund Mart. 19. March.
Alexander Conf. 6. Auguſt.
Alfred K. of Northūb. 15. Ian.
Alfred K. of Weſtſa. 28. Oct.
Algiue Queene 5. May.
Alice Prioreſſe 24. Auguſt.
Alnoth Mart. 27. Febr.
Alred Abbot 16. March.

Alricke Ermite 2. *Auguſt.*
Altho Abbot 5. *Septemb.*
AmmichadeConf. 30. *Ian.*
Amphibale Mart. 25. *Iune.*
Anſelme B. 21. *Apr.* 5. *Iuly.*
Arbogaſtus Bishop 21. *Iuly.*
Archibald Abbot 27. *March.*
Ardwyne Conf. 25. *Oct.*
Ariſtobulus Bish. 15. *Mar.*
Arnulph Conf. 22. *Auguſt.*
Arwaldi martyrs 28. *Ian* .
Aſſaph Bishop 1. *May.*
Audry vide *Ediltrude.*
Augulus mart. 7. *Febr.*
Auguſtine Bishop 26. *May.*

B

BAldred *Conf.* 29. *March.*
Barucke *Conf.* 29. *Nou.*
Bather Conf. 11. *Septemb.*
Bean Bishop 16. *Decem.*
Beatus Conf. 9. *May.*
Bede Prieſt 10. & 27. *May.*
Bega Virgin 6. *Sept.*
Benedict Abbot 12. *Ian.*
Beno Conf. 14. *Ian.*
Berectus Conf. 24. *Febr.*
Bernard Conf. 14. *Sept.*
Berteline Ermite 12. *Aug.*
Bertuine Bishop 11. *Nouemb.*
Birine Bishop 3. *Decemb.*

Birſtan Bishop 22. *April.*
Boniface B. 5. *Iune.* 1. *Nouem.*
Boſa Bishop 9. *March.*
Boſo Mart. 5. *Iune.*
Botulph Abbot 17. *Iune.*
Boyſil Abbot 23. *Ian.*
Bradan Abb. 16. *May* 14. *Iun.*
Brigit Virg. 1. *Febr.*
Brituald of Canterb. 9. *Ian.*
Brituald of VVinch. 22. *Ian.*
Burchard B. 2. *Feb.* 14. *Oct.*
Burgundoſora Abbeſſe 3. *Apr.*
Burien Virg. 29. *May.*

C

CAdocke *mart.* 24. *Ian.*
Canicke *Abbot* 11. *Octob*
Canoch Conf. 11. *Feb.*
Ceadwall King 20. *Apr.*
Ced Bishop 7. *Ian.*
Celſus Bishop 6. *Apr.*
Ceolfride Abbot 25. *Sept.*
Ceolwulph King 14. *Mar.*
Chad Bishop 2. *Mar.*
Chinede Ermite 10. *Dec.*
Chineburge Queene 15. *Sept.*
Chriſtian Bish. 18. *Mar.*
Chriſtian Virg. 26. *Iuly.*
Chriſtine Virg. 5. *Decemb.*
Clare Mart. 4. *Nouemb.*
Clintauke K. mart. 19. *Aug.*

Cogan Abbot 29. Sept.
Colman Bishop 13. Octob.
Colman mart. 8. Iuly.
Columbe Abbot 9. Iune.
Columbane Abbot 21. Nou.
Columbane Monke 28. Iune.
Comine Abbot 6. Octob.
Comogel Abbot 20. Decemb.
Coception of our B. Lady 8. De.
Congellus Abbot 6. Decemb.
Congilla Abbesse 9. Nou.
Constantine Emp. 21. May.
Conwalline Abbot 5. Octob.
Conwan Conf. 14. Feb.
Cordula Virg. 22. Oct.
Chroniacke Conf. 4. Ian.
Cuthbert B. 20. Mar. 4. Sept.
Cuthberge Abbesse 31. Aug.
Cymbert Bish. 21. Febr.
Cybthacke Conf. 20. Sept.

D

Damianus Conf. 26. May
Daniel. B. 1. Decem.
Dauid Bish. 1. March.
Dauid Conf. 15. Iuly.
Decuman Mart. 27. Aug.
Deicola Abbot 18. Ian.
Deifer Conf. 7. March.
Deusdedit Bishop 30. Iune.

Diman Conf. 19. Iuly.
Disibode Bish. 8. Iune.
Domitius Conf. 3. Aug.
Donatus Bish. 22. Octob.
Dronston Conf. 11. Iuly.
Drusa Mart. 5. Febr.
Dubritius B. 6. May. 14. Sept.
Dunstan B. 19. May. 7. Sept.
Dunstan Abbot 18. Iune.
Duuianus Conf. 8. April.
Dympna Virg. Mart. 15. May.

E

Eadgith Queene 15. Iuly
Eadsine bish. 29. Octob.
Eadware Virg. 23. Decem.
Eansled Queene 24. Nou.
Eanswide Abbesse 31. Aug.
12. Sept.
Eatta Bishop 26. Octob.
Ebba Mart. 25. August.
Ebba Virg. 2. April.
Eboam Martyr 5. Iune.
Edbert Bish. 6. May.
Edburge of Wilton 15. Iune.
Edburge of Edburton 18. Iuly
Edburge of Kent 13. Dec.
Edburge of Peterb. 21. Dec.
Edelfled Abbesse 8. Febr.
Edgar King 25. May.
Edilburge Queene 9. Iuly.

 Edil-

Edilburge of Brige 7. Iuly.

Edilburge of Barking 11. Oct.

Edilban Conf. 21. Sept.

Ediltrude Q. 23. Iun. 17. Oct.

Edilwald Bish. 12 Febr .

Edilwald Ermite 11. Iune.

Edith of Pollefwor. 14. May.

Edith of Wilton 16. Sept. 3. Nouemb.

Edmund King Mart. 10. Iune. 20. Nouemb.

Edmund Bishop 16. Nouemb.

Edward K. mart. 18. March. 20. Iune.

Edward K. Conf. 15. Ian. 10. Octob.

Edwald Conf. 29. Aug. 28. Nouemb.

Edwyn King mart. 4. Octob.

Egbert King 23. March.

Egbert Abbot of Scot. 24. Apr.

Egbert Abb of Fulda 26. Nou.

Egelnoth Bish. 30. Octob.

Egwine Bish. 11. Ian.

Elerius Abbot 2. Iune.

Eleutherius Conf. 3. Iune

Elfled Virg. 13. April.

Elfled Abbesse 20. Ian.

Elfred Virg. 12. Decemb.

Eloquius Conf. 8. Oct. 2. Dec.

Elphege B of Winchest. 1. Sept.

Elphege B. of Cant. 19. Apr. 28. Decem.

Eluane Bishop 1. Ianuar.

Emerita Virg. Mart. 4. Dec.

Engelmund Mart. 21. Iune.

Eoglodius Conf. 25. Ian.

Erconwald B. 30. Ap. 14. No.

Ercongote Abbesse 7. Iuly.

Ermenburge Queene 19. No.

Ermenild Queene 13. Febr.

Erwald Mart. 8. Iuly.

Eschillus Mart. 10. Apr.

Ethbyn Abbot 19. Octob.

Ethelburge Queene 8. Sept.

Ethelbert King Conf. 24. Feb.

Ethelbert King Mart. 20. May.

Ethelbrit ⎱ Mart. 17. Octob.
Ethelred ⎰

Ethelfrede Virg. 26. Decemb.

Ethelgine Abbesse 9. Decemb.

Etheluulph King. 14. Apr.

Ethelred K. Mart. 23. Apr

Ethelred K. Abbot 4. May.

Ethelu ide Queene 20. Iuly.

Ethelwold K. Mart. 6. Apr.

Ethelwold Bish. 1. Aug.

Ethelwyne Bish. 29. Iune.

Eternane Conf. 31. Dec.

Etto Bishop 10. Iuly.

Euftach Conf. 30. Decemb.

Ewaldi Mart. 3. Octob.

F

FAgan Conf. 8. August.
Felix Bishop 8. March.
Fethmo Conf. 12. March.
Fiaker Conf. 30. August.
Finan Bish. 17. Febr.
Florentius Bish. 7. Nouemb.
Florentina Virg. Mart. 6. Dec.
Foillan B. 3. Sept. 31. Octob.
Fremund K. Mart. 24. March.
   11. May.
Fridegand Conf. 17. Iuly.
Fridefwide Virg. 19. Octob.
Frithstan Bishop 9. April.
Frodoline Abbot 6. March.
Fugatius Conf. 26. May.
Fulke Conf. 18. Nouem.
Furseus Abbot 25. Febr. 4.
   March.

G

GAllanus Conf. 7. Dec.
Gallus Abbot 16. Octob.
Gerard Conf. 27. Decemb.
Gereberne Mart. 15. May.
German Bish. 2. May.
George Mart. 23. Apr.
Geruadius Bish. 11. Decemb.
Gilbert Bish. 11. Aug.
Gilbert Conf. 4. Febr.

Gildas Abbot 29. Ianuar.
Gislen Conf. 9. Octob.
Godricke Ermite 21. May.
Goluin Bishop. 1. Iuly.
Gotebald Bish 5 Apr.
Gregory Pope 12. March.
Gregory Conf. 25. Decem.
Grimbald Abbot 8. Iuly
Gudwall Bishop. 22. Feb. 6.
   Iune.
Guier Conf. 4. Apr.
Gunderhere Mart. 5. Iune.
Guthagon Conf. 3. Iuly. 1. Oct.
Guithelme Bish. 8. Ianuar.
Guthlacke Conf. 11. Apr.

H

HAmund Bishop 22.
March.
Hamunt Deacon 5. Inne.
Harrucke Bishop. 15. Iuly
Hedde Bish. 7. Iuly.
Heiu Virg. 30. May.
Helena Empresse. 7. Febr. 18.
   Aug.
Henry Ermite 16. Ian.
Henry of Opslo 19. Ian.
Henry of VVinchest. 6. Aug.
Henry King 22. May.
Herebert Conf. 20. March.
Hereswide Queene 23. Sept.

Higbald

Higbald Abbot 22. Sept.
Hilda Ab. 17. Nou. 15. Dec.
Heldelide Abbeſſe 22. Decem.
Hildebrand Mart. 5. Iune.
Himeline Conf. 10. March.
Honorius Bish. 30. Sept.
Hugh Mart. 27. Iuly.
Hugh B. of Ely 9. Auguſt.
Hugh B. of Lincolne 17. Nou.
   7. Octob.
Hugh B. of Roane 12. Apr.
Humbert Bish. 20. Nouemb.

I

IEron Mart. 17. Auguſt.
Inas King 6. Febr.
Indractus Mart. 5. Febr.
Inthware Virg. 23. Decemb.
Iohn of Beuerley 7. May.
Iohn Conf. 27. Iune.
Iohn Abbot 17. Iuly.
Iohn of Lewis 5. Febr.
Iohn of Birlington 10. Octob.
Iohn of Conſtance 26. Febr.
Iohn of Saltzburge 18. Febr.
Iohn of Michelmburge 10. No.
Iohn of Ely 19. Iune.
Ionas Abbot 28. May.
Ioſeph of Arimathia 27. Iuly.
Iotaneus Conf. 26. Sept.
Iſenger Mart. 21. March.

Ithimar Bish. 10. Iune.
Iudoeus Ermite 9. Ianuar. 13.
   Decemb.
Iulius Mart. 1. Iuly.
Iuo Bish 24. April.
Iuſtus Bishop. 10. Nouemb.
Irſtinian Mart. 23. Aug.

K

KEnelme King 17. Iuly.
Kentigerne Abb. 13. Ian.
Keyna Virgin 8. Octob.
Kilian Mart. 13. Febr. 8.
   Iuly.
Kilian Conf. 13. Nouemb.
Kiniſdred ⎫
Kiniſwide ⎬ Virgins 6. Mar.
Kinnebunge Queene 15. Sept.
Kortil Bish. 28. April.

L

LAnfranke Bishop. 24.
March. 3. Iuly.
Laurence Bish. of Canterb. 2.
   Febr.
Laurence B. of Dublyn 14.
   Nouemb.
Lebuine Bish. 25. Iune. 12.
   Nouemb.
Lefrone Abbeſſe 3. Iuly.
Leofgar Mart. 16. Iune.

Leuine Bish. 27. *Iune.* 12.
Nouemb.
Lewyne Virg. Mart. 24. *Iuly.*
Liephard Mart. 4.*Febr.*
Lioba Abbesse 28. *Sept.*
Luane Abbot 12.*Iuly.*
Lucius King 3. *Decemb.*
Lullus Bish. 26.*Octob.*
Lupus Bishop. 29. *Iuly.*

M

MAcharius Abbot 19. Decemb.
Macloue B. 15. *Nouemb.*
Maglore Conf. 24. *Octob.*
Maine Abbot 15. *Iune.*
Malachy Bish. 5.*Nou.*
Malcaline Abbot 21. *Ian.*
Malcus Bish. 10. *Aug.*
Malcolme King 2. *Iune.*
Marcellus Bish. 4. *Sept.*
Marchelme Conf. 14. *Iuly.*
Margaret Prioresse 15. *Aug.*
Margaret Queene 10. *Iune.*
16. *Nouemb.*
Marianus Conf. 17. *April.*
Martyrs at Lichfield 2. *Ian.*
Martyrs at Benchor 16. *Iune.*
Martyrs at Bardney 26. *Mar.*
Maude Queene 7, *August.*
Maxentia Virg. 24. *Octob.*

Mechtild Virg. 12.*Apr.*
Meliorus Mart. 3. *Ian.*
Mellitus Bishop 24. *Apr.*
Mellon Bish. 22. *Octob.*
Menigold Mart. 9. *Feb.* 15. *Iune.*
Meresine Conf. 17. *Ian.*
Merwyne Virg. 13. *May.*
Midane Conf. 26.*April.*
Midwyne Conf. 1.*Ianuar.*
Milburge Virg. 23.*Febr.*
Mildred Virg. 20.*Feb.* 13.*Iul.*
Milride Virg. 17.*Ian.*
Mimborine Abbot 14. *Decem.*
Modane Conf. 26. *Apr.*
Modwene Abbesse 5. *Iuly.*
Mono Mart. 18.*Octob.*
Motifer Conf. 29. *Octob.*

N

NEoth Conf. 31. *Iuly.*
Ninian B. 16.*Sept.*

O

OBodius Ermite 25. *Apr.*
Oda Virg. 27.*Nou.*
Odilia Virg. 18. *Iuly.*
Odo Bish. 4. *Iuly.*
Odwald Abbot 7.*Decemb.*
Ortrude Virg. 22.*Iune.*

Ofith Virg.7.*Octob*.
Ofmane Virg.22.*Nouem*.
Ofmund B. 16.*Iuly* 4.*Dec*.
Ofwald King 20.*Iune* 5.*Aug*.
Ofwald Bish. 28. *Febr*. 15.
 April 15. *Octob*.
Ofwyn King mart. 11.March
 20. Auguft.
Ofwyn Conf.18. *April*.
Otger Deacon 10. *Sept*.
Oudocke Bishop 2.*Iuly*
Owen Conf. 29. *Iuly*

P

Palladius Bish. 27. *Ian*.
Pandwine Virg. 26. *Aug*.
Paternus Conf.10.*Apr*.
Pattone Bish.30.march.
Patricke Bishop 17.march.
Patroke Bishop. 4. *Iune*.
Paul, Apoft.25. *Ian*. 29. *Iune*
Paultne Bish.10.*Octob*.
Peter Apoft.29. *Iune*.
Peter abbot 6.*Ian*.
Piran Conf.2. *May*.
Plechelme Bish. 15. *Iuly*.

Q

Q*Vemburg Virg*.12.*Sept*.
 Queran Abbot 9. *Sept*.

R

R*Emigius Bish*. 12. May.
 Richard King 7. Febr.
Richard of Chichefter 3. Apr.
 16.*Iune*.
Richard of Calabria 21.Aug.
Richard Ermite 1.Nouemb.
Robert Bish.9. Octob.
Robert Abbot 7. Iune.
Roger Bish.1.Octob.
Romwald Bish.24. Iune 27.
 Octob.
Rufin martyr 1.Iune
Rumbald Conf. 28. Iune.
Ruthius Conf.24.Decemb.

S

SAdoch Conf. 1.Apr.
 ampfon Bish.28. Iuly.
Scandalaus Conf.5.may.
Sebbe King 29. Auguft.
Senan Conf.29.April.
Sethrid Virg.10.Ian.
Sewall Bishop 8. May.
Sexburge Virg.6.Iuly
Sexulfe Bish.27. Febr.
Sidwell Virg. 23.April.
Sigene Abbot 7. April.

Sigebert King 27. Sept.
Sigfride Bish. 15. Feb.
Sophias Bish. 24. Ian.
Souldier Mart. 22. Iune.
Socrates ⎫
Stephen ⎭ Mart. 17. Sept.
Switbert Bish. 1. March.
Swithin Bishop 2. & 15. Iuly
Sunaman Mart. 25. Iuly.
Symon Apost. 28. Octob.
Symon Conf. 16. May.
Syra Virg. 23. Octob.

T

Tacwin Bish. 30. Iuly.
Tancone Bish. 16. Febr.
Tathar Conf. 23. Nouemb.
Tecla Abbesse 15. Octob.
Telean Bish. 25. Nou.
Tetta Abbesse 17. Decemb.
Theodore Bish 19. Sept.
Theorithgid Virg. 26. Ian.
Thomas of Canterb. 7. Iuly.
29. Decemb.
Thomas of Hereford 25. Aug.
2. Octob.
Thomas of Northum. 17. Aug.
Thomas Monke 16. Aug.
Tigernake Bish. 5. April.
Totnan Mart. 8. Iuly.
Tibbe Virg. 16. Decemb.

Transl. of 11000. Vir. 17. May

V

Vigane Conf. 13. March.
Vintruge Mart. 5. Iune.
Vlfade Mart. 1. Iune.
Vlfricke Ermite 20. Feb.
Vlfride Bishop 18. Ian.
Vltan Abbot 1. May.
Vnaman Mart. 25. Iuly.
Vodine Bishop. 23. Iuly.
Vrsula Virgin 21. Oct.
Vulgamius B. 2. Nouemb.

W

Waccare 5. Iune.
Walburge Virg.
27. Apr. 4. August.
Walter Abbot 3. May.
Walter Mart. 5. Iune.
Wasnulph Conf. 1. Octob.
Weede Abbesse 2. Decemb.
Wendelin Abbot 20. Octob.
Wenlocke Abbot 3. March.
Wenefride Virg. 3. Nou.
Wereburge Virg. 3. Febr.
Werenfride 14. Aug. 13. Sep.
Wiaman Mart. 25. Iuly.
Wigbert Conf. 13. Aug.

Wil-

Wilfride of Yorke 24. *April.* 12. *Octob.*

Wilfride of Worcester 10. *Febr.*

Wilfred Queene 22. *Iuly.*

Wilgife Conf. 5. *March.*

Wilgith Virg. 23. *Decemb.*

Willeicke Conf. 2. *March.*

Willebrord Bish. 19. *Octob.* 7. *Nouemb.*

Willebald Bish. 7. *Iuly.*

Willehade Bish. 8. *Nouem.*

Wilhere Mart. 5. *Iune.*

William of Yorke 8. *Ianuar.* 8. *Iune.*

William of Rochester 23. *May*

William of Norwich 25.

March.

William of Tyre 11. *Feb.*

Winfride Abbot 6. *March.*

Winibald Abbot 24. *Sept.* 10. *Decemb.*

Winocke Abbot 8. *Sept.* 6. *Nouemb.*

Wolftan Bishop. 19. *Ianuar.* 7. *Iune.*

Wolftan Mart. 31. *May.*

Wulfhild Abbeffe 9. *Sept.*

Wulfy Abbot 26. *Sept.*

Wyre Bishop 8. *May.*

Y

Ywy Deacon 6. *Octob.*

THE

THE AVTHORS
Alleaged in this Booke, out of whome the former Saintes Liues are gathered.

Abbo Floriacensis
Adam Bremensis
Ado. Alanus Copus
Albertus Crantzius
Albertus Stadensis
Albinus Flaccus
Almannus Monachus
Aloysius Lippomannus
Alredus Rhieuallensis
Andreas Leucander.
Annales Baroniani
Annales Heluetiorum
Antonius Demochares
Arnoldus Mirmannus
Arnoldus Wion
Asser Meneuensis
Aymo
Baronius Card.
Beda. Bernardus
Bernardus Guido
Breuiarium Cameracense
Breuiarium Curiense
Breuiarium Gandauense
Breuiarium Moguntiuum
Breuiarium Saltzburgense
Breuiarium Sarum
Breuiarium Sueticum
Carolus Sigonius
Chronicon Cameracense
Chronicon Cluniacense

Chronograph. Britanniæ
Chronicon Hyberniæ
Concilium Tridentinum
Continuator Bedæ
Cornelius Tacitus
Egilwardus Monachus
Extrauagans Xysti PP. 4.
Felix Crolandiensis
Folcardus Doroborniensis
Francifcus Cattanius
Francifcus Belleforestius
Francifcus Maurolycus
Gaufredus Monumetensis
Georgius Lilius
Gerardus Liegh
Gildas Sapiens
Gotzelinus Morinensis
Gregorius Magnus
Gregorius Turonensis
Gulielmus Eyfengrenius
Gulielmus Malmesburiensis
Gulielmus Neubrigensis
Gulielmus Tyrius
Gulielmus Ramesius
Hector Boetius
Hector Deidonatus
Helmodius Presbyter
Hermannus Contractus
Herebertus Rosweyde
Hieronymus Platus

Hector

Hiftoria Quadripartita
Hiftoria antiqua Scotorum
Hucbaldus Monachus
Humfridus Lhuide
Iacobus Meyrus
Ioannes Capgrauius
Ioannes Frofyard
Ioannes de Kirkftat
Ioannes Lefleius
Ioannes Maior
Ioannes Magnus
Ioannes Molanus
Ioannes Nauclerus
Ioannes Tritemius
Ioannes Roufe
Lambertus de Loos
Laurentius Dunelmenfis
Laurentius Surius
Marcellinus Monachus
Matthæus Parifienfis
Mathæus Weftmonafter.
Mombritius. Mofander
Nicolaus Harpesfield
Nicolaus Sanderus
Olaus Magnus
Ofbertus de Stokes
Paulus Diaconus
Paulus Morigia
Petrus Blefenfis
Petrus Cratepolius
Petrus Gafelinus
Petrus de Natalibus

Petrus Sutor
Petrus de Viel
Polidorus Virgilius
Profper Aquitanius
Ranulphus Ceftrenfis
Regiftrum Cantuarienfe
Regiftrum de Hide
Regiftrum Lichfeldienfe
Regiftrum Lincolnienfe
Regiftrū D.Pauli Londinéf.
Regiftrum Petriburgenfe
Renatus Benedictus
Rhenanus
Richardus Vitus
Rodulphus Agricola
Rodulphus Monachus
Rogerus Houeden
Romanum Martyrologium
Robertus Buckland
Robertus Cænalis
Robertus Salopienfis
Senatus Brauonius
Siluefter Giraldus
Sigebertus. Sophronius
Speculum Fr. Carmelitaru
Stephanus Lufinganius
Symon Dunelmenfis
Theodoretus
Thomas Walfingam
Turgotus Epifcopus
Vincentius. Vfuardus
Wernerus Rollewincke

F I N I S.

A
CATALOGVE
OF THOSE VVHO

HAVE SVFFERED
DEATH IN ENGLAND,
for defence of the Catholicke Cause ſynce the
yeare of Chriſt 1535. *and* 27. *of King*
HENRY the VIII. his raigne,
vnto this yeare 1608.

THE PREFACE

IN the yeare of our Lord 1530. King *Henry* the viij. a͡ter that he had ⸝aigned 22. yeares in great peace and proſperity , famous throughout the Chriſtian world both for Religion, learning, and proweſſe , vpon diſpleaſure taken againſt the Popes Holines, about his diuorce with Queene Catherine his lawfull wife ; began vnfortunately his breach with the Sea Apoſtolicke, forbidding by

Io. Sto. in
Annal.
hoc anno
& ſeque̅-
tibus

Aa   Pro⁻

Proclamation vpon the 19. of September, all suites to be made to the Court of *Rome*. &c. And so by little and little going forward in this course now begun , and being (through euill Counsell) incited first againſt the Clergy of England, condemning them in a *Premunire* (for relaxation wherof they were forced to giue him an hūdred thousād pounds) and then againſt the Pope; at laſt intituled himselfe *Head of the Church of Englād*, taking vpon wholy the gouerment of all the Ecclesiasticall ſtate in his Dominions, diſſoluing and ſuppreſſing Monaſteryes & other Religious places at his pleaſure. And moreouer exacting an Oath , vnder payne of death, of all ſortes of ſubiectes, *againſt their consciences*, of this his pretended Supremacy. This forſaid breach with the Sea of *Rome*, thus begun, and continued afterward vnder the raygne of King *Henryes* two Children *Edward* and *Elizabeth*, holdeth alſo vntill this day in our Coūtrey in their Succeſſour K. *Iames*, to the great griefe of all the Chriſtian Catholicke world . The names of thoſe, who for refuſing the ſaid Oath , or otherwiſe reſiſting this their pretenced Supremacy, haue ſuffered vnder theſe forſaid Princes, are ſet downe as followeth, according to the yeares , moneths & dayes of their deaths.

Sand. l. 1. deSchism. Ang.

Vnder King Henry the VIII.

Anno Chriſti 1535. *Henrici* 8. *anno* 27.

Iohn Houghton Prior of the Carthuſians at London. *Auguſtine Webſter* Prior of the Carthuſians at Exham. *Robert Laurence* Prior of the Carthuſians at Beuall. *Richard Reynolds* Monke of S. Brigits Order of Syon. *Iohn Hayle* Prieſt, Vicar of Thiſtleworth. } Theſe were put to death at Tyburne the 29. of Aprill, for denying the Kings Supremacy.

Nic. Sãd. lib.1.de Schiſin. Ang. pa. 128. 129,130.

Humfrey Midlemore *William Exmew* *Sebaſtian Newdigate* } Charterhouſe Monkes of London, ſuffered at Tyburne 18. Iune.

Iohn Rocheſter *Iames Warnet* } Carthuſians, at Yorke 11. May

Richard Bere *Thomas Greene* *Iohn Dauis* *Thomas Iohnſon* *Williã Greenwood* *Thomas Scriuan* *Robert Salt* *VValter Perſons* *Thomas Reading* } Charterhouſe - Monkes died in priſon in Iune & Iuly.

VVilliam Horne Charterhouſe Monke 4. Aug.

Iohn

Ric.Hal. *in eius* *vita.* *Staplet.de* *tribus* *Thom.*	*Iohn Fisher* Card.of S. Vitalis, & Bishop of Rocheſter, at the Tower-Hill 22. Iune *Syr Thomas More* Knight, at the Tower-hill 6.Iuly.

Anno Chriſti 1536. *Henr.* 8. 28.

Sand. ib. *l.1.pag.* *176.177.*	**I**ohn *Paſley* Abbot of Whaley ⎫ at Lancaſter *Iohn Caſtegate* Monke ⎭ 10. March. *VVilliam Haddocke* Monke,at Whaley 13.Mar. N.N. Abbot of *Sauley* ⎫ at Lancaſter N. *Aſtbebe* Monke of Geruaux ⎭ in March. *Robert Holbes* Abbot of VVoborne, togeather with the Prior of the ſame Monaſtery & a Prieſt, ſuffered at *VVoborne* in Bedford-ſhire, in March. *Doctor Maccarell* with 4. other Prieſts, at Ty-burne 29. March.

VVilliam Thruſt Abbot of Fountaynes ⎫
Adam Sodbury Abbot of Geruaux   ⎬ at Ty-burne
William Would Prior of Birlington   ⎮ in Iun.
N. N. Abbot of Riuers   ⎭

Anno 1537. *Henr.* 29.

Sand. ib. *pag. 183.* *Boucher.* *de paſſ.* *Prat.* *Franſc.* *pag.8.13.* *& 17.*	**A**ntony *Brorby* of the Order of S. Francis, ſtrangled with his owne gildle, at London 19. Iuly. *Thomas Cort* Francifcan ,famiſhed to death in prifon 27. Iuly. *Thomas Belcham* of the ſame Order, died in Newgate 3. Auguſt.

Anno 1538. Henr. 30.

IOhn Forest Frier obseruant, Confessour to Queene *Katherine*, in Smithfield 23. May.
Iohn *Stone* an Augustine friar, at Canterbury this yeare.

Two *and thirty* Religious Men of the Order of S. *Francis* being cast into prison for denying the K. Supremacy, died there through cold, stench, & famine, in Aug. Sept. and October.

N. *Croft* Priest ⎫
N. *Collins* Priest ⎬ at Tyburne.
N. *Holland* Layman ⎭

Bouch. ibid. & pag. 26. Sand. ibi.

Sand l. 1. pag. 973.

Anno 1539. Henr. 31.

Adrian *Fortescue* ⎫ Knights of S. Iohns of Ie-
Thomas *Dingley* ⎭ rusalē, at Tower hill 8. Iul.
Griffith Clarke Priest ⎫ at S. Thomas Watc-
N. *Mayre* Monke ⎭ ringes 8. July.
Iohn *Tauers* Doctor of diuinity ⎫
Iohn *Harris* Priest ⎬ 30. Iuly.
Iohn *Rugge* ⎫ Priests, at Reading, 14.
William *Onion* ⎭ Nouemb.
Hugh *Faringdon* Abbot of Reading, at *Reading* 22. Nouemb.
Richard *Whiting* Abbot of Glastēbury ⎫ at Gla-
Iohn *Thorne* ⎫ Monks of Glastēbury ⎬ stēnb. 22
Roger *Iames* ⎭ Nouem.
Iohn *Beck* Abbot of Colchester, at *Colchester* 1. Decemb.

Sand. pa. 181. 194. 197.

Anno 1540. *Henr.* 32.

Sand. ib.
pag. 216.
217.

William Peterſon ⎫ Prieſtes, at Ca-
William Richardſon ⎭ lais 10. April.

Thomas Abell
Edward Powell ⎫ Prieſtes, in Smithfield 30.
Rich. Fetherſtone ⎭ Iuly.

Laurece Cocke Prior of Dancaſter ⎫
Will·am Horne Monke
Edmund Bromley Prieſt
Giles Horne Gentleman. ⎬ at Ty-
Clement Philpot Gentleman. burne 4.
Darby Genninges Layman Auguſt
Robert Bird Layman ⎭

Anno 1541. *Henr.* 33.

Sãd. pag.
180

Dauid Genſon Knight of the *Rhodes*. 1. Iuly.

Anno 1543. *Henr.* 35.

Sand. pag.
227.

German Gardener **Gent.** ⎫
Iohn Larke Prieſt
Iohn Ireland Prieſt ⎬ at Tyburne 7.
Thomas Asbey Layman March.

Vnder Queene Elizabeth.

Anno 1570. *Elizabethæ* 12.

Nicol.
Sander l.
7. *deuiſib.*
Monarc.
pag. 734.
& 736.

Iohn Felton Gentleman, in S. Paules Churh-yard 8. Auguſt.

Anno 1571. *Elizabeth.* 13.

IOhn *Story* Doctor of the Canon-law, at Tyburne 1. Iune.

Anno 1573. *Elizabeth.* 15.

THomas *Woodhouse* Priest, at Tyburne 19. Iune.

Concert,
Ecclef.
Ang.

Anno 1577. *Elizab.* 19.

CVthbert *Mayne* the first Priest of the Se-minaryes, at Launston in Cornwall 29. Nouemb.

Concert.
Ecclef.
Angl.

Anno 1578. *Elizab.* 20.

IOhn *Nelfon* Priest, at Tyburne 3. February. Thomas *Sherwood* Gentleman 7. Febr.

Concert.
ibid.

Anno 1581. *Elizab.* 23.

EVerard *Hanfe* Priest, at Tyburne 31. Iuly.
Edmund *Campian* Priest of the ⎫
Society of Iesus. ⎪ at Ty-
Alexander *Briant* Priest of the same ⎬ burne
Society of Iesus. ⎪ 1. Dec.
Raph *Sherwyn* Priest ⎭

Concert.
Ecclef.
Ang.
Sand. l. 3.
de fchifm.
Angl.

Anno 1582. *Elizab.* 24.

IOhn *Payne* Priest, at Chelemsford in Essex 2. April.

Concert. *Ecclef.* *Angl. et* *Sand. vbi* *fupra .*	*Thomas Ford* Prieſt. ⎫ *Iohn Shert* Prieſt. ⎬ at Tyburne 28.May. *Robert Iohnſon* Prieſt. ⎭ *Thomas Cottam* Prieſt of ⎫ the Society of Ieſus. ⎪ *William Filby* Prieſt. ⎬ at Tiburne 30.May *Luke Kirby* Prieſt. ⎪ *Laurence Iohnſon* Prieſt ⎭ *William Lacy* Prieſt ⎫ at Yorke 22. Au- *Richard Kirkman* Prieſt⎭ guſt. *Iames Tompſon* Prieſt, at Yorke in Nouemb.

Anno 1583 .*Elizab.* 25.

Concert. *Ecclef.* *Angl. et* *Sand. pa.* 405.466	**R***ichard Thirkill* Prieſt , at Yorke 29.May. *Iohn Slade* Laymā, at Wincheſt. 30.Oct. *Iohn Body* Layman, at Andouer 2. Nouemb. *William Hart* Prieſt, at Yorke. *Iames Laburne* Gentleman, at Lancaſter.

Anno 1584. *Elizab.* 26.

Concert. *Ecclef.* *Ang. pa.* 127. 134. 140.143. 156. cum *Sand. vbi* *fupra.*	**VV**ill*iam Carter* Layman, at Tyburne
	  11. Ian.
	George Haddocke Prieſt ⎫
	Iohn Mundine Prieſt ⎪
	Iames Fen Prieſt ⎬ at Tyburne 12.Feb.
	Thomas Emerford Prieſt ⎪
	Iohn Nutter Prieſt ⎭
	Iames Bele Prieſt ⎫ at Lancaſter 20.April.
	Iohn Finch Layman ⎭
	Richard White Layman, at *Wrixam* in Wales
	  18. Octob.

Anno

Anno 1585. *Elizab.* 27.

THomas *Aufield* Prieſt.   ⎱ at Tyburne
      Thomas *VVebley* Layman. ⎰ 6. Iuly.
Hugh Taylour Prieſt   ⎱ at Yorke.
Marmaduke Bowes Layman ⎰
Margaret Clitherow Cittizen of Yorke, at
      Yorke in March.

Concert.
Ecclef.
Ang.pa.
203. *Sad.*
pag. 485
499,

Anno 1586. *Elizab.* 28.

EDward *Tranſam* Prieſt ⎱ at Tyburne 21.
      Nicol. VVoodfine Prieſt ⎰ Ianuary.
Richard Sergeant Prieſt ⎱ at Tyburne 20.
VVilliam Tompſon Prieſt ⎰ April.
Iohn Addams Prieſt   ⎱
Iohn Low Prieſt   ⎰ at Tyburne 8. Octob.
Robert Debdale Prieſt
Robert Anderton Prieſt ⎱ at Tyburne.
VVilliam Marſden Prieſt ⎰
Francis Ingleby Prieſt, at Yorke.
Stephen Rouſam Prieſt, at Gloceſter.
Iohn Finglow Prieſt.

Concert.
Ecclef.
Ang.pa.
204. 410
Sand.pa.
499.

Anno 1587. *Elizab.* 29.

MAry Queene of Scotland, at Foder-
      inghay-Caſtle 8. Febr.
Thomas Pilchard Prieſt at Dorceſter in March.
Iohn Sandes Prieſt, at Gloceſter.
Iohn Hamley Prieſt, at Chard.
Alexander Crow Prieſt, at Yorke.
Robert Sutton Prieſt, at Stafford.

Concert.
Ecclef.
Ang.pa.
207.

Ed-

Edmund Sikes Prieſt.
Gabriel Thimbleby Prieſt.
George Douglas Prieſt.

Anno 1588. *Elizab.* 30.

Di lacus
de Yepes
Epiſcop.
Taracon.
de perſec.
Angl.
Hiſpanicè

VVilliam *Deane* Pr. ⎱ at Milédgreene
 Henry VVebly P. ⎰ by Lódó. 28. Au.
VViliam Gunter Prieſt, at the Theater by
 London. 28. Auguſt.
Robert Morton Prieſt ⎱ in Lincolnes Inne fi-
Hugh More Gentlemã ⎰ elds by Lódó 28. Au.
Thomas Acton alias Holjord Prieſt at Clarken-
 well in London 28. Auguſt.
Richard Clarkeſon Prieſt ⎫
Thomas Felton laybrother of ⎬ at Hounſlow
 the order of the Minimes ⎭ 28. Aug.
Richard Liegh Prieſt ⎫
Hugh Morgan Prieſt ⎪
Edward Shelly **Gent.** ⎪
Richard Flower Laymã ⎬ at Tyburne 30. Aug.
Robert Martyn Layman ⎪
Iohn Rocke Layman ⎪
Margaret VVard Gent. ⎭
Edward Iames Prieſt ⎱
Raph Crochet Prieſt. ⎰ at Chicheſter 1. Oct.
Robert Wilcockes Prieſt ⎫
Edward Campian Prieſt ⎬ at Canterbury
Chriſtopher Buxton Prieſt ⎭ 1. Octob.
Robert VVidmerpoole Layman ⎰
VVilliam Wigges Prieſt, at Kingſton 1. Octob.
Iohn Robinſon Prieſt, at Ipſwich 1. Octob.

Iohn VVeldon Prieſt, at Milendgreene by London 5. October.

VVilliam Hartley Prieſt ⎱ at   Halliwell   by
Richard VVilliās Prieſt ⎰ London 5. Octob.

Robert Sutton Layman at Clarkenwell 5. Oct.

VVilliam Spenſer Prieſt.

Edward Burden Prieſt.

Iohn Hewit Prieſt.

Robert Ludlam Prieſt. ⎫
Richard Sympſon Prieſt ⎬ at Darby.
Nicolas Garlicke Prieſt ⎭

William Lampley Layman at Gloceſter.

Anno 1589. Eliʒab. 31.

George Nicols Prieſt ⎫
Richard Yaxley Prieſt ⎪
Thomas Belſon Gentlemā ⎬ at Oxford 5. Iul.
Humfrey Vp-richard laymā ⎭

Iohn Annas Prieſt.

Robert Dalby Prieſt.

Anno 1590. Eliʒab. 32.

Chriſtopher Bales Prieſt, in Fleetſtreet in London 4. March.

Alexander Blake Layman in Grayes Inne lane in London 4. March.

Nicolas Horner Layman in Smithfield in London 4. March.

Miles Gerard Prieſt ⎱ at Rocheſter 30.
Francis Dickinſon Prieſt ⎰ Aprill.

Antony Middleton Prieſt at Clarkenwell in London 6. May.

*Didac. de
Yepes
Epiſ.
Taracon.
de perſec.
Angl.
Hiſpan.*

Ed-

Edward Iohnes Prieſt in Fleetſtreet in London 6. May.

Anno 1591. *Elizab*.33.

Edmund *Geninges* Prieſt ⎱in Grayes Inne
Swithin VVelles Gent. ⎰ fields 10. Dec.

Andr. Philop. cont. Edict. Reginæ. Ang. pa. 482.

Euſtach VVhite Prieſt ⎫
Polidor Plaſden Prieſt ⎪
Brian Lacy Gentlemā. ⎬at Tyburne 10.Dec.
Iohn Maſon Layman. ⎪
Sydney Hodgſon Laymā ⎭

Momfort Scot Prieſt ⎱ in Fleeſtreet 2.
George Biſley Prieſt ⎰ Iuly.

Williā Dickinſon Prieſt ⎱at Wincheſter 7.
Raph Milner Layman ⎰ Iuly.

Edmund Duke Prieſt ⎫
Richard Holiday Prieſt. ⎬at Durham.
Iohn Hogge Prieſt ⎪
Richard Hill Prieſt. ⎭

VVilliam Pikes Layman at Dorceſter.

Anno 1592. *Elizab*. 34.

VVilliā *Patteſon* Pr. at Tyburne 22. Ia.
Thomas Portmore Prieſt in S. Paules Churchyard in London 21. Febr.
Roger Ashton Gent. at Tyburne 23. Iune.

Anno 1593. *Elizab*. 35.

Did.yepes ibi. pag. 651.

IAmes *Burden* Laymā, at Wincheſt. 25. Mar.
Antony Page Prieſt, at Yorke 30. April.
Ioſeph Lampton Prieſt at Newcaſtle 23. Iune.

Wil-

William *Dauis* Prieſt, at *Beumaris* in Wales, in
   Septemb.
Edward Waterſon Prieſt.

Anno 1594. *Elizab.* 36.

VVilliam *Harington* Prieſt, at Tyburne
   18. Febr.
Iohn Cornelius Mohun Prieſt of ⎫
   the Society of Ieſus.   ⎬ at Dorceſter
Thomas Boſgraue Gentleman   ⎪ 4. Iuly.
Patricke Samon Layman   ⎪
Iohn Carey Layman   ⎭
Iohn Ingram Prieſt.   ⎫
Thomas Boaſt Prieſt   ⎬ at Newcaſtle.
Iames Oldbaſton Prieſt.   ⎭

*Yepes vbi
ſuprà
pag.* 633.
640. 64ɼ

Anno 1595. *Elizab.* 37.

Robert *Southwell* Prieſt of the Society of
   Ieſus, at Tyburne 3. March.
Henry Walpole Prieſt of   ⎫
   the Society of Ieſus   ⎬ at Yorke 17. Apr.
Alexander Raulins Prieſt ⎭
George Errington Gent.   ⎫
William Knight Gentleman   ⎪
William Gibſon Gentleman ⎬ at Yorke.
Henry Abbots Layman   ⎪
William Freeman Prieſt.   ⎭

*Did.
Yepes in
hiſt. per-
ſecut.
Angl.
pag.* 642.

Anno 1596. *Elizab.* 38.

N *Auleby* Prieſt.
N. Thorpe Prieſt.

Anno 1597. Elizab. 39.

Yepes vbi supra. pag. 710. l. 5.

Iohn Buckley alias Iones Prieſt of the Order of S. Francis, at S. Thomas waterings 12. Iuly.

Anno 1598. Elizab. 40.

Thomas Snow Prieſt
Chriſtopher Robinſon Prieſt
Richard Horner Prieſt } at Yorke.
N. Grimſton Layman
N. Britton Layman.

Anno 1600. Elizab. 42

Relatio 16 Mart. à Th. W. edit.

Chriſtopher VVharton Prieſt, } at Yorke
with a venerable Matrone } 18. May.

Iohn Rigby Gentleman, at S. Thomas Waterings 21. Iuly.

Robert Nutter Prieſt } at Lancaſter in
Edward Thwinge Prieſt } Iune.

Thomas Sprot Prieſt } at Lincolne in Iuly.
Thomas Hunt Prieſt }

Thomas Palaſer Prieſt }
Iohn Norton Gentleman } at Durham in Iuly.
N. Talbot Gentleman. }

Anno 1601. Elizab. 43.

Iohn Pibush Prieſt, at Tyburne 11. February.

Roger Filcocke Prieſt of the Society of Ieſus. ⎫

Marke Barkworth Prieſt of the Order of S. Benedict. ⎬ at Tyburne 27. Feb.

Anne Lyne Gentlewoman widdow ⎭

Robert Middleton Prieſt. ⎫ at Lancaſter.
Thruſtan Hunt Prieſt. ⎭

Anno 1602. Elizab. 44.

FRancis Page Prieſt of the Society of Ieſus. ⎫

Thomas Tichborne Prieſt ⎬ at Tyburne 29. April.
Robert Watkinſon Prieſt

Iames Ducket Layman ⎭

N. Harriſon Prieſt ⎫ at Yorke in April.
N. Bates Gentleman ⎭

Anno 1603. Elizab. 45. & vltimo.

LAurence *Richardſon* alias *Anderton* Prieſt at Tyburne 27. February.

Vnder King Iames.

Anno 1604. Iacob. Reg. 2.

LAurence *Bayly* Layman, at Lancaſter in March.

Iohn Suker Prieſt ⎫ at Warwicke in Auguſt.
Robert Griſſold Laymã ⎭

Anno 1605. Iacobi 3.

THomas VVilborne Layman, at Yorke.

Relat 16. Mart. pag. 93. & 94.

Anno 1606. *Iacobi* 4.

EDward *Oldcorne* Prieſt of the Society of Ieſus. } at Worceſter. 7. Apr.
Raph Aslley Layman

Henry Garnet Prieſt, Superiour of the Society of Ieſus in England, in S. Paules Church-yard 3. May.

Anno 1607. *Iacob.* 5.

RObert *Drury* Prieſt, at Tyburne 26. Februarꝑ.

Anno 1608. *Iacob.* 6.

MAtthew *Flathers* Prieſt at Yorke 21. Mar. *George Gervis* Prieſt of the Order of S. Benedict, at Tyburne 11. April.
Thomas Garnet Prieſt of the Society of Ieſus at Tyburne 23. Iune.

FINIS.

CERTAINE CORRECTIONS
and Additions in the late English Martyrs, which came to the Authors knowledg after the printing of the former Catalogue.

Anno 1543.
Adde, Iohn Risby, *and* Thomas Rike.
Anno 1585.

Adde { N. Hamelton Priest. } at Yorke
{ Rob. Bicardicke layman }

Anno 1586.
Adde, Richard Langley Esquire at Yorke 1. Decemb.
Eodē anno put Iohn Sands, *&* Stephē Rousam in Anno 1587.

Anno 1588.
Hugh Morgan *Priest,* corrige, *Gentleman.*
Ibidem, Edw. Shelley *Esquire,* corrige, *Gentleman.*

Anno 1592.
Roger Ashton *Priest,* corrige, *Gentleman.*

Anno 1595.
Adde, Iohn Watkinson (*alias* VVarcoppe) layman, at Yorke.
Adde, Anno 1599. Matthew Hayes Priest, at Yorke.

Anno 1600.
Dele illa verba, with a venerable Matron.

Anno 1601.
Iohn Pibush Priest, *at Tyburne,* corrige, *at S. Thomas* VVaterings.

Anno 1603.
Laurence Richardson, *alias* Anderton Priest, *corrige sic,*
William Richardson Priest &c.

Anno 1605.
Adde, William Browne layman, at Rippon.

Anno 1606.
Richard Oldcorne, *corrige,* Edward Oldcorne &c.

Yf, besides these, any other errours haue heerin escaped, either in Names or Syrnames, or in the yeares, or places of their sufferings; I humbly desire the Catholicke Reader to pardon the same, and of himselfe in charity to amend them: To whose prudent Iudgment, & Censure of HOLY CHVRCH, I submit the whole.

I. W.